Tim Bergling

Reeling in the Years
Gay Men's Perspectives
on Age and Ageism

Pre-publication
REVIEWS,
COMMENTARIES,
EVALUATIONS . . .

"**B**ergling makes good use of current technology to converse with large numbers of gay men. In so doing, he provides the reader with reasons gay men believe a 'gay generation gap' exists. He documents the importance and relativity of the social construction of age. He is also quick to point out that ageism is not only directed at older gays by younger gays, but that older gays experience internalized ageism. This reflects the larger, more general problem that we have created and maintained—a youth-obsessed culture for both gays and nongays.

This is an engaging read not only about age specifically, but about gay culture in general. Readers will benefit from the various conversations about 'old' persons, i.e., anyone over 40. As I see it, the book serves two purposes. First it informs readers of the history and plight of older gay men, and enables one to appreciate a group of gays that is often viewed with disdain because of being in a particular age category. The book also, however, does the reverse and makes the reader recognize and appreciate what younger gays have to offer the community. Young gay men should also be acknowledged and valued by older gays, rather than being viewed with disinterest and the presumption that they have nothing to offer. There is certainly room for both young and old to learn from and value one another.

Reeling in the Years is a welcome addition to the emerging and long-overdue literature on aging gay men."

J. Michael Cruz, PhD
Author of *Sociological*
Analysis of Aging:
The Gay Male Perspective

More pre-publication
REVIEWS, COMMENTARIES, EVALUATIONS . . .

"**I** have become a Tim Bergling fan! His style is wonderfully accessible and engaging. Not that I agree with everything that he writes, but he is a wonderful storyteller who seduces you into his perspective and won't let you go. *Reeling in the Years* is a must-read for every gay man, anyone who loves gay men, and anyone who wants to understand gay men. This is an exceptional contribution to the gay aging literature."

Mark Pope, EdD
President, American
Counseling Association (2003-2004);
Associate Professor,
Division of Counseling
& Family Therapy,
University of Missouri–Saint Louis

Southern Tier Editions
Harrington Park Press®
An Imprint of The Haworth Press, Inc.
New York • London • Oxford

Reeling in the Years
Gay Men's Perspectives
on Age and Ageism

THE HAWORTH PRESS
Titles of Related Interest

Gay and Gray: The Older Homosexual Man, Second Edition by Raymond M. Berger

Against My Better Judgment: An Intimate Memoir of an Eminent Gay Psychologist by Roger Brown

Gay Men at Midlife: Age Before Beauty edited by Alan L. Ellis

Gay Men's Sexual Stories: Getting It! edited by Robert Reynolds and Gerard Sullivan

Gay Midlife and Maturity: Crises, Opportunities, and Fulfillment edited by John Alan Lee

Midlife and Aging in Gay America: Proceedings of the SAGE Conference 2000 edited by Douglas C. Kimmel and Dawn Lundy Martin

Social Services for Senior Gay Men and Lesbians edited by Jean K. Quam

Sociological Analysis of Aging: The Gay Male Perspective by J. Michael Cruz

When It's Time to Leave Your Lover: A Guide for Gay Men by Neil Kaminsky

The Mentor: A Memoir of Friendship and Gay Identity by Jay Quinn

Reeling in the Years
Gay Men's Perspectives on Age and Ageism

Tim Bergling

Southern Tier Editions
Harrington Park Press®
An Imprint of The Haworth Press, Inc.
New York • London • Oxford

Published by

Southern Tier Editions, Harrington Park Press®, an imprint of The Haworth Press, Inc., 10 Alice Street, Binghamton, NY 13904-1580.

Cover design by Brooke Stiles.

Illustrations by Joe Phillips.

Library of Congress Cataloging-in-Publication Data

Bergling, Tim.
    Reeling in the years : gay men's perspectives on age and ageism / Tim Bergling.
        p. cm.
Includes bibliographical references.
    ISBN 1-56023-370-2 (hard : alk. paper)—ISBN 1-56023-371-0 (soft : alk. paper)
    1. Gay men—United States—Attitudes. 2. Middle aged gay men—United States—Attitudes. 3. Aged gay men—United States—Attitudes. 4. Aging—Psychological aspects. I. Title: Gay men's perspectives on age and ageism. II. Title.
    HQ76.2.U5B48 2004
    305.38'9664'0973—dc21

                                              2003009795

For Andy

We danced until the night became a brand new day

Neil Diamond/Gilbert Becaud
"September Morn"

ABOUT THE AUTHOR

Tim Bergling is a television news producer and journalist in Washington, DC, and the author of *Sissyphobia: Gay Men and Effeminate Behavior* (Haworth). His work has appeared in *Genre, Out, Instinct, HERO,* and *Joey* magazines. A DC-area native, Bergling is a former U.S. Marine (1982–1990) who was among the contributors to the 2001 military short story anthology *A Night in the Barracks* (Haworth). He is currently working on his third solo effort, *Chasing Adonis: Gay Men and the Pursuit of Perfection,* and putting together a compilation of essays and commentaries called *What Planet Are YOU From? Gay Men, Lesbians, and the Space Between.* You can visit his Web site at www.timbergling.com.

ABOUT THE ARTIST

Rocketed to earth when he was just a baby, **Joe Phillips** soon found he had strange and unusual powers to capture on paper the life forms he saw around him.

At first this ability separated him from the people of this new world but he soon learned to harness his power to recreate things as he sees in his mind's eye. The results are what we know today as the art of Joe Phillips! Hahaha . . .

That's what you'd expect me to say after over a decade of drawing comics. In truth I'm as amazed by the popularity of my work as anyone. I never knew how well received it would be. I'm a very private person and prefer my work speak for itself.

I live in sunny San Diego, we have 75° weather nearly all year long, and I have a view of the bay from my apartment with the park just a block away. With this as my canvas, my current art reflects the life of men around me.

CONTENTS

Foreword   ix
Michael Alvear

Acknowledgments   xi

Introduction   1

Chapter 1. "Nothing in Common"   7

Generations   13
That Was Then, This Is Now   16
"No Oldies, Please"   19
"No Kids Allowed"   20
"Us" versus "Them"   21
Separate Ways   24

Chapter 2. The Myths of Time   27

Myth One: "Kids These Days . . ."   28
Myth Two: Caught in the Net   32
Myth Three: The Chicken Hawk Syndrome   38
Myth Four: The Menudo Complex   41
Myth Five: Let's Talk About Sex . . .   46

Chapter 3. Forever Young?   53

A Brief History of Time   54
Men at Work   58
Dressing the Part   59
Hair We Go   64
Hair We Go, Again   69
Men's Fitness   73
Like a Surgeon   80
Extras, Extras   82
"Time Marches On"   83

Chapter 4. The Untouchables   87

The Lost Boys   90
"Hatred in the Hallways"   93

You Sexy Thing   98
The End of the Innocence   101
The *XY* Files   105
"Young People at Risk"   107
No Sex, Please   111
"I Feel Like Chicken Tonight"   114
Big Brother Is Watching You   124

Chapter 5. Bridging the Gap   **129**

Legends of the "Fall"   131
When Two Worlds Collide   137
The "Twinkie Defense"   143
Friends, Indeed   145
The Eyes of a Boy   151

Chapter 6. After the Fire   **159**

"Hope I Die Before I Get Old"   162
Outing Age   165
Awakenings   168
Left Behind   174
"We Always Had Each Other"   178
Rainbow's End   182
"The Life in Your Years"   188

Chapter 7. Yesterday, Today, and Tomorrow   **195**

"Stuck in the Middle"   198
"The Truth About Money"   206
"Over" the Rainbow   212

Chapter 8. The Numbers Game   **219**

Afterword   **257**

Resources   **269**

References   **271**

Foreword

Older gay men and younger gay men rarely talk to each other. We're like Italian salad dressing in the fridge. You can shake us all you want but eventually we'll lift, separate, and retreat to separate halves of the bottle.

Why don't Generations Gay mix very well? You're about to find out in Tim Bergling's veritable almanac of attitudes. Bergling is a sort of anecdotal sociologist, using informal surveys, questionnaires, and interviews to get at the heart of what beats in our intergenerational chests.

Bergling discovered four basic kinds of younger/older relationships: the type that are repulsed by each other, the type that fall in love with each other, the type that are best friends with each other, and the type that don't know enough about each other to even have an opinion.

The real appeal of this book isn't Bergling's fact-finding, myth-busting stories. It isn't even the intellectual enlightenment of a subject that's sat in the dark too long. It's the emotional pull of his findings. Or rather, the emotions that his findings pull out of you. This is a difficult book to read because your memories keep intruding on the text.

For example, as soon as I started reading Bergling's narrative, I was immediately transported to my early twenties. I always hated older gay men when I first came out. They made me nervous. Whenever I was introduced to an older man I always got the sense it wasn't my hand he wanted to shake.

When I was twenty-four I played in an out-of-town volleyball tournament. I stayed at the house of a man who volunteered his home to visiting players. He was forty-two. He was kind, generous, and wise. On the flight home I realized he was the only "older" guy I had ever made friends with. Someone had finally broken through my belief that sex was the only thing older guys wanted.

A couple of weeks later my forty-two-year-old friend called to tell me he was coming into town on business. He sent me his itinerary, which hinted at unscheduled stops in my bedroom. Thinking I was reading too much into it, I wrote him a quick note, decorously hinting at my own expectations of his visit. It went something like this: "I can't wait to spend some time with you. You're the first older guy I've become friends with who didn't have a hidden sexual agenda. I just want you to know how much I appreciate that."

I never heard from him again. No response, no visit, no nothing.

I went through my entire twenties without a single friendship with an older man. I felt manipulated by them. There were only two kinds of older men as far as I was concerned: those who made a pass at you and those who didn't—because they were more interested in your friends.

I couldn't even come close to charity on the subject. Twenty years later Bergling found out not much has changed—a lot of younger guys have the same palpable distrust of older men that I had.

In one of the most entertaining chapters of the book, Bergling chronicles the antipathy that young guys have for older guys. For example, a twenty-one-year-old told Bergling, "Sugar daddies are something you should find on a stick in a candy store, not on your stick in bed." Ouch. But hey, never put your money on youth and beauty when the contest is about intellect and wit. Bergling quotes an older man's distaste for young guys: "I'm a man, not your daddy. . . . Don't let your son go down on me."

Underneath all the bitchy asides, the passionate relationships, the rock-solid friendships, and the hateful distrust between older and younger gay men, one question seems to pulse silently through the book, like a shadow appearing on a door right before you knock on it. It's a version of the famous question straight people have asked themselves throughout time: "Can men really be friends with women?"

In *Reeling in the Years: Gay Men's Perspectives on Age and Ageism,* the interrogative has a different spin, but the flavor is essentially the same: "Can older gay men really be friends with younger gay men?" In other words: Can you truly be friends with somebody you have the potential to have sex with? The answer might be obvious to you. Then again, maybe it's not. Perhaps this book will only confirm your opinion, but, just possibly, it could change your mind.

Michael Alvear

Michael Alvear has written for *The New York Times, The Los Angeles Times, Newsweek,* and Salon.com. A frequent contributor of commentary to NPR's *All Things Considered,* he is also the author of *Men Are Pigs but We Love Bacon.*

Acknowledgments

This book would not have been possible without the ongoing support of all the great folks at The Haworth Press, specifically Bill Palmer (for taking yet another chance on me, before my first book was even published!) and Rebecca Browne (for letting me cry on her shoulder and hold her hand on more than one occasion).

I also have to give a nod to all my "experts" in various fields and the dozens of youth and old-age advocates who shared their expertise and opinions with me, privately and for attribution, as this book was getting underway, along with the hundreds of "regular folks" out there who took the time and energy to answer all my nosy questions, and fill in the blanks on my surveys throughout the last year. Thanks also to the thousands who responded to my online polls; without those "perspectives" this book wouldn't exist.

I need to thank my former partner, Andy. There's simply no way to quantify the invaluable assistance he provided by helping to create the Web site by which we gathered a thousand pages of life stories and poll data reflected here. My newfound friend, Marc Acito, deserves kudos aplenty for all his support and advice as I banged this thing out chapter by chapter.

Most of all I need to thank my good, good friends—Christopher, Derek, Ed, Tim, Jeff, and many more—for all their steadfast support and unconditional love during one of the more turbulent years of my life. For that I will always be grateful.

Introduction

Late one night about eight years ago, when I should have been tucked safely away in bed, I was instead doing something that more and more of us are doing all the time these days: playing around on the computer. Chatting on America Online (AOL) was still a relatively new fascination for me then, and it's quaint to recall now how it seemed so magical, this ability to zip around the country at the speed of light with my ass firmly planted in a chair, cocktail in hand, safe in the company of mysterious people I'd likely never meet.

This particular night wasn't about "hooking up" with anyone—not that there's anything wrong with it—I was just hanging out, shooting the shit, and checking out the member profiles of various people as they popped into the "m4m" chat rooms on AOL. A little small talk here, some "pic trading" there, a few instant messages exchanged, all the while shuttling from DC to Denver, Dallas to Detroit, with a few layovers in Seattle, Los Angeles, Boston, or Tampa along the way. I was enjoying myself immensely in the easy wielding of this new technology, never sensing I was about to get the rude awakening which would lead, with a few detours, to this very book you're reading now.

The young man in question appeared suddenly before my eyes . . . or rather, his screen name did. I can't recall what it actually was, but I'm sure it was something like "HotSoccerJock" or "LifeGuard21," one of those names that for many gay men (myself included) evoke all sorts of powerful and lusty mental images: a cluttered dorm room with athletic gear and clothing strewn about, posters on the walls, and a good-looking young man in his loose Abercrombie and Fitch boxers, posed casually in the desk chair or atop the messy bed. A quick profile scan only supported those images, and it was enough to convince me that a hearty little hello seemed to be in order. I dashed off a greeting and after a short pause came the reply: "How old?" Not really thinking twice, I typed in "thirty-six," to which my mysterious young stranger answered, after a longer pause, "Too old. Bye." A single ensuing message from me, something along the lines of "What the hell?" went unanswered.

All I could mutter was a quiet "Wow." Apparently this young fellow wasn't remotely interested in where I lived, what I did for a living, or whether I was successful in life; he cared not a whit whether I created art or healed the sick, if I did drugs, smoked, or beat up my boyfriend when I was pissed off (or if I *had* a boyfriend, for that matter). He didn't even ask any of the most venerable of online questions, inquiries like "Top or bottom?" or "So, what are you packing?" Just "How old?" as if my age was something that defined me and categorized me in toto. And now, having exceeded his self-designated threshold—whatever that was—I wasn't fit for even a simple chat across the vastness of cyberspace.

As far as I can recall, it was the first time, the very first time, that my age was ever held against me—and I was dumbstruck.

OK, surely some of you are saying, "But that was online, and who the hell cares about what happens there? It's not like it's real. Get over it" (like that time I caught a friend of mine shaving ten years off his age in his online profile, and he offered the same reasoning in defense). Truthfully, anyone *would* be a moron if he let some random, anonymous online encounter shake his whole worldview; after all, for all I know my "HotSoccerJock" was actually some sixty-nine-year-old retiree in Tallahassee, perpetrating a fraud to collect some choice words and images for his own private pleasures. I'm fully aware that all sorts of normally good-hearted people cruise the Net looking for a particular sort of "chat partner," and ignore or dismiss anyone who doesn't meet their "needs" at any given time.

Trust me, I know all that. Just like I know that if any of us took personally all the apparent slights and outright abuse that we've endured online, we'd end up making some therapist very, very rich. I'm just saying that, like many of life's little epiphanies that arrive amidst the most trivial of pursuits, my late-night encounter opened my eyes to something I cannot say I'd ever given much thought to: the idea that there are people out there who use age as a primary qualifier for companionship, contact, or even conversation. For some people, however old they themselves might be, someone in their mid-thirties was already too far gone to have anything to do with at any particular moment. It was a lot like spotting the first gray hair or spying the first extra line around the eyes, only more so because someone else was pointing it out to *me*. It's that singular, unsettling instant when the clock becomes, not a timepiece, but a time bomb. You're suddenly moved to wonder how long it will be before—BOOM!—it's all over.

As a journalist writing for a handful of national magazines over the past several years, I've often talked about, or at least walked around the edges of, the gay community's attitudes about age, and the rites of passage associated with certain age groups. I've examined some of the problems that underage gay kids confront, and explored what the coming-out process is like for younger people today, as compared to what it was like for us "way back when." I've written articles that discussed retirement and investment issues as they relate to gay men, and profiles of older gay men, some with loving relationships that have lasted almost half a century. I've looked into the particular joys of relationships that span a generational gap as well as the problems those pairings might present. But one topic I don't think I've ever tackled head on, at least not before I took up this project, was the subject of ageism, which has to be among the oddest social prejudices we all face.

If we define the term as the dictionary does, a "discrimination based on age, especially prejudice against the elderly," then what we're talking about is an intolerance for the very people that, God willing, we ourselves will become one day. Unlike other forms of discrimination, where bigotry occurs between forever-disparate groups —heterosexual homophobes targeting gays, sexist males targeting women, or one ethnic or religious group pitted against another—ageism occurs along a strange continuum, where today's oppressor could well be tomorrow's oppressed; the aging man, his own youth far behind him, realizes only with the passage of time that he's becoming— or has become already—that which he himself may once have feared or despised. He's finally gained the hard-won knowledge and understanding that only years can bestow, just in time to become—for some people—an object of fear, suspicion, or prejudice himself.

Talk about your chickens coming home to roost!

In my first book, *Sissyphobia: Gay Men and Effeminate Behavior,* I examined the tensions in the gay community between men who fancy themselves as masculine and "straight acting," and those who have a tendency toward the effeminate or all-out flamboyant. After two years of talking to gay men about their attitudes concerning older or younger men, I'm here to tell you that I found very similar tensions at work, a "two tribe" mentality that, for many, splits the gay community into an "us" and a "them." *Sissyphobia* looked for the root causes of the hostility that straight *and* gay society often holds for effeminate men; in this book I've set out to explore this peculiar phenomenon called ageism as it exists within the gay world. Along the way, it occurred to me it might also be time to revisit some of those other age-related topics I once wrote about, to give them more examination and depth than one has room for in a magazine article.

Hence this book, *Reeling in the Years: Gay Men's Perspectives on Age and Ageism.* What *do* gay men think about such issues as ageism and "under" ageism? (For certainly there are just as many older people who look askance at today's youth—if not ignoring them completely—as there are those who blanch at the sight of a gray hair or a wrinkle; it's a river that often flows in two different directions.) I've tried to measure the gulf that age sometimes seems to put between us, to find out how gay men in different age groups view one another. And moving on from the contentious to the contemplative: How does the world look through the eyes of a gay teen as we enter the twenty-first century? What's it like these days to go to your first gay bar and make your very first circle of gay friends? . . . Then what happens when the bar scene gets old before you do? In this brave new gay world of the 2000s, powered by the Internet and wired up for digital cable, what's it like to come out at sixteen, or twenty-eight, or forty, or even seventy? How does a gay man look at midlife—as opposed to his straight counterparts—and what does he think about as retirement nears and the fabulous pace of gay life starts to slow down? Or does it ever *have* to slow down? There are a lot of myths out there about the young, the middle-aged, and the elderly; which ones are true and which ones just don't hold water? Those are just some of the questions I've looked into and I hope you'll find I've presented you with some intriguing snapshots of the prevailing attitudes about age and aging that we hold as we grow from teens to seniors. We'll also see how some of those attitudes evolve with changing times and our ever-changing selves.

Admittedly it's a tall order, and I'll ask you in advance to forgive the fact that many of the subjects addressed here will overlap more than multiple ripples on a still pond. A topic broached in one chapter is frequently looked at again later on, from a different point of view, or simply for more emphasis. That's not me being careless; that simply reflects the somewhat fractured and often contradictory or controversial viewpoints that so many of us have. Whatever age group you find yourself in, you'll likely find yourself alternately fascinated and infuriated by what you read in the pages ahead. The hundreds of people I talked with, and the thousands more who responded to my poll questions and surveys, had a lot to say on all of the topics previously mentioned, and other topics as well. Though I have sometimes changed or omitted names and geographic locations out of respect for privacy or anonymity, all of the opinions expressed herein come from real people and I present them to you as truthfully as possible.

"We do not grow absolutely, chronologically," wrote Anaïs Nin. "We grow sometimes in one dimension, and not in another, unevenly. We grow partially. We are relative. We are mature in one realm, childish in another." I found mighty proof of those assertions in all the material I gathered in the two years spent putting this book together; sometimes I found myself moved to tears by the stories my subjects related to me about their lives and experiences . . . just as often I found myself laughing at the lovable lunatics gay men can be when it comes to growing older. When all's been said and done here, I hope you'll find I did their stories justice.

Chapter 1

"Nothing in Common"

When it comes to age we're all in the same boat, only some of us have been aboard a little longer.

Leo Probst

Jeff looks both ways before he crosses the street, but it's not an on-coming car or bus he's worried about avoiding. He's checking to make sure anyone who might know him isn't around to see him duck down the alley toward the Fraternity House—or Frat House as it's commonly called—one of the handful of gay bars that populate DC's Dupont Circle neighborhood. On this cool autumn night in 1977, the Circle is already gaining a reputation as a "gay mecca," and most likely any of his straight friends or co-workers—none of whom even suspect he might be gay—are miles away.

Still, it never hurts to be sure, right?

Safe inside the club, Jeff mixes and mingles with a hundred or so other gay men spanning a range of ages; he can see kids younger than he is, and some gray-haired gents laughing loudly together at one end of the bar. Everyone is bopping to a pounding disco beat—Donna Summer, the Village People, ABBA—and the smell of cigarette smoke is pungent in the air, along with the occasional whiff of poppers drifting over from the dark shadows of the loft where the braver, bawdier souls venture. Out here in the brighter lights a few guys approach him as the evening winds on, and some offer their names in conversation. He wonders vaguely how many of those are real, how many fictitious, since he's been known to use a "bar name" himself on occasion. This is Washington, after all. Being gay in this strange new era of freedom makes you feel like a kid in a candy store—the sweets are there for the choosing—but if word gets out it can still get you fired, passed over for promotion, or knocked out of the next election.

At last one promising fellow passes by, turns, and makes his move. He's wearing hip-hugging designer jeans and a close-fitting satin shirt, a gold chain around his neck, with golden blond hair feathered and parted in the middle. He even has a ring in his right ear. Very sexy. Clearly he's someone Jeff is interested in more than just trading names with. They have a few beers together, making small talk and flirting. Jeff cheerfully declines his offer to do some lines of coke or smoke a joint in the bathroom; he's not into drugs, but he's not a narc or anything. Whatever floats your boat. Eventually, Jeff suggests a joint exit, explaining how his apartment is just a quick taxi ride away. The pair hardly even notice the knowing sneer on the cabby's face when he drops them off; they're too eager to get upstairs for some mixing and mingling of their own.

Afterward, Jeff's new "friend" excuses himself quickly, mumbling something about having to work early. He throws on his clothes and leaves without leaving a phone number. *Just as well,* Jeff thinks as the door closes. *He's probably married or a complete closet case.* It's not as if Jeff is looking for anything like a steady boyfriend, anyway; though his own closet door may be cracked open a bit, a "significant other" would make his life way too fucking complicated right now. He figures there's always time to settle down later; he got exactly what he was looking for tonight, no more, and no less.

There's far too many fish in this pond, he thinks, smiling. And there's *always* tomorrow.

Ryan looks both ways before he crosses the street, but it's not an oncoming car or bus he's worried about. He's looking for the friend who's supposed to meet him at Badlands, the Circle's largest dance club. He's not sure if he'll recognize the guy right away; though they met on the Internet weeks ago, so far he's only seen a handful of pics attached to e-mails and instant messages.

Someone taps him on the shoulder as he passes the alley that leads down to the club called Omega—Ryan has no idea it used to be called the Frat House, and it's all old men in there, anyway—and he turns to see a group of women who work with him downtown; done with dinner, they're killing time before a movie, and they're glad they ran into him so they could wish him good luck again on his date. Ryan has never had any trouble talking about his love life at work. In fact, it's never occurred to him *not* to talk about it; his co-workers know Ryan's been trying to meet this guy for weeks, and that the two have been having trouble getting their hectic schedules to gel. "Ah, well," Ryan tells them. "That's gay life in the summer of 2002."

Inside the club Ryan makes his way through a crowd of a couple hundred or so other gay men, mostly twenty-somethings, with few over thirty and virtually none over forty. The smell of cigarette smoke is pungent in the air, and it nearly makes him gag. *If only they'd pass antismoking laws like the ones in Los Angeles,* he thinks. He heads for the back room where the videos play—Britney Spears, 'NSYNC, J.Lo—since the lights are brighter back there, the music not quite so deafening as it is by the dance floor. Here and there he sees people he knows, a few that he's even dated. This is Washington, after all, a small town when it comes to being gay; everyone seems to have known or slept with everyone else (no wonder they have baskets of condoms all over the place).

Finally, he spots his Internet friend ordering a Coke from the bar. He's wearing baggy cargo pants and an Abercrombie and Fitch T-shirt, a colorful shell necklace, with dark hair just a bit longer than buzzed. He's even got two small rings in each ear. Very sexy. They introduce themselves; Ryan is relieved to find he's just as young and cute as his pictures were, and not just another aging bar boy lying to try to get in his pants (that's happened to him more than once). They start chatting, each wondering how the easy affability they'd already found online and the telephone will translate into the "real" world.

So far, so good, Ryan thinks as his date excuses himself to hit the bathroom, and he focuses on the video screens. The third successive boy-band video makes him restless, and he realizes he needs to take a leak himself; he makes his way to the bathroom, where he discovers his new friend in a crowded stall, taking a bump of something or other with three other guys. Nonplussed, his date offers him some; neither he nor Ryan is old enough to drink yet—the magic marker Xs on their hands testify to that—and you have to get your jollies somehow, right? Ryan just shakes his head, turns, and walks out, wondering how that little detail never came up in previous conversations.

Just as well I find out now, he thinks to himself sadly. Dating a druggie just makes life too fucking complicated. *All I want is a normal boyfriend. Is that too much to ask?* He's heading out of the club when he spots a good-looking guy cruising him. Ryan keeps walking, but he shoots the guy a smile, regardless.

Plenty of fish in the sea, he reminds himself hopefully. There's *always* tomorrow.

Two tales from the same city, stories taking place on virtually the same patch of ground yet separated by a quarter century in time; maybe you see yourself or someone you know in there. Then again, maybe not. I don't claim the details will ring true for everyone. There were plenty of young gay men who were totally and comfortably out in 1977, for one example, just as there are plenty of young men today who are not out at all. And lots of people weren't so casual about sex, or drug use, in the mid-1970s, just as one might argue that far too many *are* casual about both today. (We could also quibble about the merits of the fashion choices mentioned above, but that's probably a topic for another book.) Still I've cobbled them together, using pieces of anecdotes sent to me over the past two years by hundreds of gay men of all ages, and I hope you'll forgive me the device. I simply wanted to allow "Jeff" and "Ryan"—each about twenty years old on the nights in question—to coexist for a moment, the better to see some of the differences between them as they progress through one of the major formative eras of their lives.

There's a line from an old Billy Joel tune, "We are only what our situations hand us." Like any good lyric, it crystallizes a too often ignored truth, that we are all products of our times and circumstances. As I review the comments that younger and older gay men make about each other, it's clear in many cases that neither group seems to know—or care—where the other is coming from, much less where they've been or where they're going. But that doesn't stop them from talking about each other. Not by a long shot.

"Older guys? Forget it," says Jamey, a twenty-four-year-old music store manager in Detroit. "I get bored out of my skull if one of them walks up to me and tries to start a conversation, even if he isn't hitting on me, which he probably is."

"I just can't imagine what it would be like not to be able to be yourself at work, at home, wherever," says Jason, a twenty-four-year-old graduate student in Boston. "I think it's sad that there was a time when people felt like they had to be in the closet, but I can't say that experience is really relevant to me today. We have rights now. All those old people's stories are pretty boring and useless."

"I hear about these guys who went cruising for sex all the time back in the 1970s, like it was some kind of big party," says Joey, a twenty-one-year-old student in Michigan. "They're the ones who all got AIDS and died. I think a lot of older guys are still like that, and they're the ones who make it tougher for me to come out, because so many people still think gay equals AIDS now." Joey says he never goes out to gay clubs because he hates it when "all the old guys hit on me." Generally he only meets other gay people on the Internet. "It just seems to be safer than going out and meeting some random stranger in a bar. At least I talk to them for awhile first."

Attitudes and statements like those make a lot of older gay men see red. "These kids today just piss me off," says Thom, a forty-year-old painter in northern California. "And I know I sound just like my dad when I say that, but it's true. They would be nowhere without the people who came before them, people who looked at going out to a gay club like it was just as much a political statement as it was about having fun. I think it was people like me, and people a lot older than me, who made it easier for them to come out. They have a great way of showing their gratitude. And by the way . . . aren't younger people getting HIV more these days than any other group? Great job, kids!"

"Young people today seem to whine a lot more than we ever did," contends Sam, a thirty-seven-year-old salesman in upstate New York. "Yet they have so many things going for them, so much more than we did when we were all growing up alone and isolated. When I was fourteen I wasn't even sure if there was anyone else in the world who felt the same way I did. Kids today can see young gay characters on television and in the movies, and they can talk to other gay people on their computers. They start off so much farther ahead than we did, but for some reason they don't seem to do much better when it comes to relationships or making some kind of contribution to society. To put it bluntly, I think they're kind of fucking up a golden opportunity. I just don't have time for them."

"All these younger guys, the twenty- to twenty-five-year-old group, think older guys like me just want to get them all into bed," says Rick, a forty-five-year-old software consultant in Mansfield, Ohio. "Please! What an utter waste of time would that be? They could never keep up, and good lord, what the hell would we even talk about?"

Now it's hardly a newsflash to tell you that there's a time-honored human tradition of conflict between generations, whether they're gay or straight. Such behavior isn't even confined to humans. Just watch Animal Planet some time; there's always a young wolf aiming to knock off the leader of the pack, or a vicious predator lurking in the bushes, looking to make a meal out of something young and tasty. But while the younger generation of gay men usually forgoes the actual use of fangs and claws when they take over the joint, a lot of older gay men still feel bloodied by the experience; similarly, countless young and inexperienced gay men *have* been used or abused by someone a lot older and craftier than they.

Don't get me wrong. There are numerous, undeniable cases where a younger man has given "new life" to an older man he loved or be-friended, and instances where an older man has positively influenced a younger man through a loving relationship or simple mentoring. Those stories are part of the fabric of this book as well. Yet heart-warming and inspiring as they are, I can't say they characterize the sentiments of a majority of the folks I've talked with. At best, the younger and older within the gay community are frequently living al-most wholly separate lives; and when they do mix, they often find themselves casting wary eyes on each other, forever unsure and untrusting of the other's intentions.

So it might well be with Ryan, and with Jeff, who's pushing forty-five now and only rarely hits the clubs anymore. They might pass on the street these days and never know they once walked the same side-walks, each looking for whatever might make him feel happy or ful-filled. They may trade a glance or have a conversation by happen-stance, but more likely they'd simply go their separate ways.

After all, they have nothing in common, right?

GENERATIONS

The noted British essayist Samuel Johnson once noted that when a man knows he's going to be hanged, it "concentrates his mind wonderfully." Although I'm not sure turning forty is tantamount to a public execution, passing that milestone a few years back *did* make it a lot easier for me to get in the proper mind-set for this book; I finally had a "perspective" of my own from which to tackle this topic, and many others. But it's a dangerous business to ever trust our own perspectives solely. Not long after the little unpleasantness on my computer that helped inspire this project, it would have been easy for me to become convinced that ageism was rampant everywhere, not just in cyberspace. When I moved back to the Washington area in the mid-1990s, I started venturing out to the same bars and clubs where I misspent much of my youth, and there was clearly something different in the air.

For the record, I started coming out to friends in 1977, and went to my first gay bar in 1978 (the Frat House, now Omega). It wasn't long before I was hanging out at the larger discos and dance clubs around town, the late-and-often-lamented Lost & Found, the sainted Tracks, and the still-alive-and-kicking Badlands, now called Apex. Maybe it's just my mind's eye looking back through the rose-colored glasses of memory, but it does seem that such places were once giant melting pots where guys of all ages mixed and mingled. God knows there have always been various cliques in almost any bar, but in those halcyon days the groups seemed more formed by interests or inclinations than by age alone. My friends and I always moved among them with ease, able to have a good time talking to anyone, be they eighteen, forty-eight, or eighty. I'm not saying we necessarily hooked up with them; I'm not saying we didn't, either, but I can recall many a night when we'd talk with older gentlemen holding court in their comfy little corner of the bar. They were our elder statesmen and we thought we might learn something.

By the time I hit my thirties and came back home, it felt like something had shifted somewhere. I could see lines forming and barriers going up, behind which one could find small cadres of younger guys who, at least to all outward appearances, were not so anxious to mix with anyone else, especially not with guys much older than themselves. Many, in fact, seemed quite hostile when it came to being approached by men getting on in years (if any could actually be found on the premises, that is).

Maybe we were more like a "happy few" back then, and since it felt like we all had to band together for survival, a little sage advice was just what we needed. Or perhaps I'm remembering it all wrong. The mind is funny that way. For every "older gentleman" sitting there at the bar, there may well have been a dozen more hiding in the shadows, watching the parade go by but never interacting with anyone younger for fear of rejection. And who knows how many more never turned out at all, for the very same reason? Now that I am getting a bit older myself, it is impossible to be sure what the years might have done to my perceptions of the past, and how they might be coloring my views of the present.

As I started thinking about the topics this book might address, I became terribly curious, first to see if other gay men my age and older remembered things the way I did, then to find out how they see the world today; I also wanted to get inside those walls where the youngsters play, to get their impressions and talk about their experiences. And if I was really going to do this project justice, I had to do all that in as broad a manner as possible, to get in touch with those who might be just hitting puberty in Poughkeepsie, doing the circuit in South Beach, or retiring outside Reno.

It's sort of ironic, in a way, that I found the best strategy was to go back to where this all began, back to that offending little computer in my bedroom. Along with my then-partner Andy, a brilliant young Web designer, I created a Web site—reelingyears.com—where visitors could register their ages, take a poll that asked all sorts of age-related questions, then, if they wished, answer a much lengthier survey. I promoted the site on several other Web sites, handed out literature at various events, and steered folks to the site online while visiting chat rooms on AOL, Gay.com, PlanetOut, and various other areas on the Web that cater to gay men of all ages. The site was active for almost a year, and during that time about 2,000 people took the poll and more than 250 people filled out the survey. I also took in surveys and polls from people I met in the course of my travels. (A number of them actually came back to me through snail mail, some from folks I'd never met who'd seen my questions, made copies, then filled in their answers.) I interviewed dozens more in person or online when it became clear they had a valuable perspective or two of their own to share. Those polls, survey responses, and interviews are largely what make up this book.

Before we get much further, let me offer a few disclaimers. I'm not a professional pollster by a long shot, and I'm sure there are those who will wonder how accurate the numbers really are or what margin of error there might be. I would be the last to claim that the polls are, by any definition of the word, "scientific." But checking the results as they came in week after week, I noticed that, after some minor fluctuations at first, the results for each question stabilized and the percentages remained pretty much the same, no matter how many fresh numbers came in. I'll share that data with you from time to time as we go along here; you can find the entire age poll in Chapter 8. Please feel free to draw your own conclusions.

You'll also see that I make a lot of references to "younger" and "older" men, and since such terms are obviously relative, you may at times wonder exactly what I mean. Any division according to age is totally arbitrary, but we have to set the bar somewhere. For my purposes here, we can consider anyone from the age of forty and up to be older, anyone age twenty-nine and below as younger, with the men in the thirty- to thirty-nine-year-old group somewhere in between, leaning one way or the other based on their particular individual experiences or inclinations. Of course there are lots of folks who aren't going to fit within even those broad parameters; the kid who is "seventeen going on thirty"—which is what my friends used to call me, back in the day—or the mid-forties phenom who still has that "young thing" going on in his eyes, not to mention stone-hard abs and a minimum of gray hair (I met plenty in each group, and they often wondered what the big fuss was about, since age means virtually nothing to them). But I found that most men interviewed and surveyed *did* have the most in common with others within their age groups as described.

There is something else that may trouble some readers, and that is my frequent use of bars, nightclubs, and the Internet throughout this book as the major nexuses of the gay community. It would be idiotic to claim that those are the *only* places where gay people cross paths. As we all know, gay men come together everywhere: sports leagues and social events, coffee shops, book, clothing, or record stores, gyms, fast-food restaurants, theaters, business conventions, you name it, we're there (and yes, they actually meet at church, too). But when we're talking about sheer numbers, I don't think one can argue *too* strongly against the idea that more gay men will gather at bars and nightclubs on any given weekend night than they will anywhere else; unnumbered thousands are online at any hour, on any day or night.

That's where the generations meet en masse. And that's where they frequently butt heads the most, thanks in large part to the vast differences in their situations, and an often appalling lack of under-standing.

THAT WAS THEN, THIS IS NOW

When you really look at the things that younger and older men say about one another, or even to one another, it seems they do come from different worlds, speaking in two different tongues, and no one has a translator handy. Except for the passion in their words, it's not all that surprising.

A few summers ago while checking my e-mail I found one of those "forwards" that people like to send. You know the type; usually it's a chain letter, phony virus warning, or a really lame joke. This one was different. It was called "Check Your Age," and it was a list reportedly put together each year by the administration of a college, intended for distribution to the faculty and staff so they'd realize the mind-set of the incoming class of freshmen, in this case, kids who were born in the early 1980s. Reading it over, I must say it gives those of us over forty a little something to think about.

I'll share some of the highlights with you. "The expression 'You sound like a broken record' means nothing to them, since they have never owned a record player; vinyl albums predate them. They proba-bly haven't even heard of 8-track tapes, and the CD was introduced when they were in diapers . . . which, by the way, have never been made of cloth, as far as they're concerned. They can't fathom a time before everyone had a cell phone, computer, VCR, and there was an ATM on every other street corner.

"They never took a swim and thought about *Jaws*. The Vietnam War might just as well be World War II. They can't imagine what hard contact lenses are. They do not know 'who shot J.R.' (they have no idea who J.R. was or why they should care very much that he was shot). The *Titanic* was found? They thought we always knew where it was. McDonald's meals never came in Styrofoam containers. Michael Jackson has always been white, not to mention rather odd and creepy. Kansas, Chicago, Boston, Alabama, and America are *places,* not bands. And there has *always* been an MTV."

There was a lot more, but I think you get the idea. It's just so damn odd the way time seems to creep by in fits and starts; only in retrospect does its passage look like warp speed. Nowhere is that better reflected than in the blank stare of a teen or twenty-something when we make reference to what was once a common phrase or popularly known phenomenon. I can say, "I've fallen and I can't get up!" in a room of my contemporaries and they'll snicker, remembering that poor old woman in the cheesy safety alarm commercial; the same line falls with a silent and questioning thud among a younger crowd. They don't know what the hell I'm talking about.

I also remember being on the other side of the divide. I had an older friend who used to subject his party guests to semiannual viewings of *The Boys in the Band,* an early 1970s film filled with self-loathing characters, emotional desolation, New Yorkers, and really, really bitchy queens. While I did appreciate it for what it was, sort of a time capsule or snapshot of the way things used to be, I can't say the movie had much relevance at all to what the gay people *I* knew were like (none that I cared to hang out with, at any rate). The younger party guests—those of us born after 1960—would always roll our eyes and drift away from the television. Yet my fifty-something friend and his contemporaries stayed glued to the screen through multiple viewings, regarding the film as a veritable gay cultural touchstone, one that still had some kind of currency.

In the October 2001 issue of *OUT* magazine, writer Steve Weinstein addressed this growing "gay generation gap," what he and many others see as the ever-expanding lack of a common ground between the Stonewallers such as my older friend and gay men under the age of thirty-five. Weinstein called movies such as *The Boys in the Band, Auntie Mame,* and *All About Eve* part of a "matrix of received cultural references," which, along with admiration for such classic gay icons as Judy Garland, Bette Davis, and Joan Crawford, is slowly becoming a thing of the past.

> It was all part of Gay 101. Before Stonewall, secret codes—like touching your nose with your index finger, a red tie, or a nosegay in a lapel, even the locations of bars—were part of a lore passed down to newcomers. In today's brave new gay world, camp is being rejected as a vestige of outdated, closeted, ghetto-style mentality. Instead of Judy, we have Madonna; for *The Boys in the Band*, there's *Queer As Folk*, today's Maria Callas is *Cher*. (Weinstein, 2001, p. 91)

It's inevitable that musical and cultural tastes will change and evolve as time goes by, and I don't think anyone wants to take the world back to those golden days of yesteryear, where a same-sex orientation was considered so shameful that secret codes were an absolute necessity. But it's also a shame when such seminal parts of our collective history go unremembered, disregarded, and worse, disrespected . . . along with those who came of age in those difficult times.

"Everything has changed so much . . . the world I grew up in is lost in time," says Joe, a seventy-year-old retiree living in Oklahoma. "I was talking to a young man a few years ago, telling him how I had to stay hidden. He had no conception of what it was like in the 1940s and 1950s. All he could say was, 'I could never stay closeted.' And yet, in his current occupation, he wouldn't have survived two days as an out gay man. It was disappointing that he could not and would never understand." A member of what is often called the "Greatest Generation" of Americans—those who weathered the Depression, then fought and won World War II—Joe says the differences between then and now are staggering. "It's like living on a different planet." I've heard much the same kind of thing from dozens of other older gay men, many of them not nearly as old as Joe. "We all live in the 'now,' and we talk about 'then,'" says one such middle-aged fellow. "Some of us have a lot more 'then' to talk about. Would it kill these kids to listen?" I'm certainly a little embarrassed now, remembering my reaction to my older friend's taste in films. (Maybe at some point in the future I'll be boring *my* younger friends with repeated viewings of my own personal classics, like *Doing Time on Maple Drive* or *The Broken Hearts Club.*)

In his article, Weinstein laments that "if there are fewer and fewer common touchstones, what is there to talk about over cocktails?" (p. 91). But I'm beginning to wonder if the gap isn't widening, well outside the realms of culture, references, and language shared by the over-fifty set, the kind of stuff that can make a twenty-something draw a blank; it's not just the passing of "lore" or history we're talking about, but nearly any kind of social contact.

"NO OLDIES, PLEASE"

While researching *Sissyphobia,* I scoured personal ads from gay newspapers and magazines from across the country, looking for those ads that disparaged anyone with effeminate characteristics, and basically invited them to stay away. I also searched the online profiles of hundreds of gay men, using keywords such as "homo," "femme," "fag," and "swishy." Both exercises were part of my effort to justify the premise of that book, the idea that there's this seething dislike within the gay community for anyone that behaves in an effeminate or flamboyant manner.

Not long ago I went back to those same ads and profiles, and guess what? Turns out that "sissyphobia" is just one of an unholy trinity of prejudices abroad in the land. It's not just "No femmes need apply." It's also "No fats" and "No oldies, please." The ageist faction actually turned out to be nearly as high as the antisissy portion; while 40 percent of all the ads and online profiles were highly critical of effeminate men (the percentage got a lot bigger if I threw in the code words of men searching for a "frat boy" or "military man"), as much as a third indicated a serious negativity for older men as well, with about a third more expressing highly positive sentiments for anyone who might be "young," "younger," "youthful," or "a little brother type," or "a cute twink."

In *Sissyphobia,* the personal ad survey wasn't anything that claimed to be a scientific, controlled survey. But it was pretty amazing how the antifemme percentages held up no matter how many new ads I threw in the mix; much the same happened when I started looking for ads that skewed ageist, or, if you will, "youth positive." Like this ad, from someone who calls himself "Gay, Single, and Young," where the man in question says he wants to avoid "anyone who looks older than me, and I look really young." Or the "Fit Gym Stud" who says, "you better be able to keep up with me, so if you're old and out of shape, keep looking." And another from "Str8 Acting Bottom," who maintains he needs "a hot stud who's not fat, not old, and not a flamer" (at least he manages to offend everyone equally).

Signing onto the Internet to scan profiles on AOL, PlanetOut, or Gay.com was equally telling. Random searches turned up scores of profiles that said, "no one over twenty-five, please," "no one over thirty," or "my age only!!" with the vehemence increasing with the youth of the member. I'm not going to give the screen names, but here's a sampling: a thirty-something man from Texas who said, "if you're gay and gray, stay away!"; a college student in Minnesota that advised, "anyone that's not my age, you're not my type"; and another college student from Maine who said, "no old people, and if you have to ask, you're too old." I also logged into various chat rooms over the course of a few weeks, using faux profiles variously designed to make me appear young on some nights, older on others, and age-neutral the rest of the time. You can probably guess what happened. I was contacted on my "young" nights about three times as often as I was when I was "older"; on my age-neutral nights I was often asked first—say this with me now—"How old?"

I should point out here that I did come across numerous ads and profiles that totally bucked this trend, dozens that sang the praises of "mature" men, men with "some miles" on them, ads and profiles of younger men seriously looking "for some gray-haired wisdom," or the kind of companionship "that only an older guy knows how to give." I contacted several of those men and we'll hear from them a bit later on. For now, suffice to say that, in most cases, a generous helping of years wasn't exactly a preferred menu item.

"NO KIDS ALLOWED"

Although the vast majority of ads and profiles that mentioned any kind of age preference came down decidedly in favor of youth, I found ample evidence that it's not just young people, or people looking for young people, who build walls with age-negative signs plastered on them. Though not nearly as prevalent, there were a significant number of ads placed by older men that slammed the younger set. An ad placed by someone billed as "Not a Babysitter" sets his sights on anyone "thirty-plus" and advises anyone younger than that "to come back when you grow up." Another calls himself "No Kids Allowed" and says, "if you're one of those little drugged out twinkie types I don't have time for your drama."

Back online I found several more like that. A forty-something man in the New York area asks anyone "who didn't live through disco the first time" to go somewhere else, and explains, "I'm a man, not your Daddy." Another "older gent" in San Francisco tells folks scanning his profile to "move along" if they're "wet behind the ears," and, likewise critical of the dad/son dynamic, uses the following line for his quote: "Don't let your son go down on me." And one Midwestern fellow goes to great lengths to criticize anyone who uses the word "boy" in his screen name or description: "I want a man, not a boy, and if you're so desperate to be a boy that you have to call yourself that, *go away!*"

"US" VERSUS "THEM"

Useful as they are in illustrating the attitudes that many younger and older gay men have for each other, ads and profiles only go so far; to really get inside these opinions requires a different methodology.

"I get annoyed when my friends and I want to hit the club on a Friday or Saturday night, and we walk in and find anyone in there that's old," says Eddie, a twenty-one-year-old waiter in Atlanta. I ask him to define "old" and he tells me "anyone that's over thirty or looks like they're that old." Eddie goes on to say older gay men "just drag the place down, like they're sucking all the air out of the room." Another young man, twenty-four-year-old Jason from Miami, says he wonders why "older guys even go out to clubs at all, at least clubs where young guys go. You don't see me going back to high school to hang out. Give it up already."

Those comments came from live interviews, but they strongly resembled the responses I got from survey questions that asked younger gay men what they thought of the older gay men they encountered. "I really hate it when some old guy sends me a message when
I'm online," says Henry in his survey. He's a twenty-three-year-old
student in California. "They should stick to people their own age and
leave me the fuck alone."

As we've already seen, I found similar sentiments at work among
many older gay men, aimed at the younger men they run into. Mark is
a forty-year-old attorney in San Francisco. "If my friends and I are
dining out, or walking into a club, and the crowd skews on the younger side, we just go somewhere else," he says. "It's not as if we fear
rejection or anything, since we all prefer 'real' men to the twinkie
types. We just don't like the atmosphere that kids bring in with them,
all that attitude, arrogance, 'Look at me, I'm a young god,' that sort of
thing. I didn't put up with that crap when I was young and I'm certainly not going to put up with it now."

Jim, a fifty-one-year-old home inspector in Virginia, uses the same
language to describe the young people he now sees hanging out at the
very places he came of age. "It's all about arrogance and attitude. . . .
It's kind of sad because those bars and nightclubs used to feel like
home to me. Thank God I have other interests."

Again, I'm not here to make the claim that these are universally
shared concepts. I've talked with plenty of younger and older men
who seemed dumbstruck by the comments of their peers, by the
strong thread of resentment, even hostility, in their words. Like me,
they wonder where those feelings come from. As I found, there's no
shortage of theories as to what causes such discord, what it is that cre-
ates that "us" and "them" mentality. "Why should gay kids be any different from straight kids when it comes to adults?" asks Chris, a
thirty-three-year-old designer in New Orleans. "It's just the same
things that make any young person want to get away and be on his
own. The only difference is that gay people of all ages hang out at the
same places." Rodney, a thirty-five-year-old office worker in Cincinnati,
agrees. "I can't say I'm happy about the fact that I get ignored now in
clubs where I used to be popular, but that's just life, the nature of
things. We live in a society that worships youth, and young people
buy into it, so if they think you're over the hill, they don't mind telling

you. It'd be nice if they weren't such assholes about it, though." And Chet, a fifty-three-year-old professor in New Jersey, reminds me about the movies of the 1950s and 1960s, the first films that talked about "juvenile delinquents" and "rebels without a cause," films that had the curious effect of glorifying youth and yet somehow "being condescending" at the same time. "And let's not forget that old song that asks, 'Why can't they be like we were, perfect in every way?' ["Kids" from *Bye Bye Birdie*]. I am afraid 'twas ever thus, this lack of understanding between the old and the young."

In his groundbreaking book *Gay and Gray: The Older Homosexual Man* (1982), Raymond Berger talks about some of the "intergenerational attitudes" that often create barriers to any kind of meaningful dialogue. "Age segregation in the gay community often prevents older and younger gay men from checking out their possibly erroneous views of each other" (p. 42). Berger cites a number of men who never even try to make contact with those much younger than themselves, sadly confident that younger men will "react negatively to older gays" (p. 43). He suggests many older men actually feel guilty even contemplating contact with younger men, perhaps because they've absorbed the social message that once you're past a certain age, any kind of contact with someone much younger is somehow unseemly. Certainly, plenty of young men have bought into that idea, too. But Berger also unearthed a sentiment I ran into several times in my own research, an idea held by many older men, that younger men are unworthy of much attention, that they are "attractive but boring company." He talks of a commonly expressed thought that "a twenty year old hasn't been anywhere or done anything. What would we talk about?" (p. 43).

Some younger folks have their own ideas, of course. Marc, a twenty-one-year-old college student in Seattle, says he has a "few gay friends in their thirties. These are decent, quality guys. Most older guys are just trying to figure out a way to get a young guy in the sack, but of course they don't admit it." Brian, an eighteen-year-old U.S. Navy sailor from San Francisco, says as far as he's concerned, "older men come off as whorish, bitter old queens," which is why he likes to keep to people his own age, "because we all think alike." Patrick, a twenty-year-old college student in New York, says that "the older a guy gets, the more out of touch he is. . . . I don't know why thirty-, forty-, and fifty-year-old people want anything to do with a twenty-year-old, and I don't why they're surprised that I want nothing to do with them."

Some find the tension between the two groups mildly humorous. "It's only natural that young gay men ignore older gay men," says Marc Acito, a syndicated columnist who writes for a number of gay papers nationwide. "Think about it. When you were in your twenties, did you want to hang out with people your parents' age? Don't lie, of course you didn't. But why should aging baby boomers, a generation which actually survived the 1970s, care about the opinions of a generation stupid enough to revive them? Even if they insist on wearing clothes from The Decade That Taste Forgot, children should still only be seen and not heard. . . . Young gay guys need to stop calling older men trolls and gnomes as if gay life were some kind of fairy tale, but only if older men stop calling young men chicken or twinkies, like they're some kind of snack."

SEPARATE WAYS

Some of you reading this may be moved to ask what the big deal is. What's so wrong about people of different ages and experiences choosing to keep company with others like themselves? As Chet noted earlier, isn't that the way it's always been, and always will be?

"I think you're right when you say that gay people were more of a 'family' twenty or twenty-five years ago," says Kevin, a forty-three-year-old lawyer in northern Virginia. "There's so many more gay people out now, and they come out younger; they don't need to be as accepting as we perhaps had to be. It still depresses me all the same because I think it means our community is going to become ever more fractured and splintered, and there won't be anyone looking out for the older gay guys."

In his *OUT* magazine article (2001), Steve Weinstein writes of his fear that we'll lose our "institutional memory" as a community if our self-imposed segregations continue. "You don't study gay rights in high school, and you don't learn how to be gay in college. Such things are passed down, one generation to the next, and if the generations aren't mixing, then everything we had will be lost" (p. 109). Some think that any community is in constant need of fresh ideas and influences lest it grow stagnant. "Young people have a lot to bring to the table," says Jarrod, a nineteen-year-old college student in California. "But it's not going to do anyone any good if there's no one else sitting there. I wish older people would treat us with more respect, like we might have an idea or two in our heads. I'm ashamed when I see the way people my age treat older guys. We're going to be older one day, too."

As Jarrod's peers meet middle age, folks in my age group will be at or near retirement. Some experts warn that the widening generation gap, and the coarsening of opinions such as the ones you've seen here, could well have their greatest impact on those soon-to-be-senior gays. "They looked down on us when they were twenty and we were forty," says Charles, a forty-five-year-old professor in Illinois. "Are they going to wake up and treat us better when they're forty and we're sixty? I think we'll still be something they're afraid of. Maybe more so, because we'll remind them of what's waiting down the road for them."

Today's seniors already know what a tough road that can be. Mike, a sixty-five-year-old retiree in North Carolina, says in his experience "the older gay man is frowned upon and snubbed by younger guys. They'll be here someday, God willing, and I hope they're not treated the way they treat us. We need more acceptance."

Dean, a forty-five-year-old writer in Washington, DC, says he feels like a lot of kids today are setting themselves up for payback later on; he shares this "cautionary tale of karma," one he's hoping others might take to heart. "When I was just coming out twenty-five years ago I had this friend, Mikey, who was about five years older. He was so beautiful, charming, and witty, and we all used to laugh at the creative—but very cruel—way that he would shoot down anyone that hit on him if he felt they weren't young or attractive enough to suit him. He was the first guy I ever knew who used the words 'troll' and 'old' together like they were one word. Well, guess what? Mikey is bald, fat, and I have to say this, really unattractive now, especially in the way he acts. Quite bitter and jaded, and on those rare nights he goes out to a club, he's convinced that all the young guys are laughing at him and calling him an 'old troll.' I don't know if they are or if they aren't, but isn't it curious, and rather sad, that he's so certain?"

Chapter 2

The Myths of Time

We don't see things as they are, we see them as we are.

Anaïs Nin

"All young people today are looking for is their next trick, or their next drink, or drug, or whatever it is they do," says Allen, a fifty-year-old home restorer in Maine. "They'll wise up when they get older. *If* they get older."

"I think all old men want is a boy toy, which I am not," says Seb, a twenty-one-year-old college student in Seattle, who says he gets "disgusted" if anyone in the fifty-year-old age range tries to approach him. Still, he thinks they might have something useful to offer him. "I see how bitter and jaded older guys are, and I want to know how they got to be like that, so one day I won't."

Every young guy is a sexed- or drugged-out twinkie? Ask older guys if they agree and many say yes. Every older man is a chicken hawk or a bitter old queen? Lots of younger men will agree with those suppositions, and rather whole-heartedly, but ask the members of one group if they ever really spend a lot of time with the other. Ask them where they got those ideas. Something interesting emerges.

As Seb tells it, "Ninety-five percent of my gay friends are within five years of me. I don't meet older men because they're probably looking for something shallow." Allen explains that he "doesn't really know anyone gay who's under thirty, not firsthand at any rate, but I hear the stories."

Ah yes, the stories. We all hear them from time to time. Older men pawing at unwilling kids young enough to be their sons, or sulking at home and hating the world. Promiscuous young men partying down till dawn, not even knowing or caring who they're sleeping with, or even trying to be safe about it. Do such things happen? Of course they do. Does that paint an accurate picture of *all* younger and older gay men? Of course it doesn't. Yet as we've already seen in the previous chapter, the ideas and images persist, most often inside the minds of gay men who'll readily admit they're pretty much strangers to each other.

That's why I call such stories or widespread ideas "myths." Not myths in the classic sense, like some guy in a toga hurling thunderbolts at some other dude in a chariot, or even in the "urban legend" sense, like that story about the rat that got deep-fried at KFC and served up with a side of coleslaw and barbecued beans. (You mean that *didn't* happen?) I'm talking more here about the attitudes and preconceptions, based on individual facts and occurrences, that are then applied to a whole group of people so that everyone within that group is tarred with the same brush. Maybe it's not surprising, considering human nature, that many of us still think this way; it's such a timesaver to be able to dismiss an entire group. Taking people as individuals . . . well, that takes some work and some thought. Straight folks prejudge gay people all the time, just as men judge women, and butch gay guys judge the femme boys. Why would older and younger gay men be any different, even if when it comes to the battle of "us" and "them" none of us has much personal knowledge from which to speak?

As I surveyed and interviewed folks over the past year and a half, I saw several age-related myths that kept bubbling to the surface, claims and counterclaims that could bear some examination. I'm sure there are a lot more myths out there floating around than the mere handful I propose, but these seemed to be as good a place as any to start. Some of them aren't necessarily harmful, or at least, not as harmful as others. Many of them are downright dangerous, in that they perpetuate such negative concepts as to cut off any possibility of true communication.

MYTH ONE: "KIDS THESE DAYS . . ."

By far the most common statement I heard from older gay men was that gay kids have it much easier these days, in their coming out, in the way they're treated at school, etc. And who can blame older men for thinking that way? Just listen to their stories.

Grant, a sixty-year-old retiree living in Miami, says he knew he was "different, but not what the difference was" when he was just twelve or thirteen. "Once I got into high school, then college, I knew, but I couldn't do anything about it, not in those days, and not where I lived. I knew what happened to kids people thought were 'queer.'" Following the family tradition, Grant got married, settled down, had kids, later grandkids, all the while hiding the desires he felt for other men. He came out at fifty. "I guess it's better late than never, but I feel like I wasted most of my life."

Tony is a forty-four-year-old human resources recruiter in Florida who was kicked out of his home at sixteen after a raging fight with his parents when they found out he was gay. "My dad hit me for the first and only time in my life, and my mom was screaming at me," he remembers. "It was awful. I was disowned for several years and had no contact with my family at all."

Stewart, a thirty-eight-year-old accountant in Denver, says he "stumbled upon" his true sexual orientation when he was sixteen and another kid "came on" to him during "one of those *That '70s Show* pot and beer fests at a friend's apartment." The young man in question never made another move like that again, leaving Stewart "really, really frustrated. I was living in a really backward town with a family that never talked about anything sexual, let alone anything gay. I had no gay friends, none that I knew of anyway, and no way to find out if there were any other gay people around." It wasn't until he was in his "second or third" year in college that he had any male-on-male contact again, and a year after that before he went to his first gay nightclub, "just in time for all the early 1980s AIDS panic," as he calls it.

"When I think about what it would be like to be young and gay now, and just coming out, I have to say these kids lucked out not being born twenty years earlier like I was," Stewart maintains. "It's just so much easier to be out."

Oh, really? Activists tell me that for every young man who starts a gay-straight alliance at his high school, some other kid somewhere is transferring to get away from taunts and harassment, and dozens more are suffering in silence. One youth advocate says that every time she thinks we're making progress, "there's another Matthew

Shepard or Barry Winchell. It just breaks my heart." Many of the young people I surveyed complain that their older counterparts tend to dismiss their problems, convinced that anyone coming out today is greeted with a brass band and a parade complete with rainbow-colored confetti. If only.

Ben is an eighteen-year-old high school student in the Midwest. "I talk to all these old guys on the Internet all the time and they tell me how lucky I am to be so young," Ben tells me. "Well, I told my mom I was gay the other night, and she's still pissed off at me, and she's threatening to tell my dad. I've got a bag packed right now, and I'm calling friends to find out if I can stay with them because I know he'll kick me out on my ass if he finds out. Yeah, I am so lucky."

Brad, a twenty-year-old college student in Michigan, says his father did in fact kick him out of the house when he found out Brad was gay three years ago. He moved back home after spending time with relatives, then left shortly thereafter for college. "Since then it's not something we talk about. No one wants to go through that again."

James, an eighteen-year-old high school student in Missouri, says his father was "actually supportive, which kind of surprised me," but his mother, who's divorced from his father, hasn't spoken to him since. "I live with my father, so it's not too bad, I guess. I don't know what it would be like if we were all in the same place. Probably not too good."

Now, make no mistake. I came upon plenty of stories about parents who didn't reject their kids, or threaten to evict them; in fact, I found dozens of stories that showed true advances in attitudes since the gay days of yore. Jae, a twenty-one-year-old business analyst in Seattle, tells me he came out at fourteen to friends and family in Montana. "It was a very positive 'poster child' type of experience. I was very fortunate, as I was unsure how [they] would react." Barry, now a twenty-five-year-old lawyer in New Jersey, tells me he came out at seventeen to his widowed mom, and that "she's been my best friend ever since. I can't imagine what it would have been like not to be honest with her." And Dan, a seventeen-year-old high school student in Virginia, says his father was "open and honest and didn't judge me" when he came out just recently. Dan says it was actually his father who "informed me he knew, before I ever approached him about it."

But for every positive experience I encountered like Jae's, Barry's, or Dan's, I have to tell you I found two or three coming-out stories more akin to those of Ben, Brad, or James, stories that might just as well been date-stamped "1974" or "1983." Clearly, despite every social and technological advance we've made, coming out is still not easy.

"I don't believe that what young people go through when they are coming out today is any less difficult today than it was in the past," says Craig Bowman, executive director of the National Youth Advocacy Coalition (NYAC). "Young people still struggle with isolation and the feeling that they are all alone."

"Society has not transformed enough to effectively eliminate the strains of coming out," says Arthur Padilla, the former executive director of the Sexual Minority Youth Assistance League (SMYAL), a Washington, DC-based youth advocacy group. He believes the much greater public knowledge of gay and lesbian issues these days in some ways actually works *against* those coming out, in that young people today are more likely to become aware of their sexual orientation at a much younger age and to make that orientation known. "They put themselves in the position to be confronted by their peers, family, and extended communities. . . . Most young people have not had the opportunity to gain the skills and resources to effectively deal with the resulting oppression and backlash."

Christopher Dyer, an activist who founded the DC-based Youth Pride Alliance in the mid-1990s and launched the city's first Youth Pride Day in 1997, agrees that times haven't changed that much, at least not yet. Like Bowman, he maintains that gay youth today still face "isolation" from others like themselves, as well as "threats of physical and emotional violence, and fears of rejection." It may well be those kinds of threats and fears, real or imagined, that lead some to make a decision *not* to come out at all. For a surprising number of young people I talked with, it's something they're not even close to contemplating.

Consider Brandon, a nineteen-year-old college student in Texas. He realized he was gay when he was in the sixth grade and started having sexual fantasies about his older brother's friends. But Brandon is still a virgin; in fact, he's never been kissed on the lips or even been on a date with a guy. "I absolutely hate having to lie about girls and dates that I have been on just so I will appear to be 'normal' to those around me," he says. "It's hard when my family and friends back home keep telling me to watch out for 'those people' and how bad it would be if people thought I was 'that way.'"

Brandon's family has its suspicions, sure enough, that he might be "that way" after all. "It is very difficult living in a house with a homophobic mother and trying to combat those negative feelings without letting her know that I myself am gay. I've been told that if I 'decide' to be gay, I will not be welcomed back into the family until I abandon that lifestyle."

Dan is a twenty-year-old college student in Canada who "always knew" he was gay, then started having sex when he was seventeen. As of now, that activity remains a secret to all those who knew him growing up. "I am 'in' and currently thinking about the right way to come 'out.' What a pain in the ass!"

Tom, a twenty-year-old college student from Long Island, New York, has also been sexually active since he was a teenager, but he hasn't come out to anyone close to him, either. "It's tough in some ways, but I like it. I am not ready to be judged by my sexuality, and I also don't want to change the relationships I have with my friends and family because they're great just the way they are."

I have to say that sounds a lot like what some of my friends used to say fifteen or twenty years ago. The times may be a-changing, but they're a-changing real slow for some kids. We may want to hold off on that brass band for just a bit.

MYTH TWO: CAUGHT IN THE NET

Even if they're closeted, many of the young men I've talked with say they're able to meet and keep in touch with other gay kids on the Internet; without the Net there would have been virtually no way for me to ever hear their stories. A vast majority of all the age groups I queried in my poll agreed that "the Internet makes it easier to be gay" for everyone. Most people surveyed believe that gay youths benefit from the Net more than anyone; the ability to reach out to other gay people, plus the instant access to vital information, is an advantage that's hard to dispute.

"The Internet played a huge role in my making contact with other gay people," says William, a nineteen-year-old computer technician in Florida. "To my knowledge, I hadn't ever met any other gay people in my life until I started talking to two wonderful people online." Nathan, a nineteen-year-old college student in Texas, echoes that nearly word for word, and adds that he "got to see how some people came out and how that in turn affected their lives."

Andrew, a twenty-two-year-old college student in Orange County, California, says the Internet "probably saved" his life. "I found it to be a source of support and compassion unlike anything else I knew. Being in the closet offline made it difficult to share my feelings about being gay with anyone in person. The Net opened new doors for me and helped me grow." Steven, a twenty-seven-year-old financial planner in Houston, says the Internet is where, quite unexpectedly, he met his very first gay friend. "I just came across his home page one Sunday afternoon and realized that not only did he and I have a lot of common interests, but he was gay as well. I e-mailed him and introduced myself and we hit it off instantly. We became close friends and still are two years later. His friendship was instrumental in helping me accept who I was and begin the coming-out process."

Many of the older men I spoke with, many of them nearly as active online as the youngest and most enthusiastic techno geek, clearly envy the head start the Internet provides. "If I could have had, for just one week of my adolescence, the kind of positive reinforcement these youngsters have today," says Lenny, a forty-three-year-old store owner in Atlanta who grew up in Mississippi. "I had to run away from home when I was seventeen. I literally had to 'hit the road' to find a place where there were people like me. Even now I'm not really out to many people, and I think that's because I'm still dealing with the way I felt so isolated when I was young. I chat on the Net all the time now, and I can only imagine how my life might have turned out so very differently if I'd had that at my disposal then."

Walt, a fifty-two-year-old insurance salesman in North Carolina, concurs. "I had to figure it out by myself, 'step by step, inch by inch,' as the saying goes. No one to help me. No one to tell me that being gay didn't mean I was going to burn in Hell. No one to make me feel less alone. And, let's be honest about it . . . no one sending me really hot pictures that made being gay look sexy and desirable, to give me something to feel good about."

With all that it'd be easy to conclude that, for the young gay guy just starting his journey into self-acceptance, the Internet is the best thing since sliced bread met peanut butter. But sometimes I'm just not so sure, which is why I list this concept as a myth. Yes, the Internet may well make it "easier" to be gay, but I wonder sometimes if "easier" is everything it's cracked up to be.

I'm not the only one who has doubts. Art is a twenty-nine-year-old musician in Los Angeles who was barely out of his teens when the first Internet chat rooms began to spread across the land. "I think of everything in terms of song lyrics, and when I think about computers I think about that Sting song ["If I Ever Lose My Faith in You"] where he sings, 'I never saw no miracle of science that didn't go from a blessing to a curse.' That was my experience in a nutshell."

Art says after "really getting off" on the fact that he could talk to so many other gay guys on his "little old black and white laptop," he made "the hideous mistake" of trusting someone he met online, and agreed to meet him somewhere dark and deserted. "Hey, I was young and stupid, and really, really closeted, and I didn't want anyone to know I was gay. So I met this guy one night and he basically raped me. And I couldn't tell anyone about it, either. That was like ten years ago. If I ever see him again I'll probably kill him. Quote me."

Art's story, though extreme, isn't all that unique. My surveys offer up a number of similar accounts of scary encounters that followed a contact made online. John, a nineteen-year-old restaurant worker in Phoenix, tells the chilling tale of a man who met him online, then started showing up night after night outside the place where he worked. "I finally had my boss call the cops, but I still look over my shoulder a lot in the parking lot. My own stupid fault for telling him where I worked."

Billy, a twenty-five-year-old graduate student at Dartmouth, says he's still haunted by the phone calls he started getting from someone he rejected after "just one" hookup. "It was weird, kind of flattering at first, then he started telling me shit like, 'If I can't have you, why should anyone else?' I got my number changed, and I have never given it out since."

I've also heard from guys of all ages who've encountered the more benign forms of maltreatment that the cyber world makes all too easy: hopes raised, then dashed, promises made and broken, outright lies told and nasty rumors spread. For the older, more adjusted gay man those can be bad enough; for the young guy just coming out, such goings-on can have the insidious effect of undermining his confidence and making him forever distrustful of other people's motives. "All I've ever met off the Internet were freaks and losers, and for a long time I figured a lot of gay guys were just whack," says Seth, a twenty-four-year-old postgraduate student in New Mexico. "Nobody ever seemed to be telling the truth about anything, they'd all tell me different names on different nights, and the only pictures anyone online ever sent me were somebody else's. I'm finally starting to come out, but I wouldn't give any credit to talking to people online at all. If anything it set me back." Dave, a twenty-two-year-old college student in Philadelphia, dismisses the Internet totally, too. "I tried it for awhile, and it was just liars, underage kids, and a bunch of oversexed whores. No thanks!"

Others have a slightly different take on the Net's effects. "I think a lot of guys are taking their online personas and acting the same way offline," suggests Phil, a twenty-eight-year-old waiter in New York City. "It's kind of like the computer changes the way they think about people, so now everyone is just as disposable as the guy you were chatting with last night. It's like, 'Who are you again?' Except now they treat people that way even when they meet 'em in person. What a bunch of assholes!"

Certainly, all of us come into contact with shady or sketchy characters quite independent of our computers; regrettably, "assholes" in the real world have never been in short supply. But the Internet *does* make it possible for one to be an asshole on a truly global scale, and it can give unsavory folks an unblocked entryway into the lives of unsavvy young people. It can also allow those same youngsters unfettered access to ideas, images, and words they may not be able to handle quite yet.

A few years back I wrote an article for the now-defunct *Joey* magazine, a national publication aimed at gay teens and postteens. Titled "Caught in the 'Net," the article chronicled the often harrowing experiences of young men who have at times found themselves somewhat addicted to everything the Internet makes possible: fast and easy sexual liaisons, both real and in cyber form, pornography in the form of downloadable pictures and videos, and "hot" Webcam sites that allow the viewer to become voyeur. Although a number of the health officials I spoke with at the time were quick to praise the Internet for all it offers young gay men in terms of support and affirmation, they did suggest that "cybersexual addiction" was a growing problem, especially among the younger set of gay men encountering the Internet's gay content for the first time. "It's wild, seeing guys naked and having sex," says Johnnie, a seventeen-year-old high school student in California. Like many of the gay kids I interviewed, he's no stranger to the seamy side of cyberspace; to be candid, he and many others revel in their naughtiness.

When I was just a lad growing up in the suburbs, it was rare to find anything that even vaguely resembled gay porn; you counted yourself lucky if you found the occasional page torn from some skin mag. These days it's not at all difficult to go online and find a willing trade partner, and a huge number of them are teenagers. Here the coin of the realm is a pornographic pic, often taken by the kids themselves with their own digital cameras, which means that kid is likely to have his free willie stored on who-knows-how-many hard drives, not to mention posted on sites around the world. Will it come back to haunt him one day?

Others like to trade passwords to porn sites, either legitimately purchased or stolen. Whatever you think of such things, you have to admit it's one thing for someone relatively mature to peruse the best of Bel Ami, and something else if the peruser is just beginning to form his feelings about sex and love. "I've been trading passwords to porn sites for years," says one young man I know. "Mom thinks I'm just doing my homework online. I've got a lot of pics saved. You want some?" Call me naïve, maybe, but I wonder a little about the mind-set of a youngster whose romantic worldview might be informed by *Frat Boys in Heat, Part Two.*

All this presents a conundrum that may be unique to gay life. "Think about it," suggests Tommy, a twenty-two-year-old college student in Indiana. "Your parents have no idea you're gay, so they're not going to sit down and tell you that it's OK to talk to or meet boys your own age online, but that some older guy might be trying to get in your pants, so watch who you talk to. Or maybe just be careful what gay sites you go to. Yeah, right. That kind of thing isn't part of their reality . . . and if they did know about all the gay sites and chat rooms you're hanging out in, they'd probably take your computer away. I know mine would have."

"It's a really touchy subject," admits one gay activist who doesn't want her name used. "We need to keep all the portals open for these kids so they can talk with peers and get access to information, but that means that sometimes something gets through that a young person probably shouldn't see. On the other hand, if the family gets some kind of blocking software like Net Nanny, half of the really useful sites might get screened out because they talk in frank and useful terms about safe sex. I don't know what's more damaging, but we can't put the genie back in the bottle. The Internet is just too valuable for young people coming to grips with their sexuality, whatever their parents might think about it."

Numerous studies conducted over the last several years would seem to prove the assertion that, because of the initial anonymity it provides, the Internet is more often employed by gay men than it is by their straight counterparts (the sheer number of "m4m" chat rooms on AOL, the largest mainstream Internet service provider in the world, helps bear that out). Although the online experience has been demonstrably vital to countless gay men of all ages, it's clear that it presents its hazards as well, and young gay men may sometimes be most at risk. The technology of the modern age may well give them the "head starts" their predecessors envy, but it can come with a cost.

That's what puts me on the fence on this one, and it's enough to make others look back at our unwired yesterdays with a bit of nostalgia. "I thank God that I didn't have a chance to go online before I was old enough to handle it," says Rob, a thirty-four-year-old retail worker in Mississippi. "It would have been way too addictive, and God knows who I might have ended up hooking up with when I was young and kind of desperate. I actually pity these kids now because they're growing up way too fast. Maybe they have it easier in some ways, but there's one thing they'll never get back. They don't get to be kids for very long."

MYTH THREE: THE CHICKEN HAWK SYNDROME

We've already touched on this one, the idea that every older guy just wants to get in some kid's pants. I can't think of a more widespread claim among the younger men I've talked to, or a charge more firmly denied by most older men. It has to be by far the most damaging myth, since no other concept has done as much to build that wall between the old and the young.

I'm not saying the myth doesn't have its factual underpinnings. Any one of us can probably recall getting "hit on" by an older man at some point, or maybe on numerous occasions. What gives me pause is the absolute certainty on the part of so many younger men that virtually *all* older men are lying in the bushes, just waiting for a chance to cut a calf from the herd. Also somewhat telling is their palpable disgust at the prospect.

"It seems that every time I go to a club it's filled with 'lurkers,' old nasty men just trying to pick up boy toys," says Josh, a twenty-two-year-old retail manager in Ohio. "Never in my life have I been attracted to someone who's older, nor will I ever be. Sugar daddies are something you should find on a stick in a candy store, not on your stick in bed. Ick!" Allan, a twenty-one-year-old retail manager in Baton Rouge, says he's been approached by older men so many times he can't count them all. "Maybe it's because I'm blond or something, and they think I'm a slut, or worse," he says. "They are usually quite trashy, so I'm rather rude when I dismiss them."

Teej, a twenty-three-year-old college student in Denver, says he's "sick of being chased by chicken hawks." When he's approached, he thinks, "Oh shit, not again. . . . Most guys like that just want a young piece of ass or a trainable boyfriend and I am neither." Patrick, the twenty-year-old college student from New York that we heard from in the last chapter, says gay men who are thirty and above "scare the hell" out of him. "Most older gays are only interested in one thing: sex. They don't see anything wrong with making lewd comments to you or inappropriately touching you against your will right in the middle of the club."

It's not just clubs we're talking about. The same thing goes on in cyberspace, maybe even more so. Many of the young men I talked with complained mightily about the "old pervs" who crash the party, so to speak, in chat rooms or Web areas formed by or targeted at younger gay men. Like the "lurkers" Josh talked about, they tend to go where the game is.

So I grant you, yes, the myth has a solid basis in fact, but how have the loutish actions of a few come to signify the behavior of all? "I think young guys just coming out are forming their opinions about a lot of things," suggests Randy, a thirty-year-old mechanic in Pittsburgh. "This gay shit is all new to them. Like a lot of young guys, they assume a lot of things are true based on one thing they see, and then maybe another thing they hear. So one young guy gets hit on by an older guy and his friends say that happened to them, too. Soon he's going to think all older guys are like that, whether they are or not."

Chris, a "thirty-something" writer/editor in Washington, DC, says it's probably only natural that young people form such suspicions. What they know is what they see. "Just where is all this happening? In bars and clubs, right? So those older guys, the chicken hawks, who want to find someone young will hang out there for exactly that reason." John Guggenmos is a thirty-four-year-old nightclub and restaurant owner in DC who's been involved with the club scene for a decade and a half, and he agrees with Chris. "If you're a fifty-year-old man still hanging out in a bar, I think the chicken hawk syndrome is pretty accurate, at least from a young gay guy's perspective. A nightclub is not a place to share wisdom."

The problem seems to be that the places where such "wisdom" might be shared are few and far between. Michael Shernoff is a psychotherapist who practices in New York City's Chelsea district. "I think that the 'chicken hawk' stereotype, while obviously sometimes accurate, is one of the most insidious and destructively homophobic myths in our community. Of course youth is prized, but I also hear young gay men bemoan the fact that they do not have access to older gay men for mentoring, role modeling, and as older and wiser friends, family members, and confidants. I think many younger gay men fear aging precisely *because* of the invisibility of so many older gay men. Most middle-aged gay men are not in bars, clubs, and other venues where younger gay men hang out."

So where are they? "I'll tell you where you won't find me on Saturday, and that's out at some twinkie/raver/kiddie bar," says Hal, a forty-two-year-old law enforcement officer in Los Angeles. "Those places were fine when I was younger, but I think most of us outgrow them pretty fast. At least I did. The world is a lot bigger than the inside of some dance club, and just because I'm gay doesn't mean I have to hang out there on the weekends. I'm single right now, and when I go on dates we have dinner, see a movie or a show, or we take a long drive somewhere. If we do go to a 'gay' place, it's some quiet bar or pub, just some place to have a conversation. I hate shouting over music." I ask Hal what he thinks about the young people convinced that every older guy is after them. "They should be so lucky," he tells me. "Tell them to give me a call when they're thirty."

That's a sentiment shared by dozens of men I spoke with. Rick is a forty-year-old computer salesman in Texas. "At forty I find most people under thirty don't hold my attention or impress me as someone I'd be interested in dating," he says. "Most of their concerns are no longer mine. I like people with some experience under their belt, who feel more secure about themselves." Larry, a thirty-four-year-old warehouse worker in Indiana, describes the time he was approached by a younger man on the Internet. "I told him I wasn't interested and he seemed very surprised by that. He was sure that every man was attracted to someone younger."

David, a thirty-nine-year-old counselor in New Jersey, says he actually gets "uncomfortable" when he's out on the town, and young people are out there with him. "A lot of the clubs around here will let eighteen-year-olds in now, and I have to tell you, it makes me feel like I'm baby-sitting, or reminiscing about having my first beer. No thanks." Ross, a thirty-four-year-old salesman in Eugene, Oregon, says he likes men "thirty and over, and that's it. As far as I'm concerned you don't have anything to offer me until you have some miles on you. I can't imagine even having a conversation with someone in college. He doesn't know anything, but that's not going to stop him from thinking he does."

In my polling I found that clear majorities—and in some cases, substantial majorities—of men aged twenty-four to fifty-nine had rejected someone's advances simply because he was too young for them. "Youth is nice, but to me a man is at his best physically between the ages of thirty and thirty-five," says Jack, a forty-seven-year-old author and professor in Nashville. "I have always felt that and probably always will. Teenagers have never held much appeal for me sexually." Tony, a thirty-one-year-old marketing specialist in the Midwest, says he just can't take "young 'uns" very seriously. "They need to learn a little more before I can handle them. They have this 'It's either this way or that way' kind of idealism. It's not for me."

So the chicken hawk syndrome, for me at least, is simply not demonstrably true. Still, I would be remiss here if I didn't share some thoughts from the mythmakers themselves, and sure enough, several self-avowed chicken hawks were only too happy to oblige, without a trace of embarrassment or shame. "Sure I like younger guys," says John, a thirty-eight-year-old movie theater manager in Dallas. "How can you *not* like a firm body and tight butt? I suppose when I go out I tend to 'hit' on them, as you put it. But if they make it clear they want me to get out of their face, I'm happy to do so. Why waste my time?" Chuck, a sixty-one-year-old retired airline pilot in Palm Springs, California, says he doesn't "know why age is important to me, but it is. I prefer to be with younger men, have sex with younger men, usually in the twenty to forty age range. Many guys like to have a moment of role-playing or something with an 'older Dad' type . . . they need some 'Dad' time in a safe and trusting environment."

One older man who's fond of "tricking" with younger guys tells me he likes to refer to them as "puppies," because at that age, he says, "almost any guy is cute. I call them puppies because almost all the things that make them cute to me, like their energy, their innocence, and their good looks, tend to fade away over time. Then they're just dogs, like me." Dennis, a fifty-year-old administrator from Baltimore, says he's always "had a thing" for young men, and he's not shy about approaching them at dance clubs. Dennis explains that he's not looking for a relationship, just some harmless fun, the same as anyone else on a Saturday night. "Look, I know going in that I'll get shot down several times a night. It's no big deal . . . as long as he's legal. He can always say 'no.' All I need is one 'yes' and I'm a happy camper. Trust me, the kid will have a great time."

MYTH FOUR: THE MENUDO COMPLEX

This myth addresses the idea that, whatever passes for gay culture these days, it by and large worships at the altar of youth, in its hottest clubs, music, fashion, and media marketing. While you're young—and hopefully beautiful, or at least giving it your best shot—you're welcomed in with open arms and occasionally, reasonably priced drinks. But once you're past a certain age, it's "geezer be gone."

I've named the phenomenon for the 1970s/1980s Puerto Rican pop band Menudo, famous on these shores mainly for two things: spawning the career of Ricky Martin, and for regularly kicking its members out once they hit the grand old age of sixteen, replacing them with newer, younger kids. It's an apt comparison, I think, to the way scores of men tell me they started feeling 'round about thirty or so. That's when the big chill started setting in, when they first noticed the crowds in their favorite clubs were getting younger—and surlier—the music started changing into something they didn't much care for, and all at once their "homes away from home" didn't feel so much like home anymore. Talk about your *vida loca;* one man likened it to "some gay version of *Survivor* where you get voted off Fire Island by the rest of the tribe, except they're all a lot younger and hotter than you." Others say it's nothing like *Survivor.* It's more like *Lord of the Flies* and every older man is Piggy.

"I think if one more young punk shoves me off a dance floor, or pushes me aside at a bar rail, I'm gonna just throw down," says Theo, a thirty-six-year-old management consultant in San Diego. "I've had it up to here with the snide comments about 'Work it, Grandpa!' and 'It's a great time to be silver!' Fuck, I'm not even forty yet, and these kids go way outta their way to try and make me and my friends feel like we're over the hill. I wanna remind them 'we built this city.'"

"Gay culture is incredibly youth centered," says Lee, a thirty-two-year-old projects manager in Atlanta. "The gay bar I used to go to has afternoons when older gay men gather there. It's referred to as 'Jurassic Park.' The bars down here seem desperate to attract a younger crowd of people. I am gay and successful and have more money than the kids, but somehow the gay nightlife doesn't want me."

It's not just the nightlife some find lacking. They point to the highest-selling national gay men's magazines, their covers and the lifestyle features and advertising within; rarely do you find models who appear to be far removed from their thirtieth birthday. Korey, a forty-three-year-old operations manager in San Francisco, claims it's even worse than that; he thinks the folks that market to the gay community start turning a blind eye toward anyone on the high side of twenty-five. "The Abercrombie and Fitch boys, the guys in their early twenties, are the ones that advertisers spend their money on. I think *they* think if you're over thirty, well, you're just used meat. You're no longer part of this new and upcoming community." Dov, a forty-seven-year-old AIDS educator next door in Berkeley, agrees. "Youth and beauty are the gold standard. I think it's a sad shortcoming the gay community has. There's just no space for older, wiser, mature folks."

Indeed, my polls do reflect similar beliefs. Overwhelming majorities of every age group say gay culture—as a whole—is friendlier to young people than it is to those older, and tends to marginalize those not regarded as young. Even most young guys seem to buy into the idea. "When you're young like I am now, and you're fairly good looking and you know how to dress, it's like you're the 'golden child,'" says Will, a twenty-two-year-old student in New York. "Just about everyone kisses your ass. Guys buy you drinks, doormen let you in for free, you see your picture in the local gay rags, the deejays play the songs you like. It's *your* gay world. But I like to think I'm smart enough to see how shallow all that is, even if I enjoy all the attention. Tomorrow there'll be someone younger and cuter, and it'll be 'Will who?'"

So why on earth, you might be asking, would I call this a myth with all the apparent consensus? I have to admit, this one *is* closer to full-on fact status than the rest, but I still hear a lot of dissenting voices out there. Maybe not quite enough to stick it up there with the deep-fried rat, but *just* enough to call it a half-myth at best. I just don't think it's accurate to say gay culture worships youth; I think it's probably fairer to say that *all* of our culture, straight and gay, tends to admire that which is youthful and vital, sometimes to the point of excluding or ignoring the older crowd.

Ken South is an Aging Initiative Fellow at the National Gay and Lesbian Task Force's Policy Institute. An ardent activist on behalf of gay seniors, South agrees that Western society, and American society in particular, "puts a tremendous value on being young. Being young is good, being old is bad. Young people are respected for their energy and productivity, while older people are seen as a drain." South says that general societal view undergoes something of a transformation within the gay community. "The power of ageism is so profound for gay men that they actually experience what social scientists call 'accelerated aging,' that is, some men in their forties think of themselves as washed up and find no hope for their future, as if they're close to death."

"Gay society is just like straight society, except we take things to extremes," suggests Dave, a forty-year-old teacher in Ohio. "That's why most trends in music and fashion are usually a product of gay people." But Dave isn't convinced that gay people are any more extreme in their views about age. "I think some people take youth and put it on a pedestal, but that's not true for everyone. I don't think you can even claim there's any one gay culture. We're a lot more complicated than that."

Hell yes, we are. Many of those "dissenting voices" I heard came from members of what some might think of as fringe groups inside the gay community: from those hirsute and often rather large men known as "bears," to other men of all ages, shapes, and sizes who favor the leather scene, to the men who tell me how they "love a man in uniform"—and I think they mean that literally—and elsewhere from men who don't really think of themselves as part of the "community" at all. They don't generally frequent clubs or buy the mass-market gay magazines. Several reported to me from rural locations, but just as many came from urban and suburban locales.

Barney is a forty-two-year-old construction worker in Kentucky. "I belong to a motorcycle club. Most of the members are gay, some bi. We get together socially, bang back some beers, and some people hook up. Youth is the last thing anyone cares about in our circles. Men turn us on, not boys." Fred, a thirty-eight-year-old shipyard worker near Norfolk, Virginia, says he made the three-hour drive to Washington, DC, recently for the Mid-Atlantic Leather Convention, and noticed how few young people were in the crowd. "People say the gay community is all about youth, but that is such bullshit. At MAL, there were thousands of guys packed into hotels and bars . . . it was all about some of the hottest middle-aged and older guys you ever saw. Hardly a twinkie in sight. Just about every ad or magazine or poster or video for sale there was all about the older crowd. I really felt at home. Actually, I felt like the baby in the family."

Even those well within what you could call the gay "mainstream" admit that perceiving a favoritism toward youth is all a matter of where you're at and how you look at things. "If all you know about being gay is getting drunk and dancing your ass off, then hooking up with someone for the night, of course you'll think 'gay culture' is all about youth," says Perry, a librarian in Richmond, Virginia. "That's what young people *do,* and that's who the bigger clubs want. If you're an older man hanging out at 'college night,' I guess you're going to start feeling old and somewhat marginalized at some point, because the party isn't for you. But there's so much more out there, more things for gay men to do, especially in the bigger cities. I think a lot of gay guys just don't want to grow up and adjust their lifestyle to something a little more meaningful than one endless party. It's kind of sad." As for men's magazines, the librarian scoffs. "If you want to call those rags culture, fine, but how about picking up a book? How about reading some of the classic gay authors or classic books about gay life?"

People in the business of marketing to the gay community deny the idea that they target youth exclusively. Just like their heterosexual counterparts, what they target is money, and face it, younger gay men tend to spend cash like drunken sailors on a bender in Bangkok. "Men over thirty don't go out as much as the younger generation," says DC's John Guggenmos. "Kids in their twenties are our future, but we still cater to the thirty-year-olds because they have the most disposable income, and the least long-term obligations. So we've always paid attention to them. From our experience, forty- and fifty-year-olds don't go out to dance clubs. Even if we do a retro night, we still find the majority of the people who attend are overwhelmingly young. Ageism has nothing to do with it. It's simply a smart marketing plan. If the [older gay men] were partying in the same way that the younger generation is, of course there would be some businessman that would find a way to cater to that need."

Many older men tell me that's exactly what's happening, that scores of travel agencies and resorts find a way to make them feel welcome. "The circuit party scene definitely targets the midthirties to midforties types," says Al, a forty-six-year-old promoter in San Francisco. "You also find a lot of fifty-year-old guys in great shape and looking to party." And contrary to the assertions of many older men, that youth is king, many young men, especially those in their early twenties or late teens, tell me they feel anything *but* catered to. "I don't drink, I don't like club music, and I don't really know how to dress," says Arnie, a twenty-three-year-old college student in New York. "I don't feel like anyone in the gay community gives a shit about people like me." Paul, a nineteen-year-old living in Florida, was surprised anyone thinks the gay community is devoted to youth in any way. "The gay community doesn't care about young people," he declares. "Especially if you're young and you don't live in a city with a lot of gay people . . . but even if you do it seems like the clubs don't want younger people there."

"Gay culture isn't youth centered, it's 'impossible beauty' centered," avows Chris, an eighteen-year-old college student in Boston. "I am disgusted by the constant bombardment of pictures of hard bodies by gay men's magazines. This is the same thing that has generated so many eating disorders and distorted body images among heterosexual women. Gay men are supposed to look one way or else they're not attractive. We have made progress over the last few years. We've caught up to straight people in that now *everyone,* gay and straight, can feel bad about their bodies."

"I don't mind going out to clubs. I like seeing hot guys in magazines, but I guess I'm starting to wonder if that's all there is," says Stephen, a twenty-two-year-old in San Diego. "It just feels like there aren't many chill places to go to meet people that aren't about looks and clothes and drinking. I guess I just haven't found my place yet, and I don't know if it even exists."

MYTH FIVE: LET'S TALK ABOUT SEX . . .

There's this old saying—I'm not sure where it comes from—that a "slut" is simply "anyone who is getting more sex than you are." I bring it up because (1) it makes me laugh and (2) it reminds me of the things I hear a lot of younger and older guys whisper behind each other's backs. (I can't really hear them whisper, of course. It just comes off that way when I read the surveys, like the catty comments you might lower your voice to make at some *chi chi* cocktail party, such as "Oh, my God, who *hasn't* he slept with?")

Myth Five is a dual myth, in that a goodly portion of each group says it about the other; to wit, they're calling each other a bunch of sex-starved 'ho bags. "Sex is all the older guys ever think about," says Justin, a nineteen-year-old college student in Wisconsin. "I mean, I like sex, too. Trust me, I whack it a couple of times a day, but it's not the only thing I think about or talk about. Every time I talk to an older guy online or out somewhere the conversation always becomes sexual. When I talk to people my own age it doesn't happen as often." Stan, a twenty-two-year-old student in Indiana who says he's occasionally attracted to older men, tells me that many seem taken aback when he doesn't want to "hop in the sack" with them on the first date. "When I see older gay men out at clubs they act like they're more willing and anxious to hook up than the younger guys I know. They seem really surprised that I say no, let's get to know each other first."

"All the younger guys do is have sex, sex, and more sex," says Frank, a thirty-nine-year-old consultant in Los Angeles. "Followed by still more sex. I wasn't nearly as promiscuous when I was growing up, and I didn't do all the drugs they do. I wonder if there'll even *be* a next generation of gay men by the time they unfuck themselves. They're too busy fucking each other." José, a thirty-seven-year-old musician in south Florida, tells me how the younger men he meets are often very forward with him. "I guess I should be flattered when they come on so strong, but it's scary to me the way they wear their desires on their sleeves." It's happened often enough that José worries that far too many young men are making such advances pretty much every chance they get. "When I see them in clubs pawing at each other, it makes me wonder who they were with the night before and where they'll be tomorrow night. Not with me, they won't."

As I said earlier, it's sad when the actions of a few come to represent for some an entire grouping of people. The reality is that no majority of either group is nearly as slutty as the other seems to think; that much seems plain from the surveys, polls, and interviews I've conducted. Truth be told, some older guys *are* still acting like kids in the candy store, reliving those pre-HIV days when one could hit on anything that moved without fear of many repercussions besides the clap, or a slap in the face. Certainly some younger men, far removed in space and time from the funerals and memorial services men my age had to go through in the 1980s and early 1990s, are behaving as if the risk of sexually transmitted diseases, some of them still quite deadly, are just part of the game, if indeed the risk ever crosses their

minds at all. (My polls unearthed a few curious and contradictory
trends on that topic. I won't get too much into the specific age break-
downs here, but I'll tell you that of all the men over the age of twenty-
four questioned, fewer than half said they used protection every time
they had sex; just over half of the men twenty-three and under said
they always used protection. Obviously that leaves a large segment of
the gay population unprotected, and still huge majorities of each
group said they "worried about getting HIV/AIDS." To which I can
only reply, with all the seriousness and compassion I can muster,
"Duh!")

Although most younger and older guys really don't have much
trouble keeping it in their pants, for some reason they keep pointing at
each other, yelling, "Slut!" Looking at the poll results, it turns out a
sizable majority of each group *would* prefer to be involved in a stable,
monogamous relationship. But the figures also show that younger
men, those twenty-nine and below, would be somewhat more reluc-
tant to have sex outside of that relationship than those above the age
of thirty. Similarly, younger men said they'd be less likely to have sex
with someone on the first date than their older counterparts. So if my
numbers have any accuracy attached to them at all, it would seem true
that it's the older men who are more likely to play tomcat than their
younger counterparts.

Still, I'm not sure that makes us older guys de facto sluts. Some
suggest it's simply a matter of life experience and self-confidence.
Gay men are coming out at younger ages than ever before, and while
many are rather anxious and eager to get out there and explore, others
are a lot more reticent and don't have their footing yet. They see an
older man's more playful attitude toward sex and mistake it for
"sluttiness."

"I think you have to remember that a lot of us came out before sex
became dangerous," says Jack, a forty-year-old IT manager in northern
California. "Or at least we came out, dealt with the dangers, and
moved on to find some balance. I don't really have much sex at all
outside of a relationship (well, maybe oral sex, but everyone does
that!) and I still love to flirt the way I did back in the early 1980s. I
think I'm much more at ease with the idea of flirting and seduction
than the younger ones probably are. Somewhere they got all these
really negative ideas about sex, and that translates into acting either

like total prudes if they still want to please Mommy, or total sluts if they wanna piss Mommy off. Doesn't seem to be much in between."

In the Winter 2000 "Sex" issue of *XY* magazine, publisher Peter Cummings—who's roughly my age—sounded off on the topic of flirting and sluttiness after having the scarlet "S" placed on him when he told a younger man online that he happened to find him attractive, not realizing what a shit storm that innocent comment might cause. "I am tired of this thing where nobody is allowed to flirt, where nobody is allowed to express interest in anyone for fear of being labeled a slut," he writes in his editorial (p. 12). "It makes me so sad. Can we just get past that?"

Writer/actor Craig Chester, writing in the May 2002 issue of *Instinct* magazine, couldn't agree more.

> It's something that my 30-something friends and I talk about: Why is it, we wonder, do so many of the 20-somethings we meet have such complicated hang-ups about getting laid . . . why all this guilt about sex if we are supposedly more accepted by society than ever?" (p. 70)

Chester—you may have seen him in his role as the gay roommate in 1997's *Kiss Me, Guido*—suggests that "all these young gay boys" are "scared of their own wanton desires, of what I'm sure they think is their 'dark side'" (p. 70). As a gay man in his thirties, Chester says he knows well "the difference between making love and sex," and that love is always the more rewarding of the two. "But right now I'm single, and until I find someone to make love to again, I'll have sex if I feel like doing so. Call me a slut, call me a sex addict, call me a two-door garage, I think sex is good" (p. 70).

But Terry, a twenty-four-year-old postgraduate student at New York University, bristles at the suggestion that he has any kind of hang-up about sex, just because he's extremely choosy about whom he chooses to bed and when he chooses to bed them. "I'm willing to flirt with someone if I find him attractive, and I'll go a lot further than that if I feel like it. I just don't feel like it as much as a lot of the older guys seem to. I'm picky. That makes me smart, not scared." Jeremy, a twenty-year-old student and "proud virgin" in northeast Georgia, is more passionate. "Excuse me if I don't jump into bed with the first dick that comes in the door," he says. "I don't think that makes me a 'prude' or anything. I want to wait until I get a boyfriend, or at least until I am in love, as corny as that probably sounds to everyone out there. I think some of my friends are a lot more sexually active than they should be. I don't want to be like that, getting drunk in clubs, flirting with everyone and going home with anyone."

I'd be the last one to suggest that staying true to one's heart, or waiting for someone special, is in any way prudish; in a lot of ways I find it rather admirable in today's sex-soaked society. But I have to say that I've talked to many young men who look upon almost any sexual activity with a jaundiced eye, and that just can't be healthy to the heart or soul. I'll let Peter Cummings sum it up:

> People should do what they want and if people want to have sex and both parties are happy, that's cool with me. . . . The question is whether you intend to be nice to that boy after you pick him up, or whether you intend to be a user and not give a fuck about anyone's feelings. The proof is in the actions that come afterward, not in the "way" that you "flirt." I don't understand why liberated gay people have to act like teenage girls in the 1950's, and I for one won't do it. (Cummings, 2000, p. 12)

That seems like sound advice to me, but who knows? Maybe I'm just one of those bitter old queens all those youngsters talk about. I could stay home and sulk—us old guys are really good at it—but I think I'd rather go looking for a twinkie to take advantage of.

If I can find a nightclub that'll still let me in, that is.

Chapter 3

Forever Young?

To get back one's youth one has merely to repeat one's follies.

Oscar Wilde

In the first-season finale of Showtime's *Queer As Folk,* a character turning thirty is awakened by friends who throw him a surprise birthday party, complete with black confetti, balloons, and a casket; at one of my favorite DC restaurants the whole wait staff comes out and serenades you when they find out it's your birthday. . . . When they get to the part where they're supposed to insert your name, they sing "Happy birthday, *you old queen,* happy birthday to you" as they deliver the cake and candles. (It doesn't seem to matter to them how old you actually are. Any birthday will do.) And a few years back on my then-boyfriend Christopher's birthday, I came home and went back to the bedroom to give him his card and presents. I found him lying on the bed in a near catatonic state. I seriously thought he might have ODed on something; it turned out he had, in a way. He'd had too many birthdays, as far as he was concerned, and was therefore feeling ancient.

Christopher had just turned twenty-five.

Not all gay men have such oddly humorous or downright depressing ways to look at aging, but I'm here to tell you that quite a few do. John is a just-turned-forty ad executive in New York City who says the "clock just seems to tick louder these days" now that he's reached the big 4-0. "Almost any man takes stock of his life at forty, and sometimes he's going to have that middle-aged angst thing happening. But a gay man who's forty, especially a gay man who's single, is often going to start worrying about how long he'll be socially viable. He's got kind of a double burden to carry."

"I think a lot of gay men have, for some reason that escapes me, adopted the worst attitudes of straight women when it comes to getting older," says Charles, a thirty-three-year-old executive in Los Angeles. "When a straight guy turns thirty it's barely a speed bump. For a lot of gay guys, turning thirty or—gasp!—forty is like the worst thing they can imagine. For them it's like a roadblock."

Charles tells me that he's the kind of guy who prefers "mature" men, and hardly even notices his own birthdays, but he says he has "tons of friends that are really obsessed about their age. It's like all their birthdays are on the calendar, circled in black. I guess, like a lot of women, they fear that as they get older they'll be less and less attractive to potential mates . . . and trust me, these guys do a *lot* of mating. So getting older just freaks them out."

"Gay men are always concerned with age. Men as a whole become more distinguished than women as they age. But gay society has placed them as obsolete after the age of forty," notes Pierce Mattie, men's grooming editor for *Instinct* magazine and author of *Groomed for Success* (Allured Publishing, 2002). "Yes, your chicken virgin status is lost at age twenty-five placing you in your prime at thirty, then moving you along as a spectator at thirty-five and retired by forty. Naturally the gay man who turns thirty-five will be going through what a heterosexual man would at the age of fifty-five. You could say that gay men are twenty years ahead of the game. This is a lot of pressure to be young forever."

A BRIEF HISTORY OF TIME

Whenever we find ourselves contemplating whether we're "over the hill" or not, many of our friends and friendly acquaintances will take us aside, tussle our hair, and remind us that "age is just a number." (Most of them, I've noted wryly, are rather a lot younger than I am when they say that to me.) Yet even if it's true, age is a number that many of us have trouble wrapping our brains around; we can talk about budgets in the billions of dollars and hardly blink, or discuss interstellar distances in the trillions of miles and never bat an eye. But remind us that it's been twenty-five years since high school or college and our minds shut down, unable to comprehend just how that time got by us so fast. One friend of mine says he often feels like he climbed into a time machine at twenty and jumped into the future a quarter century. He doesn't resent his age in the slightest; he's actually amazed he's lived this long and well. His comments are simply made with a kind of wide-eyed wonder, with more "wow" than woe.

I'm certainly not immune to any of this, though for some reason it's usually someone else's years that give me pause. I stopped going to high school reunions years ago, and not because I was worried about how my so-called career might stack up against the doctors and lawyers in the group; it was just too damn depressing to see how badly my former classmates were deteriorating. Just the other day I looked up at the calendar and saw that it happened to be the birthday of the first boy I ever had sex with: "Billy" was my next-door neighbor, one of those too-beautiful-for-words, straight-but-curious-and-horny sixteen-year-olds, while I was just a horny gay boy of eighteen, looking-waiting-praying for a chance in his pants. One night it finally happened, thanks to some fine weed and a couple of six-packs, and off we went to mix it up for virtually the whole summer, making some of those memories you carry for a lifetime (at least I carry them; can't say if Billy does). Lost as I was in the reverie, it took me awhile to do the math and realize my beautiful young Billy was, that very day, celebrating his fortieth birthday.

My own birthdays I can deal with fine, but thinking about that young boy of summer frozen forever at sixteen in my memory, and picturing him contemplating middle age . . . all I could utter was "Wow." Now *that* made me feel old.

In Chapter 2 I examined the commonly held idea that gay culture lionizes youth above all else. I still believe that's a myth in most important respects, but as we've seen already, many gay men have bought the party line to the point where they find themselves cringing with every extra candle on the cake. And though "youth worship" is by no means a universal aspect of the gay community, there's still a hell of a lot of professed "youth envy" out there, even among those who tell me they're not necessarily interested in pursuing younger men.

Jeff, a twenty-eight-year-old bartender in Denver, says he hears it all the time from his customers when the night wears on and the crowd dwindles down to a drunken, nostalgic few. "Even though some of these men are really successful, dress well, and drive nice cars, I hear the way they talk about 'If I could go back and do it all again,' that kind of stuff. I guess everyone wouldn't mind having more life to play with, that whole 'If I knew then what I know now' sort of thing. Sometimes I catch them looking at younger guys, and not in a cruisy way, more like 'I wish I had his years *and* his looks' way. Like they wouldn't mind trading places, despite everything they have, if they could be that twinkie boy for awhile." Robert, a thirty-year-old salesman in Houston, says he misses very much being the center of attention that he was in his youth. "I am not the most attractive person in the world, but I am not ugly, either. I miss the attention I could garner when I was younger. If I could be younger again, I would be."

In my polls and surveys I tried to sound men out about this very topic. I asked gay men in every age group if they were "happy" with their ages. The vast majority of those already forty and above responded affirmatively, some quite enthusiastically. "I am proud of every wrinkle, every gray hair on my head," says Larry, a fifty-year-old stockbroker in the Northeast. "With my age I've gained so much wisdom and experience. Why wouldn't I be happy about it? Why should I be afraid to show it?" Russell, a forty-seven-year-old banker in Arizona, agrees. "It's like you trade youth for wisdom. What lasts longer in the long run?"

I have to say I also noted some curious, almost contradictory responses that reminded me of Jeff's late-night clientele; substantial numbers of the men who said they were happy with their ages also expressed the idea that, if given the chance, they'd be younger if they could. Not just for the chance to go back, start over, and take a different path. Many of us would be intrigued by that opportunity, of course. These men simply wanted to have the vitality and enthusiasm they associate with youth. "I hate to sound like a traitor to my over-forty and over-fifty friends," says Steve, a forty-one-year-old medical professional in upstate New York. "We all say how great we feel these days, how great this ride has been, and how we're looking forward to what comes next in life, but I for one would love to be a young gay boy again, just coming out and discovering the world for the first time. I wasn't like a lot of my friends who didn't get comfortable with being gay until after they'd been married and divorced. . . . I was 'out' to most of my friends in college. I wouldn't change much of my life, even if I had the chance. I'd just like to have that youthful energy again, that excitement. It's hard, once you're in a career track with bills to pay and all that, to remember what it was like being young and cute and relatively carefree. It'd be a riot if I could live like that again."

And many of those who said they wouldn't necessarily want to *be* young admitted they wouldn't at all mind *looking* young. "I know I'll never have the body of an eighteen-year-old again," says Roger, a thirty-eight-year-old marketing specialist in the Midwest. "But I know I'd like to. To be young and cute on the outside, but have substance and a little wisdom about the world on the inside; I think a lot of us dream about that, even if we won't always admit it."

Something struck me about those comments, and it wasn't just their nostalgic wistfulness. It's funny how when I started asking folks what looking young meant for them, the words "young" and "cute" were so often used together that for some people they seemed synonymous. Sure enough, there are a lot of attractive young guys out there, but that's hardly the norm, is it? Christopher, a thirty-four-year-old government employee in Ohio, doesn't think so. "Take a look at most of the nineteen- and twenty-year-olds out there. They are gangly, effeminate, or overweight," he says. "Many of them aren't having a very good time of it. When a guy says he'd like to look younger, like the guys back in high school, chances are he's thinking of the football or track jock with the overdeveloped body, and not the tuba player or the Chess Club captain."

I can't argue with him. The other day I found myself surrounded in downtown DC by a bunch of high schoolers in town for a field trip; I can't remember the last time I saw so many flabby bodies and bad skin (actually I can; it's when I was back in high school myself). James, a thirty-seven-year-old entrepreneur in south Florida, tells me he laughs when he hears people say they wish they could "go back" to their youth. "I myself wouldn't be sixteen or seventeen, or even twenty or twenty-one again, if you put a gun to my head. Forget about the fact I thought I knew it all when I didn't know dick, I'm still trying hard to forget what I looked like then (let's not even talk about the acne). It took me years to put on some decent size, get a decent haircut, and learn how to dress."

What many of us seem to be infatuated with isn't so much youth per se as it is some near-impossible standard of youthful perfection. It's a concept with only the most tenuous connection to reality, a product of mass-marketing and MTV *Spring Break*-style hype. All those narrow waists and washboard abs, the well-rounded rear ends and pecs, those unlined faces and flashing smiles . . . rarely do they all come together except in music videos, in the pages of some teeny-bopper magazine, or the *A&F Quarterly.* It's the kind of beauty that only a handful of young men ever actually possess. We never seem to stop and consider an art director's brilliant work with lighting and makeup, the shadings of light and dark that make abs and chests jump off the pages into our eager eyes, or the postproduction touch-ups that conceal an ill-timed zit or whiten teeth.

The fact that it's all something of a fantasy doesn't stop us from seeking out those "youthful" attributes in others, or trying to create them in ourselves. Oddly enough, many men tell me they came by their "youthful looks" only as their actual youth itself began to fade, when they looked in the mirror one day and didn't care much for what they saw looking back. That's when they set about the task of reclaiming their younger selves or, in some cases, creating a youthful look they never had before.

MEN AT WORK

Derek, a thirty-four-year-old advertising executive in New York City, says he started dying his hair when he was twenty-seven. "I don't like being gray. I'll probably always dye my hair. . . . I don't know if I'll ever get a face-lift. I used to joke I'd get a big surgical overhaul at thirty, but thirty came and went and I'm still the same. Maybe I'll do it at thirty-five. As soon as I'm unhappy with the way I look, I'll probably take measures to correct it."

Steve, a thirty-three-year-old higher education professional in Oklahoma City, admits to some "touch-up" surgery. "I've also changed my lifestyle of eating and exercise. I feel it's helped my self-esteem greatly." Tom, a forty-eight-year-old television reporter in Michigan, says he went "the whole nine yards" recently and had liposuction on his tummy and chin, a nose job, and had his eyes tightened up. "I have to say it's made all the difference in the world, not just in my day job where suddenly I find myself getting a lot more air time, but also in my social life where I find myself getting a lot more dates." And Alan, a thirty-four-year-old designer in Wisconsin, says he has a gym membership that he uses to help stay in shape, but so far he hasn't taken any drastic actions. "I'm not a vain person overall, but I think I might consider cosmetic surgery with age to make me feel better about how I look. Ironically, I'd consider plastic surgery before I'd consider wearing 'younger' fashions. There's nothing more embarrassing than seeing a person who is obviously too old trying to act young."

Whether it's with a bottle of hair dye, a closet filled with youthful clothes, the hours they spend in the gym, or in a plastic surgeon's operating room, thousands of gay men every year are taking on Mother Nature and Father Time, and greeting them with a unique salute: a raised middle finger. Their reasons and methods are as varied as the individuals themselves. Some simply want to hold on to a boyish self-image; they're not quite ready to, in the words of the *Desiderata,* "gracefully surrender the things of youth." Others find they do better on the social scene or within their careers if they have that "youthful thing" going on.

"I don't think the gay world puts pressure on me to look young," says Paul, a twenty-nine-year-old teacher in Portland, Oregon. "I put that pressure on myself. Whether we like it or not this society, gay and straight, values youthfulness and vitality. If I'm going to be successful in anything I do, I'm going to need energy and imagination, and staying fit gives me that. Does that make me look younger? Probably it does. Does it make me more attractive to a potential mate? Of course it does and I'm not complaining!"

DRESSING THE PART

"I'm a banker, so when I'm at work it's all about the suit and tie," says Stephen, who's thirty-five and lives and works in Los Angeles.

"But when I go out I rarely wear more than jeans and a T-shirt. The shirt's going to come off almost as soon as I get inside anyway." John, a forty-year-old lawyer in Chicago, has a similar approach to bar wear. "The last few years I've taken to A&F cargo pants and one of those wife-beater tanks. Summertime, it's just shorts and sandals. I work out all the time and I have a pretty good body, so I just show it off a bit. Haven't had many complaints."

Neither John nor Stephen says he picks his clothes out of any conscious effort to look younger. "I'm just dressing the way I always have," says John. "If it makes me look young, great, but I'm not really trying to go there." Still, I've talked to a number of gay men who say they *do* make such choices consciously.

Bob, a forty-seven-year-old doctor in the Midwest, says he's "as buttoned down as they come" when he's at work or when he's attending social functions with mostly straight colleagues. "But I wouldn't dream of going to a gay bar or club dressed so conservatively. I'd look like an old fogy, somebody's sugar daddy. I like to fit in with the younger crowd. I always have." Brian, a forty-two-year-old engineer in Tampa, takes it a bit further. "I watch some of the television shows younger people watch, and I see how they dress. When I go out I see how the kids dress there, too. I try those styles out to see how they work for me. I've always looked a lot younger than I am, so I guess it's still working."

If indeed "clothes make the man," then many gay men are making and remaking themselves all the time, a lot of them with an eye toward showing off their gym-bodied physiques, others trying hard to remain part of the "young and hip" crowd by keeping current with fashion trends. But I have to say that the effort isn't always successful, or even much appreciated at times by its intended audience.

Dan, a twenty-two-year-old student in Georgia, tells me he gets "embarrassed" when he sees an older guy "trying way too hard" to look young by dressing the way he thinks a younger guy does. "They just don't seem to realize that some clothes look odd on an older person. It's like he's trying to be someone else, and it just looks fake to me." Gary, a nineteen-year-old student in Indiana, says older men dressing like younger men looks "pathetic and I wish they'd just stop."

Now "dressing younger" isn't just a gay phenomenon. A few years back in his nationally syndicated column, political commentator George F. Will was bemoaning what he saw as a troubling trend in Western culture, the fact that popular taste was skewing younger than ever before, and nowhere was this more evident than in fashion choices. There was a time, he wrote, when "children enjoyed dressing like adults. Now adults increasingly dress like children. In airport concourses you see them, men wearing jeans and T-shirts and running shoes, holding the hands of small boys dressed similarly" (2001, op-ed page).

I'm rarely one to agree with Mr. Will. He's a Republican, which is bad enough, but he's been spotted wearing a bow tie in public, for heaven's sake, and therefore should not be allowed to comment on anyone else's fashion sense. Still, I have to say I've seen the same trend. I'd even suggest quite a few gay men "dress younger" and not just when they're late for a flight or heading down to collect their matched set of Louis Vuitton from the baggage carousel.

I think a lot of us simply don't "grow up" quite the way many of our straight counterparts do. For whatever social, cultural, or biological reasons, we get to a certain fashion mode and stay there, and for many of us it's a decidedly casual mode, especially when we hit the town. Sure, we have our "dress up" bars, where you'll see lots of khaki or dress trousers, button-down shirts, even a smattering of ties and sports jackets. (Where else would the Log Cabin Republicans go for happy hour?) But when you head over to the bigger dance clubs that cater to the "hip" crowd, you'll find a much different style sense at work, and it's often one that "skews younger." Older men who go to such clubs often wear the same outfits they did when they first came out; others race to keep up with the fashion du jour.

Wayne Northcross is an editorial assistant for fashion at *Esquire* magazine, as well as a contributing fashion editor at *Genre* magazine. "For some older gay men it's less a challenge of how to look younger than an inability to look grown up. It's also harder for gay men to dress appropriately because many of us don a gay uniform that we believe communicates sexual attractiveness," he says. "The gay uniform, tank and jeans worn with boots or sneakers, for example, also contains political and social meaning and it should be acknowledged that certain gay men dress in a uniform because it nostalgically reminds them of the struggle for gay rights, when the look of a butch aggressive man dovetailed nicely into the image of a sexual revolutionary. Clothes that are imbued with such emotional significance—sex and politics—are harder to discard as one ages."

As for those older men who try and ape the style of the club kids out on the dance floor, they do so at their peril. "The club kids wear these *huge* baggy pants, big ol' boots, and shiny shirts, or they're all dressed up and glittering," says Aaron, a thirty-eight-year-old advertising manager in Dallas. "If they are wearing jeans, they're a wild off-color like berry or orange, or tight white things that I defy any man over thirty to try and slip into." Any older man trying to fit in by imitating that style sense, he says, is likely going to look utterly ridiculous. "My friends and I in Detroit growing up at the height of punk and new wave wore the most outlandish outfits that were more like costumes than clothes," says Wayne Northcross. "But we didn't know who we were, what we wanted, and we sure didn't have any idea of what was sexy. We were awkward, and young fashion deflects attention away from our inner selves. Most of us thankfully grow out of that as we get older."

Some men tell me they do try to retain a sense of youth from the clothes they choose, even if it's by happenstance. Tim, a fifty-year-old Web site master in the Northeast, says his field just lends itself to a casual style of wear. "All the people I hire, many of them young gay guys in their twenties, dress the same way they did in school. In some ways, I guess I am emulating them, and it does make me feel a bit closer to their age if we're all dressed alike. Sometimes we go out after work and hit a bar or two and I feel just like one of them, which is rather nice, to tell you the truth. At least until the check comes and they all look to me to pick it up."

Other men tell me after years of dressing the way they always have, they've traded in their well-worn looks for something fresher and felt better as a result. "I thought I was dressing fashionably, and I guess I was—for 1982," says Eric, a fifty-two-year-old writer from Philadelphia. "I had a closet filled with Izod Lacoste shirts and Members Only jackets, Jordache jeans, you get the idea." Eric says he never noticed the smirks on the faces of the younger crowd until a friend gently suggested a shopping trip to replace some of his more vintage items. "I'm never going to look like anyone's fashion plate, but it is nicer to look a little more current. At least I don't look like a relic now."

Some men tell me they get downright defensive, if not downright angry, when anyone decides to tell them they're not dressing "the right way" for their age. Sam, a forty-five-year-old restaurant owner in Sacramento, California, rejects the idea that he has to get "approval" from "any young punk who doesn't think it's appropriate for an older man to dress in the clothes he likes or finds comfortable. So what if he dresses that way because it makes him feel younger? Who is he hurting?" Ike, a sixty-four-year-old retiree in Virginia, says he sometimes worries about the scrutiny of "the younger crowd" when he ventures into gay venues. "One does feel like a visitor from another world already," he suggests. "My thinning silver hair and generous midsection make me stand out, and I feel like the younger ones are aghast to see an 'older gentleman' in their midst. The idea that my clothes are being put under a microscope too is a little galling."

Yet some older men themselves say their contemporaries need to keep watch on their wardrobes, lest they stray into some kind of hazardous Thread Zone of criticism or unintended mirth. "Nobody wants to see some fat old guy trying to dress like a twink," submits Kent, a fifty-three-year-old retired Navy man in San Diego. "It's like any other look, really, and almost doesn't have to do with age at all. I don't care how old you are, if you have a good physique at sixty you'll look just fine in a tank top. If you're fat and flabby at twenty-five, you'll look just as sad if you try and squeeze yourself into tight jeans."

Wayne Northcross of *Esquire* and *Genre* concurs. "I do believe in age-appropriate dressing because it reflects a life lived as well as growth and change," he says. As for the 200-pound body trying to fit into a 150-pound outfit, he says it's not so much a problem of trying to look younger as it is a problem of not understanding one's body. "If you're an older guy whose body is still in shape and things are where they're supposed to be, an athletic look works. If you don't have a fit body, you must accept how your body moves in clothes and make adjustments."

The biggest mistake some men make, he says, is in their assumption that younger men don't find older men attractive. Many do. "The rub is that younger guys are attracted to older guys who look their age," he says. "It's nice to see a guy looking forty, that is, appearing mature, stable, in control, and self-assured. I suspect younger guys are turned off by someone who has an obvious need to look sexy. That slavishness to pimping your body for viewing pleasure seems desperate. By the time you're forty, you should have personal issues of style and appearance sorted out."

Admittedly it can be a fine line to walk. I myself have grown fond of the A&F/Structure/American Eagle/Old Navy look of late, mainly because they all make clothes that are comfortable and pretty easy to throw together when you're late for the subway (they're a lot cheaper, too, compared with all the ridiculously expensive clothes out there). I've also been known to wear a tank top or two on occasion. As John said up near the top of this section, so far I haven't gotten any complaints. Still, I can't help but recall a guy I used to see out all the time, back when I was first coming out a quarter century ago; he was an older gent who insisted on wearing athletic-style gear to the clubs, despite the fact that, charitably, he was the furthest thing from athletic imaginable. I have begged my friends to tell me, should I ever fail to note the inexorable effects of gravity on my aging body—when things are no longer "where they're supposed to be"—to *please* let me know it's just not working anymore.

I can always start sporting a bow tie.

HAIR WE GO

In all my interviews about staying young or looking younger, one of the most oft-mentioned words was "hair" ("tight abs" was up there, too, along with "firm butt"). Many men associate a thick head of hair—or hair that has yet to see a silver thread among the gold, brown, or red—with that youthful image they love so much. And alongside fashion choices, a little hair manipulation is probably the most common strategy that some men use to try and hold back the advancing years.

Some gay men, being, in fact, gay, take this to extremes. After all, nothing says "young" like those fine magenta hues overlying your natural mousy brown or hair bleached to such a shade of platinum it's almost literally screaming "Blond Ambition." Since I've been such a shady character myself on occasion—I've dyed my own hair so many times I've lost count—I have no room to criticize. Go for it, I say. If you find your bliss in a bottle of Clairol Ultra Blue, or if painting your head a fierce shade of fire engine red makes you happy, you've got me as a fan.

Others aren't so charitable. "I think older guys that try to look like trendy club kids by dying their hair unnatural colors are really grasping," says Jason, a twenty-two-year-old student in Seattle. "That stuff looks stupid on younger guys. I think when an older guy does it he's showing how unstable he is, and unhappy with his age." Will, a thirty-five-year-old warehouse worker in Lansing, Michigan, says he wouldn't even think about approaching an "obviously older" guy if his hair was "colored some really weird" shade. "I think that says he's trying to be something he's not, and I'm attracted to reality, not fantasy."

But I do hear from other men who say a middle-aged man is actually saying something rather positive when he adopts such a new look. "Too many men just wear the same hairstyle their whole lives," says Brian, a thirty-year-old physician assistant in Rochester, New York. "They get stuck in a rut, and they tend to criticize anyone who tries to break the mold. I think it's a bold statement when someone says, 'To hell with what society thinks, I'm going to do what I want.' If a guy suddenly bleaches his hair, or makes any other kind of daring change in his appearance, he's probably a lot more interesting to know."

I haven't touched up the hair in quite awhile; I've been considering maybe getting some highlights put in, but lately I've noticed that Nature, in her wisdom, is already providing me with an ample supply of those. Of course we're talking about *gray* highlights, not blond, which brings me to the main reason some men turn to the "bottle." Adam, a forty-year-old retail manager on the West Coast, tells me his own hair started turning gray when he was in his early twenties, and he's been a faithful Just For Men client for the last several years. "I know there are lots of guys who find gray or graying hair attractive, but it just doesn't fit my own self-image." John, a fifty-year-old tech manager in Boston, used to stare at his ever-graying head of hair every morning in the mirror while shaving. "I just couldn't stand looking like my own grandfather," he says. He took the same tack as

Adam, and now his silver mane is concealed with the help of a little Grecian Formula. He's pleased with the results. "As long as the color looks natural on me I'm going to keep using it."

Adam and John aren't alone. Far from it; I saw a report on CNN the other day that said men spend something like $130 million on hair coloring products, three times what they spent just ten years ago. In my own polls I asked the men in my five different age groups if they'd ever dyed their hair to look younger; less than 10 percent of the folks ages twenty-four to twenty-nine had—or admitted as much—but from there the percentages increased. Nearly one-fifth of the thirty- to thirty-nine-year-olds said yes, they've put a little dressing on their salads; almost a quarter of the men ages forty to fifty-nine replied in the affirmative as well. A little color is clearly going a long way for these guys.

"I started real slowly, just added a little here and there," says Ken, a thirty-seven-year-old news photographer in Fresno, California. "I didn't want people at work to make fun of me, or people in my social set to notice. I don't think there's much worse than someone with a bad dye job." Ken says he started going gray just a few years back, and that his hectic profession probably doesn't help. "It's pretty stressful. At least that's what I tell myself when I think about my gray hair." But except for his weekly applications of hair color, he doesn't think about it much anymore. "It just looks like it used to. Maybe when I get to be forty or something I'll let it all grow out, I don't know. At least it's not falling out. Yet."

Oh, yes. The heartbreak of hair loss. Few things tend to rattle a man's self-image more than a collection of his once-prized hair clogging the shower drain or clinging to a brush, especially when he fancies himself as a still-virile stud muffin. Tom, a forty-three-year-old marketing executive in Sacramento, tells me the one thing he misses the most about his youth is his hair, "great, flowing locks" of golden hair, as he puts it. "As I got older the flowing thing just went away, and long thinning hair doesn't look good on anyone." He considered the various remedies available: a hairpiece, a hair weave, or some kind of hair restoration project. In the end he rejected all three, and simply cut it off, down to a very butch stubble. "I was amazed," he still marvels. "I actually looked younger."

Tom stumbled on something that more and more men with thinning hair are finding out. You can sport a buzz cut and attract less adverse attention these days than you could back when a thick head of well-tended-to hair was all the rage. Take a look out on the dance floor at any urban mega disco, gay or straight, and you'll see what I mean. There are any number of shaved or close-cropped heads, bobbing up and down right there with the well-coiffed 'dos. Since those heads belong to men of all ages, older men who take the plunge tend to blend. "You can't beat the maintenance, either," says one older man who says he started getting a "Marine cut" years ago. "It's like I comb my hair with a towel, now. I haven't used a blow dryer or hair gel in years."

Unfortunately it's not a strategy that works for everybody. Harry, a twenty-seven-year-old medical student from New Mexico, suggests that when it comes to cutting it close or shaving it off, African-American, Asian, and Latino men have one up on their white counterparts. "Especially when it comes to the shaved look. A lot of those guys can look really cool or exotic if they have smooth heads. *We* tend to look like convicts or cancer patients." Steven, a thirty-five-year-old bartender in southern California, says he doesn't want to look "like some skinhead Nazi fuck, or a crazy punk skater refugee from 1993." Steven tells me he's only recently started noticing some hair loss, but he's concerned from this point on it's going to be an accelerating process. "I know I sound stupid obsessing about it, but hey . . . people see me, you know? I just can't stand the idea of going bald and looking like my dad before I'm even forty."

Sure enough, not everyone's going to look like Vin Diesel or Yul Brynner sporting a smooth 'do; I remember boot camp at Parris Island and that fateful first night when we were all herded into the barbershop for a shearing at the hands of a sadistic crew of head shavers. Some of us recruits were fortunate enough to possess noggins of relatively pleasing shapes, mostly free of scars, or discolorations à la Gorbachev, but there were lots of guys who didn't. These were the dudes who looked handsome and hunky on the plane ride down with their luxurious manes of brown or blond, but once the barbers got to them they looked downright alien. Where once was hair there now lurked all sorts of unsightly moles and bumps and dents, and they gleamed pale and spooky in the harsh fluorescent lights. It was like an episode of *The X Files.*

Besides cosmetic considerations, some men simply value their hair too much to let it go lightly; like Samson they see it as the source of their strength and virility. So where do they go when the hair starts going? Many head for the drugstore in search of a little minoxidil or to their doctor's office for a Propecia prescription. (Just in case you're not familiar with those two, minoxidil is a topical liquid you apply daily; Propecia is a hormone-based pill.) While several men tell me they do see the results they want, they also tell me either remedy can have some side effects; minoxidil can dry your scalp out and give you dandruff, and Propecia has been known to cool off the libido in some cases. (Ironic, isn't it?) And for many men the products don't achieve the desired results; they may help hair regrow up on top of your head, but that receding hairline will keep on trucking. Some men see no results at all.

Paul Cotterill is a board-certified doctor in Toronto who's specialized in hair restoration for eighteen years. He's treated gay and straight men alike, and guesses that gay men are probably more often concerned about hair loss than their heterosexual counterparts. "I'd say that roughly twenty percent of my patient base is gay. The ones I know about, at any rate. I also have five transgender patients having feminine hairlines planted."

Cotterill tells me when he gets a relatively young patient concerned about hair loss, he usually recommends one of the two medications above, along with as much reassurance as he can muster since not everyone looks bad with a bald pate. Still, he admits this is often a youth-oriented and hair-centric society we live in. "That loss of the frontal hairline, the one that frames your face, can add ten years to one's perceived age. . . . Given the choice between having hair and not having hair, most men would rather have it," he says. "Studies have even shown that in job interviews with all else equal, the man with the hair will more often get the job."

If the topical applications or pills don't work, Cotterill says he'll often recommend restoration surgery if the situation warrants. Hair is taken from the still-growing areas of the patient's scalp and transplanted into thinning areas. Unlike previous eras where the surgery often left visible scars, today's procedures are frequently undetectable. But it doesn't work for everyone. "Some patients' hair is just too thin and they don't have enough donor hair, or some are too young and it's too early for the procedure." But he maintains there can be success stories. "I do not know of any other cosmetic procedure that can yield such dramatic results." He tells me about the "Baseball Cap" guy, a young man who came in depressed and shy, and so despondent about his hair loss that he never took off his hat. "The skin under his cap was pale and white, while the rest of his forehead was tan." Cotterill says after three sessions over a year and a half, the man was back in his office, open, happy, and with a girlfriend in tow. "I don't mean to imply that that's the case with all my patients, but it's great when it happens."

Like any other medical procedure, hair restoration has its drawbacks. Not all surgeons are equal and some might botch the job. Even with the finest doctors sometimes the transplants just don't "take," and there can always be postoperative infections or complications. Maybe the biggest drawback is the cost, anywhere between $2,000 and $15,000 a session, depending on the surgeon or clinic.

If you're not willing to shoot the moon on surgery, there's always hair "replacement." You've probably seen the infomercials, where they claim they can take a man bald as a cue ball and "bond" replacement hair to his remaining strands and achieve a "full, natural look. You can go swimming, shower, work out . . . no one will ever guess it's not your real hair!"

I know I sound skeptical, but it's only because I am. I've worked in television, and I've learned not to believe much of anything you see advertised at 3 a.m. Still, I did find a few men who've tried it out and now swear by it. "It really does work, you know?" says Chuck, a fifty-three-year-old insurance agent in central New York. "I didn't like the idea of anyone cutting into my scalp. They matched the hair to my old hair exactly, and trust me, no one knows I'm bald."

HAIR WE GO, AGAIN

While on the subject of hair I'd be remiss if I didn't mention the "other" hair some men dwell on in their quest for eternal youth.

That's the hair below the neckline, the stuff that grows on chests, shoulders, backs, even way "down there."

"I started 'going smooth' a few years back, after I started getting more serious about weight training," says Jeff, a thirty-year-old police officer in northern Virginia. "I guess I started noticing that most of the really buffed up guys at the clubs hardly had any hair on them. . . . Then I realized they looked buff because they had no hair on their chests. Muscles just stand out better. Your abs look hotter. I'm pretty hairy naturally, and it does tend to make one look older. Now I shave my chest and abs every few days, and I get my back waxed once a month. Smooth looks younger, and I have to say I like the way it feels. So does my boyfriend."

"All that hair just had to go," says Sam, a forty-year-old lawyer in Georgia. "I had it everywhere, and it made me look like an aging caveman. I used to use Nair, but now I get waxed every few weeks. I look like I did back in high school, except I have a bigger build. It really takes the age off."

In the interest of full disclosure, let me admit that I too have done the smooth thing from time to time. Like Jeff I've been known to shave the fuzzy growth off my chest and stomach on occasion, and yes, it does feel strangely pleasant. The first time you do it it's almost erotic, since your body doesn't feel quite like your own anymore. That, as much as looking younger, is part of the appeal, and as Jeff notes, muscles do stand out better.

I can't say I care much for the stubble that pops up after a few days, though, and that led me to try waxing a few years back. I'd been told it was much better than shaving; since the root of the hair is pulled out, the hair that grows back does so much more slowly. I was also told there'd be much less skin irritation and much less chance of ingrown hairs.

Sad to say that wasn't the case. That honey/wax stuff they put on me really did quite a number on my skin; it was days before the redness faded (I also got a number of nasty ingrown hairs that took weeks to heal). And the pain . . . well, when anyone puts hot wax on you, applies a cloth for a few seconds, then rips a wallet-sized patch of hair out of your tender chest area, it's not going to be a walk in the park. Honestly, I've had tattoos and wisdom teeth that hurt less.

Maybe I'm just hypersensitive, but if you've never done it before, be warned.

I also tried electrolysis once, where the attendant zaps your hair follicles one at a time, but as you might imagine it's rather unpleasant and time consuming, and at least in my case, not at all permanent. A much less painful but much more expensive alternative is *laser* hair removal. Electrolysis or waxing can set you back anywhere from $50 to $100 a session, depending on the size of the area you're having done and the pretentiousness of the salon that's doing it. Laser is playing on a whole different level; we're talking hundreds of dollars per session, and likely thousands spent by the time all's been seared and done.

Laser hair removal attacks the offending follicle itself while it's in the growing stage, basically using thermal energy that passes through the skin to destroy the follicle's ability to produce hair. You can target much larger areas in a single session than you can with electrolysis, and it appears to be much more effective in permanently removing that annoying growth. It's also reportedly less painful, though patients describe a mild to moderate "burning" sensation during the treatments, and the treated area can be red and tender for a couple of days afterward.

There are a few other caveats. Since laser only works in the growing stage—and all your hair follicles are stubbornly uncoordinated in their growth cycles—you have to go back for repeated sessions until all the growing hair has been treated. Since the procedure targets darker areas more effectively than lighter ones, those with dark hair on fair skin are more likely to experience success than people with lighter hair. Redheads and blonds will likely find themselves out of luck. And it doesn't always work for even the best of candidates; some hair just refuses to go gently, and keeps coming back, vampire-like. Still, most patients will tell you they have less hair after undergoing treatments than they did before.

If none of this is for you, if you just can't stand shaving or waxing, and you can't countenance the cost of electrolysis or lasers but you still want that hair gone, take heart. You still have options left, like all those new hair removal creams and lotions. If all else fails, there's always tweezers.

However they make their hair go away, many men tell me they miss the days when such measures weren't so commonly employed. "I remember when a hairy chest was considered sexy," says Joe, a fifty-one-year-old factory manager in Michigan. "I remember Burt Reynolds in *Cosmopolitan* and Tom Selleck in the 1980s. Hell, even some of the Village People were hairy. But I guess that's not considered *en vogue* anymore."

"I'll tell you whose fault it is," says Barry, a thirty-six-year-old advertising executive in New York. "It's Bruce Weber's and Herb Ritts' [both photographers], and all those other guys who created this 'perfect male body' image we have now," he says. "Ever since the Calvin Klein ads of the 1980s, all the way up to the Abercrombie and Fitch catalog and the 2Xist ads we have now, the idealized image we've bought into is this smooth, hairless youth thing. It's the 'in' thing right now." Like any other style, Barry says hair "will definitely be back, you mark my words."

Of course, many men tell me that hair appreciation never went anywhere. "I can't, for the life of me, understand the obsession in the magazines for the shaved look," says Duke, a forty-seven-year-old lawyer/consultant in Norwalk, Connecticut. "I like hair, not necessarily a 'bear,' but I happen to think body hair is unbelievably sexy."

"These smooth guys kill me," says Art, a forty-three-year-old shop owner in eastern Pennsylvania and a leather bar enthusiast. "They think everybody in the world does the same thing or likes the same kind of guys they do. You check out the Bike Stop in Philly or the Eagle in DC and it's hair galore. We're just not into the circuit party-smooth twink scene. We're not afraid to be ourselves. We're not afraid to show our age."

But many men are. "I wouldn't be caught dead in a club, or at least I wouldn't take off my shirt, if I hadn't had the body hair done," says Ted, a thirty-nine-year-old self-avowed "circuit boy." He says he has a good reason. "About two years ago these gray hairs started popping up all over my chest, so now it's like snow all over. It really gets obvious if I have a tan, it's like BAM, in your face, instant daddy. No, I have to take it off, if I'm going to 'take it off.'"

That's especially true, some older men tell me, of the "hair down there." "Nothing is less sexy than gray hairs in the nether regions," says Lionel, a forty-seven-year-old from Florida who started noting that particular phenomenon a few years ago. "At first I just trimmed it, to make it less obvious. Finally I just said the hell with it and started shaving it. I found I liked it . . . it made me feel more sexy, somehow."

Admittedly, that sort of "smooth" thing isn't always just a province of the older guy trying to look not-so-old. It's not even just a gay thing. I know some fairly young guys, gay and straight, who shave off all their body hair, including the short and curlies. My twenty-four-year-old straight bud Jack, who's built like a professional wrestler, explains that he started shaving his chest and tummy as soon as the hairs started sprouting at seventeen or so. He also confides that his girlfriends like him smooth "in that area" and he's happy to oblige. (Judging from the other guys in the gym locker room, most of them presumably straight, he's not at all alone.) I've had many younger gay friends tell me they think body hair of any kind, especially pubic hair, is just "kinda gross," and they have no problem at all trimming it to almost nothing, or shaving it off altogether. For some it's like a kind of advanced hygiene; for others it's almost like a fetish, or as if they're looking to achieve some kind of androgynous, gender-neutral approach to sexuality.

Whatever floats your boat, I tell them, and anyone else so moved to remove. Personally, I find a little tinsel around the Christmas tree to be a perfectly nice decoration, so long as it doesn't get in the way of the presents.

But that's just me.

MEN'S FITNESS

There was a time, John says, when he could walk into a bar or restaurant and almost feel the wind whip up from everyone's heads turning to see him. "I know how shallow and egotistical that sounds, but it's true. My parents gave me some good genes, and I took them and ran."

A dedicated athlete in sports from soccer to lacrosse to crew, he developed a chiseled, flawless physique, and all through college he was often regarded as a "golden child." He's not sure when things started going south on him. Maybe the legal career he pursued became too time intensive or he fell in love too much with rich foods and wine. "Maybe I just got too fucking lazy when it came to taking care of myself," he says.

In any case, what was once a chiseled physique became over the years a paunchy shadow of its former self. Now in his midforties and quite a successful attorney living near West Hollywood, he could walk into bars and restaurants and barely cause a ripple. "Unless one of my clients was in there and needed my advice."

Then one day—he's still not sure what the specific motivation was—he simply stopped eating "all that fatty crap," joined a gym, found a personal trainer, and got lean again over the course of a year. He watches what he eats now fairly religiously—"I only cheat on the weekends"—and he says his self-esteem hasn't just bounced back, "it's better than ever before. I also look about ten years younger. If I'd have known it could be like this, I'd have hit the gym a long time ago."

John's story is fairly typical of many of the older men I interviewed, men who've discovered that joining a gym, or getting involved in any kind of regular athletic activity, is like discovering your very own Fountain of Youth. They tell me that, with some discipline and attention to diet, they're uncovering the once-fit frat boy within. Others find that though their actual youths were spent inside bodies that were never quite fit—they were too thin and awkward, or a bit overweight and clunky—their workouts have provided them with an opportunity to remake themselves, inside and out.

Some, like John, engage the services of a personal trainer; others use videos, books, or workout magazines for inspiration. Whatever the spark, they've taken a look in the mirror, and fired up a desire to look and feel better.

"I think what pushed me over the edge was seeing all the kids in the clubs," says Roy, a thirty-year-old consultant in Connecticut. "It just occurred to me how I'd really let myself go, and I wanted to see if I could have the same kind of washboard abs and chiseled pecs. I'm not all the way there yet, but I'm getting there fast. I'm not sure if it makes me look younger, but I'm sure it makes me more attractive to younger guys, which is sort of what I'm into."

By some estimates, more than half of the general American population is overweight, with many bordering on the dangerously obese. As the late *National Journal* writer and syndicated columnist Michael Kelly wrote in the August 1, 2001, edition of *The Washington Post,* after a summer vacation during which he'd observed crowds gathering at the beach:

> My fellow middle-aged Americans, we are some kind of fat. . . . As a people, we have never been this fat. Probably, no people has ever been this fat. . . . We are great, soft bins of finest quality lard, a nation of wide loads wallowing down the highway. We have thighs that look like sacks of parkerhouse rolls. We have stomachs that can shelter entire kindergartens from the glare of the noonday sun. Our bottoms dwarf the seats of our poor suffering chairs as the mind of God dwarfs the mind of man. We do not walk; we shake, jiggle, and roll. (p. A17)

It's a popular conceit that gay men tend to take better care of their bodies as they age than their straight counterparts and my polls would tend to indicate there's at least some truth to that. Nearly half of my youngest group, those ages thirteen to twenty-three, said they were gym members or at least work out regularly; almost two-thirds of twenty-four- to twenty-nine-year-olds turn out to be gym rats. The numbers take a dip after that; I guess the majority of those career-minded thirty- to thirty-nine-year-olds, like the formerly fat John just mentioned, have somewhere else to be. But the postforty group rebounds back to a full third, as I suppose many take stock of themselves, or the latest mortality tables. The last group, the senior set, is least represented at 18 percent, but I imagine that's at least as many as similarly aged heteros.

In some of the bigger cities you can find health clubs that rival the bar scene as a place where gay men socialize. "I'd rather meet a guy by spotting him on the bench press than spotting him by a urinal in some dark bar," says Gary, a thirty-six-year-old software designer in Boston. "I think it's just healthier having a group of friends that I work out with than a group that only goes bar hopping all weekend." Jerry, a twenty-eight-year-old gas station worker in Alabama, says the gym he goes to is "just about the only place in town" where you *can* find gay people. "It's not like we talk about it real openly, but you get the idea pretty quickly if that guy you're working out with might be 'family,'" he says. "It's guys anywhere from twenties to fifties, but everyone is in pretty good shape. I hope I'm in shape like that when I'm in my fifties."

All social aspects aside, as someone who's been a gym rat himself since the age of twenty and an occasional fitness trainer over the years, I can tell you that, when it's done properly, weight training or regular exercise has to be the most effective of all the youth-restoring strategies gay men pursue. Unlike a new wardrobe or haircut, those hours spent in the gym, on the bike path, or on the tennis/basketball court provide a lot more than cosmetic changes. I've watched thin guys bulk up and fat guys slim down, and nothing matches that look in their eyes when they see the transformation in their bodies. I've seen guys once cowed into shyness by embarrassment over how they were built turn into outgoing, confident people in the space of just a few months; they weren't just building muscle or trimming fat, they were often restoring a damaged sense of self-esteem. Even if looking younger isn't a priority, you're going to look better, feel better, and be healthier.

It doesn't just happen inside a musty gym. Stan, a thirty-five-year-old journalist in New York, says he never wanted "to be one of those big muscle-head guys, I just wanted to drop all this excess poundage." Stan says he never picked up a weight, just a new set of running shoes. He started slowly, as one should always do, just jogging around the block in his neighborhood. Eventually those few blocks turned into miles, and within the year Stan says he had "freed the thin guy who was trapped inside me." Barney, a forty-two-year-old truck driver from Minnesota, says he wasn't drawn to the streets; he started swimming regularly after watching the U.S. men's team win multiple gold medals at the 2000 Olympic Games in Sydney. "I knew I wasn't going to get their physiques . . . they're just kids, you know . . . but I figured I could give it a shot and see what it did for me." Like Stan, Barney says that inside a year he'd dropped nearly thirty pounds, and now he tells me his health is improved, and he feels better than ever. As for his social life, Barney says when he rolls into almost any town with a gay scene he "doesn't have any trouble meeting folks. I guess an older guy who stays in shape can still be appealing."

Rob is a thirty-two-year-old fitness trainer in the Midwest. He applauds guys such as Stan and Barney for getting serious about improving their bodies, but he tells me it's important for anyone considering a return to fitness to remember a few key points. "First, talk to your doctor and make sure he agrees you're up to it. Just about anyone can do some kind of workout safely, but you want to make sure you're not going to aggravate any kind of underlying physical problem. Once you get the go ahead, *go ahead!* There's just no reason not to pick up a weight or a tennis racquet, or to start pedaling that bike or hitting the pool. Don't put it off, or ever think you're too far gone. If you started once and stopped, start again. Forget yesterday, you have a world of tomorrows to think about.

"What a lot of tired, overworked guys never seem to realize is that exercise goes a long way toward restoring your energy level," he explains. "The more you exercise, the more energy you get. The more muscle mass you have, the more calories your body burns up just to maintain it. It's all win-win, as long as you don't start too fast or go too hard. The really sad thing is that so many guys sit around pining for the bodies they used to have, but never lift their butts off the couch to make it happen. Sure, it's true not everyone can look like he's eighteen again, but if you're forty-five, would twenty-eight or even thirty-eight look so bad? Not everyone can look like a bodybuilder, but everyone can look *better.* It's the closest thing to magic I know and everyone has that power inside him. You just have to find the will to use it."

If Rob's enthusiasm for working out and fitness is palpable, so is the disgust many other gay men have for people who spend all those hours pumping iron or sweating it out on the StairMaster. A gay colleague of mine once remarked that he thought that older men who worked out and stayed in shape were "kind of creepy," as if it was somehow more proper that they should just go off somewhere and slowly deteriorate. Chris from Ohio thinks the gym rats are surrendering the substance to the superficial. "Many guys in their thirties want the brains they have 'now' and the bodies they had 'then.' What I find sad is that being 'out' once stood for being who you actually are. I think the message now is it's OK to be gay . . . now go work for the washboard abs, tight butt, and boyish wardrobe." In a hysterical parody of the gym rat culture called "Trapped in the Body of a Circuit Boy" in the June 2002 issue of *Instinct* magazine, Camper English wrote of waking up to find that he's now inhabiting "the body of a circuit queen." Though at first he thought having such a finely turned-out body is bliss, he soon found himself staring into mirrors for hours:

> I start to worry that my arms and chest are out of sync, that my calves are too small and that my butt isn't bubbly enough. . . . It's amazing how much you can find wrong with yourself when you're this close to perfection. (p. 94)

Not too long ago, the *Washington Blade* installed a feature called "Bitch Session," an anonymous half page of reader kvetches and commentary about the city's gay scene, and gay life in general. The page has been a never-ending source of fascination and entertainment for me and a valuable resource besides, since so many of the topics I talk about in this book are chewed over and debated in heated fashion. The subject of men who go to great lengths to stay young, or younger looking, has been a mainstay; not a week goes by when someone isn't throwing in his two cents, or throwing darts, at something or someone that gets his dander up. Gyms—and those who frequent them—have been a virtual epicenter of vitriolic discontent. Sometimes the comments are narrowly targeted: "To the stuck-up trendoid (yes, we all see your goatee, your Florida tan, etc.) who always gets a locker near mine late mornings at the Y: I'm not a specimen in a cage for your visual scrutiny" (May 24, 2002, p. E-3). Others are more general in nature, if no less caustic: "Would all the muscle boys stop working out long enough to notice their emotionally empty selves, then try to work on their personalities just as hard as their bodies?" (July 26, 2002, p. E-3). And this one: "For all you arrogant musclemen . . . sure you're beautiful, but how long do you think *anyone* is going to put up with your attitudes? You'll have perfect abs and never know real love" (May 24, 2002, p. E-3).

"People who write those kinds of things are probably insecure about *their* looks," says Jesse, a thirty-one-year-old friend of mine who frequents the same gym where I work out. "They really want to believe that guys in great shape must have some kind of shitty emotional life. I've got news for them. A lot of us are doing just fine, thanks. Sure, some guys are arrogant . . . but most really aren't. We're just proud of how we look, and these couch potatoes with the pot bellies can't stand the idea that we could be hot *and* happy."

It's undeniably true that some men do take their concept of fitness to extreme and unhealthy levels, and I'm talking about mental health every bit as much as I'm addressing the physical. Where some men find their self-esteem improving along with their bodies, others become almost anorexic while they chase Adonis (I've taken to calling the phenomenon "abs-session"). They can never get lean enough, or big enough, for their liking. Whatever they're looking for, they're never going to find it in a gym.

One man with a unique perspective on all this is "Moody" Mustafa, a forty-four-year-old physician in Washington, DC. He's also a well-known charity fund-raiser and avid photographer who travels widely, documenting the circuit party scene on his Web site <www. moodypics.com>. As an HIV/AIDS specialist, and a rather fit individual himself, it's fair to say he regularly sees gay men at their best *and* their worst. "I like to say 'terminal vanity' is the number one diagnosis in my practice," he says. "Many of my patients are very obsessed with going to the gym, getting very 'cut up,' using far too many nutritional supplements, and using illegal steroids. There is a lot of pressure in the male gay community to be physically 'perfect,' while overlooking other important aspects of humanity such as kindness, compassion, and humility."

"It's like anything else; you always have a handful of guys who define the edges of proper behavior by behaving badly, or ignorantly," says Pete, a forty-one-year-old self-described gym rat and circuit party goer in San Francisco. "Sure, you always have your 'body Nazis' who refuse to have a conversation with anyone who doesn't look like he can bench his own weight. But I don't think you can judge the majority of us gym rats so harshly, any more than you can assume that just because someone is on a diet, they're also sneaking off to the bathroom to stick a finger down their throat. I've never done steroids in my life. I just pump iron and party hard. . . . I also have a boyfriend of ten years who I'm totally committed to."

"Look, I joined a gym to work out, get in shape, and just feel better about myself," says Yuri, a forty-year-old businessman in southern California. "I just want to be as healthy as I can, and look as good as I can, for as long as I can. Tell me exactly what's so bad about that?"

LIKE A SURGEON

This being America, some men just aren't content if they can't find a shortcut or a quick fix to their fitness woes. Why spend all those hours on an elliptical trainer to burn off fat, they reason, when an hour and a half in a doctor's office will get you the same result?

Enter the man with the hose, in this case, the plastic surgeon who uses liposuction to remove in mere minutes stores of fat that could take months to exercise or diet away. It's just one of a number of surgical procedures that more and more gay men are indulging in these days. There's also Botox—an injected substance that can erase years of wrinkles off your face—and of course, the time-honored face-lift, eye job, collagen injections, chest and calf implants, you name it. If there's a cosmetic imperfection, someone's got a plan and procedure that can lop it off or pump it up.

According to the American Society for Aesthetic Plastic Surgery, more than half a million men underwent some kind of surgical or nonsurgical cosmetic procedure in 2000; in the past few years male liposuctions alone have increased by about 90 percent over their mid-1990s level. My polling doesn't exactly indicate that we're *all* setting aside time in our day planners or PDAs for a little side trip to the surgeon; percentages in my three oldest age groups are still in single digits. But my lengthier surveys indicate that many gay men *would* have the procedures done, if only they could afford them.

Keith is a fifty-year-old former surveyor in the Midwest. "I spent so many years out in the sun and wind, and I started seeing some facial sags here and there I just didn't care much for. I had a little cash put aside, and went to have things tightened up a little. It was amazing, and totally worth it." Frank, a forty-three-year-old stockbroker in Manhattan, says his liposuction a few years back was the "best thing I've ever done. I'd been dieting and exercising for years and I still couldn't lose those love handles. Now I look like I did the summer before I went away for college." And Ernie, a forty-five-year-old writer in Louisiana, says he hasn't had any work done just yet, but he's planning ahead. "It's going to be my fiftieth birthday present to myself. I think I'll have a total makeover. Of course I'll probably have to move, because I just know my friends will give me all kinds of shit about it!"

A lot of gay men aren't even waiting that long. In the January/February 2002 issue of *Instinct* magazine, editor Parker Ray profiled a number of younger men who've become big fans of Botox. He quotes Eric, a twenty-eight-year-old "aspiring actor," who was already getting regular injections to smooth out his "imperfections." As Eric put it, the injections were just like "going in and getting your eyes corrected, or your teeth cleaned, or your hair cut." As an actor, Eric told *Instinct* that it's his job to keep up his appearance, because "if my face is ever going to be on the big screen, the size of a semitruck, those imperfections are going to be obvious" (p. 52).

None of this comes cheaply, of course. If you think the cost of hair restoration or laser hair removal is steep, your plastic surgeon's fees can make those look like cab fare. Liposuction procedures usually start in the $2,000 to $3,000 range, as always, depending on the amount of fat removed and the size of the area being treated. A face-lift—and I hope you're sitting down—often starts in the $6,000 to $10,000 range, and can exceed $20,000. (Botox is relatively cheap, which probably helps explain its newfound popularity; most doctors charge between $100 and $300 a session.) Recognizing the high cost of most procedures they offer, many doctors are only too happy to arrange financing.

Moody Mustafa tells me he's seen plenty of "success stories" when it comes to plastic surgery, but there are "nightmare" tales as well. "There's always the risk of death from general anesthesia or from postoperative infections. I saw one patient who developed a severe infection of his chest after he had chest implants. He had to have one removed and had an open draining wound for about three months. Now he only has the one implant and is still considering whether or not to have the second one put back. His chest looks stupid. Then there are the patients who had liposuction but didn't stick to a regimented diet and exercise program, only to gain all the weight and love handles back. What a waste of money!"

And *Instinct*'s Pierce Mattie cautions that, though many gay men who undergo a little surgical makeover will find their lives subtly changed for the better—or more than subtly changed—there may be no *drastic* change. "The job, man, or house you always wanted will not knock on your door the day after you have surgery. Nor will you become a Ford supermodel. You may, however, feel a lot better about yourself and your situation. . . . Too much surgery says that your self-esteem may need some serious soul searching, journal writing, and self-exploration."

EXTRAS, EXTRAS

Holding on to youth may be simply a matter of "repeating one's follies," as the sainted Oscar Wilde once remarked; youthful clothes, attention to fitness, a little help with the hair or a nip and tuck here and there may serve many gay men's interests. But I talked with a number of gay men who had different strategies, sometimes rather subtle.

Lloyd, a thirty-seven-year-old shop worker in Kansas City, Missouri, says he simply started wearing the earring he once wore back in college days. "I guess I just associated it with all the fun we had in school. I doubt anyone else even notices it . . . so many people these days have piercings in so many different places. But when I see it, it sort of takes me back." He tells me he's thinking about getting "something else" pierced, but he's not sure yet what body part to target.

Anson, a thirty-nine-year-old lawyer in Minneapolis, says he just tries to "stay current with what's going on in music and popular culture. I think a lot of guys start feeling old once they lose track of what's going on with younger people, in terms of their fashion, what kind of music they listen to, the different things they're into as opposed to the stuff we did when we were their age." Anson says he doesn't always "get" the new trends, but he's always willing to give them a look or a listen. "At least I don't feel totally 'out of it' when someone mentions a new band or videogame."

Phil, a forty-five-year-old municipal employee in Austin, Texas, says he and his partner exchanged gifts a few years back when they were celebrating their birthdays, which they happen to share. "We agreed to try and be creative, and we went to a tattoo parlor. He had one of those tribal bands done, while I had an abstract design put on my lower back. I know a lot of guys of all ages have tatts nowadays, but none of our friends do. They were sort of taken aback, and maybe that's why it made me feel like a kid again, doing something kind of 'out there' and unexpected."

"I guess I've just never been one of those guys who gives up as he gets older," says Bob, a forty-seven-year-old writer in New Mexico. "When I was living in Minneapolis I knew several guys who withdrew into themselves as the years went by. It was like, 'Okay, I'm an older guy now, so I can't do this anymore. I can't wear that, I can't go there, it's not my scene anymore.' What rubbish! At forty-seven I think of myself in exactly the same way as I did at thirty-seven or twenty-seven. My life circumstances may change . . . one year I may have more money to play with, the next I may have to tighten up . . . but the inner me stays the same. I keep being curious about life. I keep wondering what's waiting for me around the next corner, and I keep waking up like a kid on Christmas Day. If you want to know the best strategy for staying 'young,' I think that will do it."

"It's a cliché, but some things are clichés because they're true: age really is just a state of mind," says George, a fifty-three-year-old professor in the Northeast. "My partners and I over the years have always been the active sort (I wouldn't be with anyone who wasn't!) and we've traveled, camped, hiked, and biked all over the place. Besides the level of fitness that gives one, it keeps the mind focused on the positive. I'm also fortunate that my job keeps me close to the younger set, and I think I absorb some of their energy and enthusiasm for life." Indeed, dozens of men I talked with suggest that simply hanging out with a younger crowd, or even dating someone younger, has helped them shave the years off their mental outlooks, if not their physical bodies. That's a theme I'll revisit in more depth in later chapters.

"TIME MARCHES ON"

"An aging body tells the story of your life—the number of times you've smiled, the meals you've eaten, the miles you've run, the car

accident you had, the virus you survived," wrote my friend Marc
Acito in his nationally syndicated column.

> And those features that don't tell the story of your life, inherited
> traits like varicose veins and liver spots, tell the story of the an-
> cestors who preceded you. To be ashamed of your balding head
> or saggy jowls is a dishonor to the genetic material that got you
> here in the first place.

Marc's column calls to mind the current of "youth rejectionism" I
found afoot in the land. A significant number of men I surveyed think
this fascination with looking young is fatuous at best, and dangerous
at its worst. "Age catches up with all of us," says Jerry, a fifty-four-
year-old doctor in Arizona. "I'm not sure if some of these guys have
really considered where their obsession is leading them to. At some
point the clock will hit 10:30 or 11 . . . I don't think they're going to be
'ready' to be old, unlike someone who has let himself 'grow old
gracefully.'" Matt, a forty-two-year-old contractor in Kansas, agrees.
"You have to make your peace with a lot of things in life, and one of
them is your eventual demise. In the end, gravity wins. I don't say that
in any kind of morbid sense, in fact in a lot of ways it's a blessing to
those who can see the value of a clock ticking. You get motivated to
do things, get things done, move on to the next thing, instead of just
letting life happen to you. Along the way, you're going to start showing your age. I don't have anything against people who make sure
they look their best, or keep themselves in shape as they age. I do that,
too (though maybe not as much as I could). But when looking young
starts becoming everything to you, or when you're just obsessed with
the superficial, you really risk looking, and acting, rather pathetic."
On the *Blade*'s "Bitch Session" page, one man left this comment:

> We need to grow up and accept the fact that we're growing older.
> Stop wasting your time and energy trying to look like you're
> still in your 20's. No amount of creams, lotions, hair implants
> and pec implants is going to change that. Time marches on, and
> it's time you recognized that it's marching across your face.
> (July 19, 2002, p. E-3)

Others simply grow tired of the whole youth business. Bill is a fifty-eight-year-old retiree living in California. "When I first came out at the age of thirty-nine, I tried to make up for my lost youth when I should have been simply enjoying being gay," he says. "I went to the gym, got contact lenses, dyed my hair, the whole nine yards. It seemed to work for awhile, and it did do wonders for my self-esteem; feeling more confident about myself made me more confident with others. But after I met my first lover and fell into a long-term relationship, all that youth preserving just went out the window. It's too exhausting!"

I also talked with men who told me they wouldn't look younger for anything, even if they could; it would cut their social lives in half. "I discovered a long time ago that while 'twink' is temporary, 'daddy' can last a lifetime," says Charlie, a forty-seven-year-old businessman in Florida. "I never had half the action at twenty that I've had since forty. Do I look my age? At least, probably older. Hasn't kept me down yet. Talk to me in ten years."

Chapter 4

The Untouchables

Is there something more than what I've been handed?
I've been crawling in the dark, looking for the answer.

Hoobastank
"Crawling in the Dark"

"I was really, really upset, and I needed someone to give me some advice." Marco, a sixteen-year-old high school student in California, is telling me about a conversation he was having the other night on the Internet. His parents, both military, had just gotten orders for an overseas transfer, and Marco was facing the prospect of having his whole life uprooted. "I'm a Navy brat, so it's not like it's never happened before, but we've lived here a long time. Since the last time we moved I've come to realize that I'm gay, made some gay friends, and I have this one boy that I like a lot."

He says he doesn't want to come out to his parents, doesn't want his life to change; he's not certain how happy he'll be cooped up on a Navy base in some strange foreign country. With no relatives he could stay with here, flying the coop was beginning to look like the only option. "I just couldn't stand the idea of living like that for two years until I could get back here to school. So I was online, chatting with different people . . . I just wanted to hear some ideas."

Marco tells me that, with all due respect to kids his own age, he's just not much interested in what they think when it comes to major life decisions. "I'm pretty grown up, I guess, in a lot of ways. Most kids just have a lot of romantic, unrealistic ideas." He was trying to seek out advice from someone with a few years on him, someone who had been around the block a time or two. "But all I found was two kinds of people in the chats. A few guys seemed like they were really interested in helping me, but the longer I talked to them it was like, 'Hey, I'd really like to hook up with you.'" And the other kind? "They were nice to me for a few minutes, until I told them how old I was. Most of them just stopped talking to me. One guy who didn't stop talking got real angry with me, told me to get offline and stop trying to get older guys into trouble."

Of all the young guys I've talked with, Marco's story really sticks out in my mind because it symbolizes the different attitudes many older men manifest when they find themselves confronted with a gay youth, especially one who's underage. Some see the youngster as vulnerable, someone ripe for the picking. Others get as far away as they can, as fast as they can, lest they be accused of anything improper; many of them seem downright hostile to the kid, as if the very fact that he's an underage gay boy is something dangerous and volatile.

But most just seem to look the other way. "I never, *ever* talk to anyone I think might be too young," says Michael, a forty-four-year-old designer on Long Island. "I know they have it rough sometimes, but so did I. I survived, and trust me, the world wasn't half as accepting then as it is now. I'm sure they'll find their way without any help from me."

It's rather odd timing that I would start this chapter just as the headlines scream of "pedophile priests" run amuck in parishes from coast to coast. (One friend of mine the other day nudged me, and said in his inimitably sarcastic fashion, "Where were these guys when *I* was in Catholic school? At least they would have made it *interesting!*") In the past few days I've read a half-dozen stories of older men who've arranged on the Internet to meet someone younger, often across state lines; of course, when the unwitting sap arrives for his nookie at the Motel 6, it's the Feds who are waiting there to drop the hammer on him, not the willing and able sixteen-year-old he was expecting. (He's fucked, all right, just not in quite the manner he was hoping.)

I'm not making light of sexual abuse, nor am I pleading the devil's case here. I have little sympathy for anyone who preys on kids who have no idea what they're getting into. I think people who joke about such things (as my friend above does) do so to make the best of situations that give all of us a case of the squirms. For truly these nefarious goings-on create a climate of suspicion—and prosecution of such withering proportions—that you almost can't blame an older gay man for running like a scalded ape whenever a gay boy walks in the room. And I'm not just talking about men over thirty. Jonathan, a twenty-year-old college student in Gainesville, Florida, tells me about the time a few months back when a twelve-year-old kid instant messaged him when he was online, asking him questions about what it was like to be gay. "I played it safe and started ignoring him. What if his mother happened to walk in the room? I don't want to come across as a pedophile. It's not that I don't care about him being opened up to gay culture, it's that I'm not going to put myself in the position to get into trouble. Kids that age should be looking to their peers for support. . . . The second an *over*age guy steps in, they become a role model for the youth, and in today's society that's not accepted."

"There's just too much risk these days to get involved with a gay kid, even if it's just being his friend or mentor," says Carey, a twenty-eight-year-old engineer in Atlanta. "As soon as anyone finds out that *I'm* gay, they're going to assume I'm after him sexually. I would never do anything inappropriate with someone who wasn't old enough, but for some people, gay man plus gay boy equals a scandal, and it doesn't matter what the truth is. They're sure I'm 'doing him' when no one's around. So I'm sorry, kid. You're on your own. Call me when you're legal. Right now you're untouchable."

I fear attitudes like that—and according to my surveys, they're sadly common—are creating a sad and dangerous situation for many of America's gay kids. Certainly there are resources available online for gay youth—I've listed several in the resources section of this book—and a number of gay youth organizations are up and running in cities large and small across the nation. But as helpful and vital as they are, formal institutions and Web resources can only go so far. There's really nothing like the give and take between human beings that occurs in day-to-day, unstructured life, and the wisdom that might be passed down from one generation to the next . . . not to mention the new "perspectives" an older man might gain from seeing the world through younger eyes. From what I hear from young and old alike in my surveys and interviews—we've already touched on some of it—there's a real disconnect out there between conception and reality.

Isolated from real and positive interaction with someone older, far too many gay adolescents have no idea that happy and worthwhile lives may well await them just a few years down the road. Without the guideposts a well-meaning and positive adult can lend them, it's possible they just might lose their way. And far too many older gay men simply have no concept of what it's like to be a "queer and questioning" thirteen- or fourteen-year-old in junior high school or a closeted sixteen-year-old high school student. Absent that perspective and an intimate knowledge of what these kids are going through, they do little or nothing to help.

THE LOST BOYS

Cris is twenty-one, and a waiter at a restaurant in Seattle. He had dreams once about going to college and pursuing a degree in design or art, but that's on hold for a few more years. Right now, he's just getting himself back on his feet after what he says were "four years of hell on earth," during which he was kicked out of his house and forced to live on the streets, then came "way too close" to getting HIV from a "drug-addicted dude" he lived with for a few months a couple of years back.

He tells me it's funny I would run into him online to talk about experiences like his, because he's just now scraped up enough cash to buy a used computer. "It's a piece of shit, and runs so slow . . . but now I finally feel like I have a link to the outside world, and a nice stable situation to live in. The group house where I have my room . . . it's like being in a family. But not like my *real* family. They just couldn't deal with me."

By his own admission Cris says he was probably "way too much" for his mother and father in west Texas to handle; by junior high he was already wearing outlandish clothes—"at least they were crazy clothes by local standards," he says—and by the time he was in high school he was dying his hair bizarre colors and getting pierced in places most people work very hard to keep sharp objects away from.

He always knew he was gay and also knew his family would never accept it. "I think I was acting so wild to keep the focus off my sexuality and more on my behavior. I was getting picked on at school . . . I guess I invited it by acting so wild. When kids would call me fag or fairy or queer I told myself they were picking on what I *did,* not who I *was*."

At sixteen Cris says he "hooked up" for the first time, with a local boy he met off the Internet. "It was so fucked up. His brother caught us, my family found out, and my mother started searching my room for anything that might have 'made me that way.' They took my computer, threw away all my club clothes, and told me I had a choice: keep being gay or keep being their son. I told them I was their son whether I was gay or not. I guess they didn't see it that way."

Cris says his father packed him a bag and told him to go live with his "gay friends." Trouble is, Cris didn't really have any. "I think that other kid's family sent him off to military school or something. Whatever, I didn't have anywhere to go, but I left anyway. I hitched rides, sometimes for free, sometimes in exchange for blowing a guy, and I ended up in San Francisco because I'd been told that's where all the homeless gay kids go. To be honest I actually enjoyed being out on my own at first, which sounds so stupid now. I met some really cool people, all just drifting . . . but there were a lot of really fucked up people, too, and it was like 'Watch your back!' since you never knew who was going to be your friend, and who was going to try and rip you off."

It reads like a movie script, doesn't it? Certainly it's a drama that's playing out in countless towns across the country every day. We already heard a number of tales a few chapters back, stories from kids which demonstrate that, for all our apparent advances, the world hasn't changed all that much when it comes to growing up as a gay kid. Though the majority don't find themselves kicked out of their homes by stony-faced parents, thousands do find themselves facing daunting challenges all the same. Most of the older gay men I've interviewed seem blissfully unaware of this.

According to the Sexual Minority Youth Assistance League (SMYAL), gay youth today feel more isolated from their schools, family, and peers than their straight counterparts; they might hear, on average, about twenty-five antigay epithets each day. (It doesn't matter whether they're the targets or not; just hearing the words can be damaging enough.) SMYAL says gay kids are more likely to smoke, try dangerous drugs, and engage in risky sexual practices out of ignorance or indifference; they have a higher incidence of HIV and other STD infections, along with a higher rate of depression. Almost 30 percent are homeless, either from running away or from being tossed out on the street. And although some studies have rendered the topic controversial, nearly all gay youth activists attest to the fact that gay kids are more than twice as likely to attempt suicide than heterosexual adolescents.

"From my freshman to senior year in high school I made multiple suicide attempts," says Mikhail, a seventeen-year-old student in New Jersey. "Over fifty-six of them—fifty-six different unique ways that I kept track of. There were more—I just didn't write them down. I was so afraid of admitting it to myself—I would cry myself to sleep hoping I would die that night. To make it all worse, when I was fourteen my mother sat me down and said, 'As long as you live in our house, under our roof, and we pay for your bills, and your college tuition—you're not allowed to be gay.' From that point on I hated myself for liking men—I hated every waking moment and spent every moment, every day, month, and year for six years to try and end my life. Sorry . . . I'm starting to cry as I write this."

"It is still very frightening to a young person to be so different," says Craig Bowman of the National Youth Advocacy Coalition (NYAC). "Today there is really no place to hide. I stayed in the closet all through high school and college. That's really not an option for most young people today. Some of them have terrific support, others don't. Those who are isolated feel alone, and that isolation can become desperation. When you're that desperate, all kinds of things can happen. We are just beginning to see research that shows clearly how young people who are struggling with their sexual orientation or gender identity often value their lives much less than straight youth. They take risks. They act out. They run away. They kill themselves. Not because they are lesbian, gay, bisexual, transgendered, or questioning, but because of how society treats them when they are perceived to be."

Jason Rich is the author of *Growing Up Gay in America* (Franklin Street Books, 2002) in which he chronicles many of the hazards gay youth face as they come of age while struggling with their sexual identity. Rich says in all his dealings with gay and questioning teens, he kept hearing the same stories. "Too many gay teens are being abused, mentally and physically, and this leads to extremely high levels of depression, alcoholism, fear, drug abuse and even suicide."

As Rich contends, gay teens simply don't have the resources and support available to them that they sorely need. "They have nobody to talk to openly about their sexuality, concerns, and fears, and they are unable to obtain honest and accurate information to make intelligent decisions. Instead, they wind up trying to deal with the negative gay stereotypes and misconceptions that most people have, and they base important decisions on inaccurate information."

Rich says, despite all the problems they confront, he still believes it is "very possible" for a gay teen today to lead a happy and healthy life if he receives true support and love from those around him. "Especially if it comes from family, relatives, teachers, and friends he can trust," Rich says. "In many cases, it is a lack of love and support that pushes a gay teen into unsafe and unhealthy behavior as he searches for acceptance."

"HATRED IN THE HALLWAYS"

Take a look at just a handful of stories culled from local and national media over the past few years, and it's easy to see why any gay kid might be made to feel marginalized, belittled, or even threatened. There's the story from the November 2000 issue of *XY* magazine, where a high school senior in Visalia, California, protests a teacher's use of the word "faggot" in reference to his earring. Humiliated in front of his class, the student goes to the principal, who counsels him that he shouldn't be going "over the teacher's head"; he then begins to endure such a torrent of abuse from classmates that he is eventually driven from school into an independent study program (McIntosh, 2000, p. 11). Consider a survey, jointly conducted by a Hamilton College research class and MTV, that brings to light the fact that 88 percent of high school students admit to using the phrase "that's so gay" in reference to something they don't like; the same survey shows that only 31 percent of respondents would be "comfortable" interacting with gay and straight couples at a party, and just 38 percent would be comfortable with a gay lab partner (O'Briant and Moylan, 2001, p. 5).

Here are two items from the April 19, 2002, issue of the *Blade:* Three members of the Bay County, Florida, school board refer to homosexuality as "a sin" during a meeting with local parents, saying they would oppose any curriculum that promotes or condones it, despite the fact that no such action is in the works; the same issue talks about pledges to the Pi Kappa Phi fraternity at Michigan State University, who were seen on campus wearing T-shirts bearing the slogans, "I Like Little Boys," "Capt. Gay Sex," and "Fag Hairstylist" (although the national chapter temporarily suspended the frat's charter, the paper reports that several frat brothers were unapologetic in a confrontation with gay students after the offending shirts came to light) (p. 18).

From the Gay.Com/PlanetOut.com Network on May 29, 2002, comes word of a research study that queried 9,000 high school students about taunting, hazing, and abuse, along with "risky" behavior, like drug use and unsafe sex; the study shows 28 percent of the gay and lesbian students reported a "high" level of victimization, compared to just 7 percent of heterosexual students. Those same gay and lesbian students were also more likely to engage in risky behavior. Then there's the widely reported study by Human Rights Watch in the spring of 2001, which documents the widespread bullying inflicted on gay students by their peers, and their teachers' stolid indifference; the study, called "Hatred in the Hallways: Violence and Discrimination Against Lesbian, Gay, Bisexual and Transgendered Students in U.S. Schools," suggests as many as two million young people nationwide are regular victims of repeated abuse. According to the study, a result of in-depth interviews with 140 young people and 130 teachers, administrators, counselors, and parents in seven states, the affected students have to spend an "enormous amount of energy" just figuring out how to get to and from school safely, how to avoid hallways when other students are present in order to escape "slurs and shoves"; the same students routinely cut gym classes so they won't get beat up. They do everything they can to become "invisible" just to survive. The most damning part of the report is the utter lack of concern many school administrations seem to have about policing such behavior. In fact, the study shows that several instances of abuse come from the teachers, coaches, and counselors themselves (Human Rights Watch news release, May 2001).

It's not just that no one's watching the store. It's that no one seems to be watching the folks who run it, making sure the doors are locked and the alarm gets turned on at night. That means precious and irreplaceable commodities—trust, hope, self-esteem—are stolen from the gay kids on a regular basis. And beyond that sad and tragic prospect—the thousands, maybe millions, of youngsters suffering abuse and indifference in relative silence—there's a blood-chilling phenomenon that's beginning to rear its head; fed up, backs against the wall, some kids are firing back, literally. A feature story in the June 19, 2001, edition of *The Washington Post* reports antigay epithets and taunting were often aimed at the eventual assailants in five of eight school shooting incidents that occurred between 1996 and 2001. "Columbine shooters Eric Harris and Dylan Klebold were called fags. So was Andy Williams, who sprayed a San Diego high school with gunfire last March, killing two people" (Step Sessions, 2001, p. A-7). It's not the truth behind the taunting that matters—Williams, who was sentenced in August 2002 to a fifty-years-to-life sentence, may or may not be gay; we'll never know for certain about Harris and Klebold, who took their own lives along with the lives of thirteen others, but rather the fact that the power of the accusation may have been just enough to help push them all over the edge.

The story suggests the use of words such as "fag" arrives in the student lexicon by elementary school, and is so common by middle or high school that few straight students even contemplate its actual meaning or its effects on students who might be secretly gay, insecure about their sexual orientation, or just isolated from the school mainstream. One eighth grader told the *Post* "there's 'a big difference' between anti-gay slurs and other derogatory terms." She explained, "if we were to say other words which we all know are wrong, someone would stop us" (p. A-7).

Daniel, a twenty-year-old music store manager in Roseville, Michigan, tells me about the time such slurs were directed at him. "In high school I sat next to this kid in art class. He was a very cool guy, always nice to me. But after I came out he started hating me and all my friends. He went so far as to spray paint 'kill all fags' on the street in front of my house." Daniel says he began to encounter such a torrent of abuse at school that he "finally had to drop out and take night classes. It was a very hard time for me."

I've always likened "fag" and "faggot" to the word "nigger." (Made you flinch, didn't it, just seeing it there in print?) A few years back while promoting *Sissyphobia* I was a guest on a television talk show that was discussing hate lyrics in pop music as manifested by one Marshall Mathers, a.k.a. the rapper Eminem. The teens who called in were shockingly nonchalant about what I call the gay "f" word and defensive about Mr. M's usage of it. "It's not like he uses it to hurt anyone," one young lady cried. My suggestion was that she mentally replace "faggot" with "nigger" and see how she likes the songs now. There was a long silence, then she said quietly, "That's messed up." Another young man was defiant in his defense and hit me with all sorts of references to the First Amendment and such. I asked him if he'd ever considered how painful it might be to be a young gay kid in school to hear classmates mouthing along to such wonderful compositions as "Criminal" from 2000's *The Marshall Mathers LP:*

> My words are like a dagger with a jagged edge.
> That'll stab you in the head whether you're a fag or lez.

He admitted the true meaning behind such words wasn't something he ever gave a moment's thought to. I asked if he had any gay friends; he said "no." I told him I wasn't surprised.

Confronted with such apathy or hostility from their peers, and neglect from those who are supposed to keep watch over them, gay kids have the double burden of dealing with attacks from without while they struggle with the apparent demons within. "I don't want to kill myself anymore, but a few months ago I was really tempted," says Bobby, a fifteen-year-old in Madison, Wisconsin. "I didn't want to be gay and get picked on all the time. It wasn't like anyone cared if I lived or died anyway." Bobby says he found a gay youth area on the Internet; now he e-mails regularly with other gay kids his age, and no longer feels so alone or helpless. "I wonder about the other kids out there. I worry about them sometimes. . . . This sounds really stupid, I know, but when I go to bed at night I pray for all the gay boys out there who don't have anyone to help them, or anyone to love them. I get real emotional about it. It makes me cry when I think about it."

Fortunately, the news isn't *all* grim. Gay students aren't without allies or activists within their own ranks. The Gay, Lesbian and Straight Education Network (GLSEN), a national organization dedicated to fighting antigay bias in schools, hounds educators and legislators to open their eyes and see what's going on; GLSEN also makes sure parents and students are informed about what they can do to further the cause. (In April 2002 GLSEN helped stage a national protest called the "Day of Silence," where thousands of students in more than 1,700 schools coast to coast kept quiet for nine full hours to bring attention to the plight of gay students.) A spokesman for the Human Rights Campaign (HRC) assures me that HRC is also pitching in by supporting GLSEN wherever possible and working to pass "safe school" legislation at the state level. The National Education Association, the nation's largest teacher's union, is leaning on school districts to stop the harassment of gay students and teachers. Various gay rights and gay advocacy groups, among them Parents, Friends, and Families of Lesbians and Gays (PFLAG) are lobbying local schools to include more gay-themed books in their libraries. All across the country, with varying degrees of success, gay and straight students are coming together to create Gay/Straight Alliances or GSAs. They often face stiff opposition from schools and local school boards, which sometimes mount legal fights to keep GSAs from meeting on school grounds; some school districts have banned *all* school-related clubs—like the chess club or Spanish club—just to keep GSAs off campus. But the fact that such clubs exist at all, and that ever more gay and straight students are working to form them, reflects a major sea change in American attitudes among those who'll form the next few generations of teachers, administrators, parents, and concerned citizens.

Some kids are mounting challenges all by themselves. That student who was humiliated by his teacher for wearing an earring? He sued the school district for damages; his settlement was well over $100,000, along with a pledge to create a get-tough policy on antigay harassment. Other students who suffered even more outright abuse have successfully launched similar actions and won. Efforts such as those, as much as anything else, may well serve as a wakeup call to apathetic administrations: Antigay means you pay.

Answering the calls of their adult counterparts who believe that visibility is our best weapon against ignorance and intolerance, a growing number of gay students are simply making themselves known, on campus and off, and in so doing providing other gay kids with powerful inspiration, hope, and role models. Sometimes that happens in rather unlikely places.

Stephen, a high school student in Austin, Texas, was just seventeen when he started sporting a T-shirt that read, "Let's get one thing straight: I'm not." He says he never felt he was at risk, since he was already one of the more popular kids at school. Events soon bore him out. By the end of his senior year he'd been elected homecoming king and was captain of the varsity basketball team.

Michael is a nineteen-year-old grocery store worker in Greenville, South Carolina, who hopes to start college soon, but as he tells me his story, it's clear this kid could teach his own lessons in guts and perseverance. Michael, you see, is hell-bent on staging his city's first ever Gay Pride parade and rally. "Even though we're such a small community in the Bible Belt, that doesn't mean we don't deserve the right to show who we are in public without feeling ashamed," he says. He's approached local gay rights groups, gay and gay-friendly local and national media, and city leaders to try and launch his vision. Michael admits it's an uphill battle, but he's used to those. "My high school wasn't exactly friendly to gay people," he recalls. "I was threatened with being shot, spit on, you name it." What got him through was the support and love of his family and friends, and now he wants to do what he can for other gay people, kids and adults alike. "My hope for the future is that we as a community can learn to love and help each other, and that one day we'll be able to *show* that love and affection we have for each other, our partners, and our community."

YOU SEXY THING

"I thought I was really lucky," says Desmond, a sixteen-year-old high school student in Passaic, New Jersey. "I came out to my family (my parents, I mean—we haven't told Nana yet!) and they handled it really well. My dad was just the best, better than I ever thought he could be. . . . He came over (I was crying!) and he put his arms around me and told me I would always be his son, that he would love me for who I am, and if gay was part of that, it was cool." As Desmond tells it, everything stayed "cool" until the topic of sex came up. "I started seeing this guy Donny, and we were fooling around a *lot,* and it was like, 'So you wanna do it?' and we both really wanted to. I picked up some condoms and Dad found them in my room, and he went nuts. Suddenly the idea that his kid was gay, and was thinking about having sex, was like too much for him."

As Desmond sees it, his father's reaction seems more than a little out of sync, since he gave his tacit approval when his mother took his sister to get birth control pills when *she* was sixteen. "It was a total double standard and I thought it was really unfair. I know I can't get pregnant, but I know I could get AIDS or something else. Donny and I haven't had sex yet (well, not *that* kind of sex) but I'd like to. Dad made me promise I wouldn't, but I don't know how much longer I can keep my word."

It's not exactly a surprise that any father might blanch at the prospect of his son becoming sexually active with another guy. We've come a long way in the good ol' USA, but it's still hard for parents, however socially evolved they like to believe they are, to see their children as sexual beings, whatever orientation they happen to have. "I have two sons, seventeen and sixteen," says Barry, a forty-two-year-old attorney in New York. "My seventeen-year-old is straight and has a girlfriend. . . . My sixteen-year-old came out to us as gay a year ago and he has one boy he brings over a lot. I guess you could say they're dating. I love both of my sons like I love my life, and I've told them both that if I ever hear that they're having sex I will have their hides on the wall. They're still too young." I ask Barry how old he was when he had sex for the first time. "I was seventeen," he admits. "I was too young, too. Thank God we used protection."

"When my son told me that he was gay, it wasn't too long before I began to learn that it was just fine to be gay," says Ruth, a psychologist/counselor from Washington, DC. "But the sex part, the anal sex part, haunted me. I have been a sex educator most of my professional life. How could this be? I was having lunch one day with a friend and was sharing how uncomfortable I felt about anal intercourse, my *son* having anal intercourse. (I found it helped me to just repeat the word over and over. As I did the dishes, it would be a kind of mantra:

'Glass, anal intercourse; plate, anal intercourse; knife . . .') My friend suggested that we look around the café and imagine all the couples having intercourse—the fat people, the old people, the ugly, the 'regular' people. . . . Needless to say, between the giggling and the anxiety it was a very healing lunch. I realized that when my daughter had a serious boyfriend I didn't go to the 'sex' place—I didn't have to, I've been there—but my son's sex life was different."

"It's a very strange situation you find yourself in," admits one mother, whose sixteen-year-old son told her that he was gay a year and a half ago. "Part of you, honestly, doesn't want to think about your baby boy 'doing it' with someone else. All parents sort of go through that one. Then your son tells you he's gay, and that just takes so much guts. . . . I love and admire my son so much for his courage, but just because he does come out to you, doesn't mean he can go off and start having sex. You can't reward his honesty with some kind of blank check. I'm still his mom, so I have to look out for him."

Remembering back to a conversation I had with a mother I interviewed for *Sissyphobia,* I ask her about the time-honored teenage sleepover. I didn't necessarily want to rain on her son's parade—my own sleepovers as a gay teen, filled with experimentation as they were, are still the stuff of fond, fond memory—but I ask her if she's ever given a thought to what might be going on behind the door when it closes and he has a friend over. "It's funny you ask, because we just had that conversation the other day. I suppose I'm lucky we can talk about that sort of thing so openly. I told him I was trusting him to be responsible with his sexuality and respectful of our house rules. His sister can't have a male friend in her room, but he of course has lots of friends over. I don't ask him what 'kind' of friend they are. I just have to trust him, I suppose, and hope he makes the right decision."

"Gay kids aren't any different than straight kids when it comes to sex," says Patty, a forty-seven-year-old mother of a gay teenage son in northern California. "Okay, there's *that* difference, but I mean in terms of getting the same urges, and acting on those urges, like any heterosexual teen would. My son sat down with me one night—he's sixteen, by the way—and we talked about everything he's going through . . . it really opened my eyes.

"What a gay kid has to face is really scary. . . . A straight boy might approach a girl, ask her out, and if they're attracted to each other things can happen. But the gay boy? If he's attracted to someone it's often very painful, because odds are the kid he likes isn't even gay. If he befriends someone and they start to hang out a lot, the gay kid can develop strong romantic feelings that often aren't returned. Sometimes there can be anger and violence if someone's attentions get misinterpreted. If there *is* some kind of chemistry, one boy may be overcome by a desire to 'try something' that the other isn't ready for."

I ask her what rules she's set down for her son when it comes to sex. "No rules, really, I just ask him to have some common sense. I think in a lot of ways—I have no scientific basis for this, but it's how I feel—I think gay kids grow up faster than straight kids. They realize they're different so early, and so many of them end up feeling isolated in their own homes. They have to become their own people pretty fast. My son is extremely mature for his age. That really comes home for me when I see other kids in his class. They just seem years behind."

And how does she feel about the sleepovers? "Oh, good heavens, I've never thought about it. Now that I have . . . wow, I'm not sure. I certainly can't watch him twenty-four/seven, if that's what you mean. I worry about telling him not to do anything. I don't care how mature your kid is, you make something forbidden and you can give it more allure than it had before. And I do want to give him room to discover himself, and he needs some privacy for that. But yeah . . . I worry, like any mom, that he'll have sex with someone before he's ready to handle it. Kids seem to start a lot earlier these days than we did."

THE END OF THE INNOCENCE

The idea that "kids these days" are having sex at ever-younger ages turned out to be, like so many other notions older people have about younger people, rather common in the interviews I've conducted and survey responses I've received. It's undeniably true that the last few generations of youngsters have been exposed to more sexual imagery and concepts than any who've gone before, and they get it everywhere, from pop music and movies to television programming and mass media advertising. Hell, they even get it on the news; thanks to former President Bill Clinton, oral sex became a topic of conversation over the dinner table. ("Please pass the potatoes. Mom, what's a blow job?") How that exposure might translate into actual behavior is really an open question, and it's just about impossible to measure.

It's a simple proposition, however, to ask, "How old were you when you first had sex with another guy?" So I included that question in my polling and put it before all my age groups. (For my purposes, I defined "sex" in non-Clintonian terms, i.e., any touching or manipulation of the body that means to create sexual arousal/satisfaction; I did not then, nor will I ever, define gay sex solely as "anal penetration.") As always, you can read the detailed statistical breakdown in the final chapter, but for now let me just say the numbers took an interesting turn. The youngest age group—thirteen to twenty-three—did in fact seem to be rather sexually active by the time they were seventeen; more than half reported having had gay sex by that age. The next two age groups seemed to fall off a bit, and in ever-increasing numbers; if I'd stopped there it would have been easy to conclude that today's youngsters are in fact bumping uglies at a much higher rate than previous generations.

But something funny happened on the way to confirming conventional wisdom; the two older groups, all gay men over forty years of age, actually had comparable numbers to the youngest set; the senior set reported the highest amount of underage sex of *any* group. (The most commonly cited age for their initial sexual act was thirteen, followed by fourteen!) The numbers really floored me, until I started talking to some of those randy old geezers and viewed those sex acts in context. "You have to remember that the world was very, very different then," says Jack, a seventy-two-year-old retired naval officer in Flagstaff, Arizona. "We didn't know we were having 'gay sex,' or that it was really any kind of sex at all. It's only looking back that I realize how bold we were with each other. I myself had two, maybe three friends that I regularly 'played with' in such a manner, and that play included mutual masturbation, oral sex, and on a few occasions, anal sex, almost always to the point of orgasm. It wasn't something we ever planned, certainly it wasn't something we ever talked about. Usually it just happened after we shut out the light, someone would quietly crawl into someone else's bed, with nary a word spoken."

"In my day when we'd fool around with each other it was like being in a secret club," says George, a sixty-five-year-old retired electrical engineer in Florida. "We all know how clubs are . . . there are always all sorts of dares and initiation rites. Some of these kids think they 'invented' things we were already past before the time their parents were born! I think the fact that kids today know what 'gay' means at such an early age probably prevents them from being as adventurous as we were." Luke, a sixty-two-year-old postal worker in Missouri, puts it fairly succinctly: "It was a lot easier to go down on that hot boy who lived down the street *before* he knew that having a guy going down on him might mean that either of them could be 'gay.' When we were thirteen or fourteen we just didn't talk about stuff like that. I never even heard the word 'queer' in a sexual connotation until high school."

It may well be that today's youngsters aren't having sex at anything approaching unprecedented levels. But, as Luke suggests, those who are sexually active can't cloak their activities as innocently or as easily as our seniors did when they were but lads; when a twenty-first-century teen makes a play for another, pretty much everyone knows what the score is. "I knew a boy at school who was just so hot, and I thought he liked me too," says Leon, a sixteen-year-old high school student in northern Virginia. "It took me awhile to work up the nerve to ask him if he wanted to hang out sometime. (I wasn't necessarily trying to sex him, but if he had said yes I wouldn't have hesitated, even though I'm not what you call 'experienced.') He looked at me funny, then later started acting very weird around me, like avoiding me, really. I guess he thought I was gay just for asking him to hang out." Jon, a seventeen-year-old high school student in upstate New York, tells me he used to "fool around" with his next door neighbor when each was thirteen, but by the time they turned fourteen things changed. "We used to wrestle around first, then start 'playing' with each other, but one night when I went to grab him he stopped me and said, 'No gay stuff. I ain't into that shit!' It pissed me off and hurt my feelings. It was a long time before I met someone else to have fun with."

Derek, a nineteen-year-old student/server in Providence, Rhode Island, says "fun" wasn't really part of the equation for him, at least not at first. "As far as I can remember I always had some sort of attraction to guys, even when I had a girlfriend," he says. "During the summer of the year I was fifteen, I met my 'first' (and it happened to be online). He used to come over maybe once a week and we'd mess around, but every time he left I felt dirty and would ask myself, 'What the hell am I doing?! That's disgusting!' I would take *hot* showers and brush my teeth till it hurt. I felt dirty." That mind-set, Derek tells me, lasted only until he met his first true boyfriend, with whom he had a happy, and monogamous, two-and-a-half-year relationship. "After awhile I gave up denying myself and just accepted the fact that I'm gay," he tells me.

Many older gay men I've interviewed, though, seem to have trouble accepting sexually active gay youth. "I have to say the prospect of all these gay boys having sex with each other just gives me the shivers," says Craig, a forty-year-old office manager in eastern Tennessee. "I think somehow they got the idea that being gay means you *have* to have sex with another guy. It's like they don't know, most of them, that sex should wait until you're emotionally ready for it." Jerrold, a thirty-three-year-old graduate student in Boston, echoes that. "I would hate to be one of those guys who was sexually active when he was young, then starts preaching to the kids about 'keeping it in your pants' once he's grown up. But honestly, with everything I read these days, it seems like they are throwing caution to the wind."

And it's not just the older men. William, a nineteen-year-old computer technician in Florida, says he realized he was gay at "thirteen or fourteen" but hasn't had sex yet. "Strange concept, huh? A nineteen-year-old virgin," he says. It's not for lack of opportunity, he explains, but rather a desire to make the experience something special. What's hard is finding anyone who agrees with him. "It's exceedingly difficult to find anyone my age who's interested in a relationship and not just sex." Josh, an eighteen-year-old college student in Miami, says he was a "teen slut. I'll just admit that now." Josh says he started having "hookups" with kids his age he'd meet online, usually late at night when his parents were asleep. "I would sneak out, and have them meet me around the corner. Usually we'd just fool around in the car or go make out on the playground." Josh says he's probably had "fifteen or twenty" different partners since he started hooking up at the age of fifteen, but that's not something he's proud of. "I promised myself when I got to college I would make a change and so far I have. I'm not saying it's easy—there are lots of really hot guys here. But I think I started way too young and I want to see sex as something better than I did before."

Arial, a seventeen-year-old high school student in Connecticut, says people such as Josh annoy him. "You have these guys just fucking around, then they get tired of it, and now they want to be virgins again. Sorry you feel bad about yourself, bro, but don't tell me how to live. I've had a boyfriend since I was fifteen, and we started having sex last year, and it's been the greatest thing ever for both of us. I guess some guys can't be responsible, like some people have to drink and drive. My boy and I have always been safe, and no one is going to tell us we shouldn't be having sex because we're too young. We know what we want, OK? Mind your own fucking business."

THE XY FILES

One place where I find an extremely interesting take on all this is inside the pages of *XY* magazine. I won't pretend to be objective about it; I'm a big fan, if for no other reason than the magazine has been an invaluable resource, for this project and for many others. *XY* is the only national publication for and about gay youth, and since its inception in the mid-1990s it's rarely been less than controversial. Publisher Peter Cummings isn't afraid to sound off on issues other magazines hardly dare to touch; pick up a copy and there he is, railing against the injustice of age of consent laws, lobbying to lower the drinking age, detailing the plight of homeless gay kids . . . or teaching people how to flirt the right way.

Any of those stands—and trust me, the dude *loves* to take a stand—might and do draw fire from social critics. But what really seems to grate on people's nerves is your typical *XY* photo layout, where young men are often shown in provocative and playful poses, sometimes alone, sometimes with each other. Mind you, it's nothing you haven't seen in any of the other gay mags, except these are *young* people we're talking about, not some runway model between gigs in Milan. Though *XY* never shows anything more explicit than perhaps a hint of pubic hair—something you can see regularly in a Calvin Klein ad or that scandalous *A&F Quarterly*—from the magazine's critics you'd think America's gay youth were sprawled out in their full, tumescent glory for all the world to see.

I did a quick Google.com search, and found entire sites dedicated to *XY* bashing. Almost every criticism targeted the photos. "The models are obviously in their late teens, have no body hair, are often built, and dress in skimpy outfits," wrote one poster. "They are objectified and sexualized in the most horribly patronizing ways one can imagine." (The same writer was highly critical of what he saw as "slight" editorial content, then admitted he usually flipped past the articles to ogle the hot pictures.) Another took the magazine to task for being a publication "obviously aimed at older gay men who just want to look at cute boys."

Apparently the same readers haven't picked up any of the magazines aimed at our youthful female set lately or the soft-core porn that passes for the *Sports Illustrated* swimsuit edition. Do we not find the same sort of pictures of youngish girls clad in skimpy outfits? Do we not see the same kind of "objectification" of well-built female forms? Don't believe for a second that older straight men won't browse through such magazines on occasion while waiting for the missus to finish her grocery shopping, that they will not turn to a swimsuit layout and breathe a very quiet "holy shit!"

I'll admit I'm on the fence when it comes to the topic of exploitation of beautiful faces and bodies; I can see the danger of creating a world where only the beautiful gain entry and anyone who's merely average feels left out. (Appropriately enough for *XY*'s often contradictory nature, many of the magazine's own writers and biggest fans sound off on this a lot, too; the very first issue questioned gay men's fixation on beauty in an article sandwiched between some extremely hot photo spreads.) But from where I sit I'm not afraid to say that, yeah, I like looking at cute men, young or old, as much as the next gay guy; I'll be damned if I feel guilty for getting a rush when I flip a page and find a gorgeous, heaven-sent creature smiling back at me. If we as a society have managed to accept the healthy sensuality of a just-past-her-teenage-years pop star—and I'm talking about you, Britney—or a heterosexual teenage cheerleader—*American Beauty,* anyone?—then why on earth do we have a problem with similarly situated young gay men or a magazine that dares to show them, as one *XY* fan aptly put it, "flaunting youth's unbridled sexuality"?

Perhaps it's that old demon at work, the internalized homophobia which lies at the root of so many of our ills, that makes some middle-aged gay men look askance at a youth so clearly comfortable in his gay sexuality, because we see our desire as a lesser, somehow dirty thing. Maybe it's some kind of latent regret some of us have at our own loss of innocence, some belief that gay boys who are sexually active, or actively flirtatious, have somehow surrendered their precious childhoods and entered the adult arena far too early. Hell, maybe it's just jealousy that we didn't grow up in an era that makes some allowance, however tiny, for a gay kid to express the sexuality stirring in his loins in such a public way. Whatever it is, it's made it tough going for *XY,* which barely survives month to month—the magazine is almost entirely dependent on subscriptions and newsstand sales—because too many potential advertisers see sensual and sexual gay youth as a hot potato they don't want to handle.

"I encountered some of this when I was writing the Jack character [who came out as gay in high school] on *Dawson's Creek,*" said writer-director Greg Berlanti in an *XY* interview published in the November 2000 issue. Berlanti, known best for his work on television's *Dawson's,* as well as writer-director of 2001's wonderfully crafted feature film *The Broken Hearts Club,* suggested there's something about "youth and being gay and being sexual" that upsets some people.

> It's considered the most risqué, because God forbid if boys are eighteen years old and sexual and different. That's many risky conversations at once. But I say what a great fight to have! It's a good fight to have now, because we win. We're right. (Nguyen, 2000, p. 81)

"YOUNG PEOPLE AT RISK"

"Since you're writing about young gay guys who have sex, maybe you can answer a question for me," inquires Andrew, a seventeen-year-old high school student in south Texas. "I had sex with this guy, who told me he hadn't had sex with anyone else before. He said it would be cool if we didn't use a condom. Do you think he was bullshitting me?" Another high school student, sixteen-year-old Bradley from Pittsburgh, also figures since I'm writing about kids and gay sex, I might actually know something about the topic. "My boyfriend says you can't get HIV just from sucking a guy's dick and I want to know if that's true." And one more gay high school student, fifteen-year-old Cameron from Arizona, says he's not sexually active yet but can't wait, especially since he's heard "they have drugs that can cure HIV now."

That sound you're hearing is me banging my head against the nearest hard surface. Not because the questions are being asked—for God's sake, kids *should* be asking these questions—but because they had to ask *me*. (For the record I told them (1) always use a condom, and run like the wind from anyone who says, "We don't have to"; (2) yes, you can get HIV from oral sex, just not as readily as you can from anal sex; and (3) yes, there are *treatments* for HIV/AIDS, and people who can afford those treatments are living longer, but as yet there is no *cure* in sight. I also referred them all to the Centers for Disease Control Web site at <www.cdc.gov>.)

Some of us may not like the fact that underage gay kids are having sex with each other or that any underage kids are having sex for that matter, whether they're gay or straight. But obviously they are, as they always have; nothing short of chastity belts, hand restraints, muzzles, or locking them in their rooms at night will stop them (and I'd give you odds they'd find a way to do the nasty, anyway). If they are going to be sexually active, it seems like simple common sense that we, as a society, would provide our youth with every tool available to make the right decisions to protect themselves, not just from HIV/AIDS, but from the whole host of sexually transmitted diseases abroad in the land.

Oh, wait a second. I forgot where I was for just a moment. I live in a country where kids such as Andrew, Bradley, and Cameron are posing life-and-death questions to random, curious writers because that place where they go to learn stuff five days a week, the place with the blackboards and chalk and algebra books, is largely doing an abysmal job of teaching them what they need to know. I think they call it school.

How bad a job are schools doing? Well, if disease rates are any measure, pretty damn bad. Let's just ask the CDC. "In the United

States, HIV-related death has the greatest impact on young and middle-aged adults, particularly racial and ethnic minorities," reads the CDC report on its Web site. The fact sheet, called "Young People at Risk: HIV/AIDS Among America's Youth," states that, in 1999, HIV was the fifth leading cause of death for Americans between the ages of twenty-five and forty-four.

> Among African American men in this age group, HIV infection has been the leading cause of death since 1991. . . . Many of these young adults likely were infected in their teens and twenties. It has been estimated that at least half of all new HIV infections in the United States are among people under 25, and the majority of young people are infected sexually.

The report indicates that, even though the overall incidence of AIDS cases appears to be declining, there has been no decline in HIV infections among young people ages thirteen to twenty-four.

Clearly something's gone awry here. "They just don't have the memories we have," says Eugene, a forty-four-year-old artist in Seattle. "I've buried so many friends, so many lovers. Sometimes it feels like the late 1980s and early 1990s were just one long, ghastly funeral." (I know exactly what he means. I used to go through my old address books, find names of people I hadn't spoken with in ages, and look them up with directory assistance or on the Net. I don't do that anymore; it was just too painful to find out how many old friends who came out with me in the 1970s and 1980s had passed away.) Bill, a forty-seven-year-old Webmaster in San Diego, says the epidemic has wiped away a large part of a generation of gay men who might have served as mentors for troubled youth coming out today. "In a lot of ways they're like fatherless kids and there's too few of us left to make any difference. Now with all the new drugs and treatments that have people living longer, young people have deluded themselves into thinking that 'AIDS is over.' Maybe all the new drugs will give them longer lives, but I'd rather sell prevention than buy into the idea we're going to cure this thing anytime soon."

I don't believe that young people have convinced themselves that "AIDS is over"; my own polling indicates that no more than 2 percent of any age group I queried thinks we've licked this epidemic. My polls also show that 80 percent of young people thirteen to twenty-three years old have a real fear about contracting HIV. So where's the disconnect between how they feel and what they're doing out there? "I never thought I could get HIV," says Larry, an HIV-positive twenty-two-year-old in New York City. "To tell you the truth, I never thought about it at all. I was one of those guys who walked right by the condoms they lay out in clubs. I saw all the safe-sex ads and never thought it applied to me. I was eighteen, just out, and having fun. To this day I can't tell you how I got it or who gave it to me. I just know I have it and I have to deal with it."

"I have a lot of friends that I go out and party with," says Jason, a twenty-year-old college student in Chicago. "We're all hooking up with someone, usually someone different every weekend. I use a condom most of the time if I do anal. I never use condoms for oral sex. I get tested every few months, and every time I worry this is going to be the test that comes back positive." I ask Jason if that worry ever translates into taking more effective precautions or perhaps cooling off his red-hot love life. "Hell, no," he says. "I'm having too much fun." (Pardon me while I bang my head again. OK, that's better.)

Why aren't kids getting the message? In study after study on its Web site, the CDC says that only a comprehensive school-based regimen of sex education is likely to provide youngsters, in the company of their peers, the information they need to make the safest choices. AIDS activists I've talked with suggest that such education needs to take place at the earliest age possible, so that the ability to make those choices is already in place when youngsters arrive at the stage in their lives where their sexual curiosities begin to wake. "I am not advocating telling little kids how to fuck," says Tony, a forty-four-year-old activist in northeastern Florida. "But they need to be made aware of the issues that fit with the age they're at. I've been doing this job since the early 1980s, and it breaks my heart when I have to tell a young person—gay or straight—that they're HIV positive. I think we need to revamp the whole issue of sex ed and teach them age-appropriate material, make it part of the educational process."

Just how likely is that? Sydney, a thirty-four-year-old teacher in Missouri, tells me not to hold my breath. "It is hard enough sometimes to get school districts comfortable with the idea of teaching 'normal' sex education—and I use 'normal' only to illustrate the attitudes we have to deal with. Too many people think that talking about same-sex sex ed is no different than 'promoting' it, as if just talking about homosexuality is going to make it appealing to the students, like advertising stylish clothes or a new car. It's ridiculous when you think about it, and it shows you how little our society knows about sex."

NO SEX, PLEASE

Perhaps it's that lack of knowledge that's behind a Kaiser Family Foundation survey published in September 2000; that survey, called *Sex Education in America: A View from Inside the Nation's Classrooms,* shows a huge gap in what schools teach and what parents and students want to know. Kaiser talked with more than 1,500 parents/students; the study shows that most parents think schools have a lot further to go to bring their sex education up to a workable level. About 85 percent of parents surveyed said schools should do more to instruct students on the use of condoms; 76 percent believed talking about homosexuality was a good idea and nearly as many—74 percent—agreed that when such topics come up, they need to be discussed in balanced ways that present different views of society.

Young people I talked to had a lot to say about what they're taught, and not taught, in sex ed. Daniel is a seventeen-year-old high school student in Michigan. "It's a joke, here. I sat through a whole semester waiting for them to talk about gay people. I'm still waiting." Kevin, a sixteen-year-old high school student in Indianapolis, says he wants to hear his sex ed class talk about "the stuff that guys do with each other. I don't mean they have to go into details, but I'd like to hear why gay guys get HIV more than straight guys do." (That's only in the developed world, Kev, places like Western Europe, Canada, and, of course, the good ol' USA. According to the CDC, the vast majority of HIV/ AIDS patients globally are heterosexuals. Most are about your age and just a few years older, and they don't even know they have it. Too bad no one's teaching you that.)

"Look, I think it's through sheer stupidity that young men ignore health warnings, but we're not educated about them from a gay perspective," says Chris, an eighteen-year-old college student in Boston.

"In school we hear about heterosexual sex and learn about it, but really, I'm not going to need to know about the vagina because I never intend to have to deal with one. So the mind-set is this may not apply to gay men because all they teach is heterosexual relationships." Jon, a twenty-one-year-old engineer in Texas, says he thinks most people, including the parents of kids just coming to terms with their own sexual orientation, don't understand what being gay is all about. "They hold to the premise that, when you're young, you can't really *know* if you're gay or not, because you may be just experimenting. So they just dodge the subject entirely. There has to be more widespread information available in schools, and school sex ed classes . . . at least the ones that still have sex ed classes." But like Chris in Boston, Jon also takes youngsters to task for ignoring health warnings. "There's a lot of reasons for that, I guess. The invincibility of youth, the fact that young people are surrounded by people who don't care a lot about their needs . . . and the fact that HIV medication ads are pretty deceptive . . . they always show people who look healthy and happy, and you can't blame young people for thinking that the disease has gone away. They don't show what sometimes comes along with taking the medications advertised . . . daily vomiting and nausea, fat accumulation, and weakness. I think that gives kids some pretty mixed messages."

"Our society today is much more open about sex than at any point in our history," says NYAC's Craig Bowman. "Generally I believe that's a positive development, but we haven't kept pace in terms of providing young people with the tools they need for healthy and safe sexual decision making. We still have a president who believes that abstinence only, despite the lack of even one study showing it to be effective, is worthy of high priority in his administration." A spokesperson for the Human Rights Campaign echoes that, calling abstinence education unrealistic and unproven. "We need to arm young gay people with the facts and impress upon them the dangers of unprotected sex," he says. "They will form their own judgments about when and if to engage in sex, but they should be taught the facts about HIV transmission in a nonjudgmental way. Many gay young people think AIDS is an old gay person's problem and that they don't have to worry about it. Public and privately funded prevention campaigns need to more aggressively reach out to this vulnerable group."

You can't argue with those who point out the need for better education; the infection statistics alone sadly support that dire necessity. But some gay activists tell me that such criticism of abstinence education is becoming problematic. "What happens is we tend to say 'abstinence only' in very dismissive tones, and forget about the root word," says one activist who speaks to me only on condition of anonymity. "We give the idea of 'saying no' lip service, then bury it in calls for more education and access to protection and counseling. That stuff is fine, but I don't think we stress abstinence nearly enough. It's as if we don't want to be in the position of advising them not to have sex. . . . I think a lot of activists feel that in so doing we'd be invalidating the natural urges they're beginning to feel and want to express like any adolescent, and by extension, invalidating their newly-discovered orientation."

Another regrettably anonymous activist says much the same thing. (If you're wondering why so many don't want to speak on the record, and for attribution, you have a thing or two to learn about Washington, sex, politics, and anyone who dares to criticize the current party line.) "So many other social avenues are closed to these kids, and no one wants to say, 'You can't have sex until you're eighteen,' because then they might feel totally abandoned. But if their schools aren't including same-sex orientation in their sexual education curriculum— and many aren't—then someone has to step up and let gay kids know their lives and their sexuality have a value. It's true that few believe the 'abstinence only' approach works. I don't know anyone who thinks it does, but I also think that in bashing those programs wholesale, we're devaluing the idea that abstinence can *ever* work."

Someone who isn't afraid to wade into the debate by name is Chris Crain, executive editor of the *Washington Blade*. In an editorial in the April 26, 2002, edition, Crain submits that, like it or not, the best way for young people to avoid HIV and other STDs is to abstain from sex. Just because the idea is also supported by right-wing conservatives and religious ideologues, he reasons, doesn't mean it's lacking in merit. Though he too takes care to distance himself from those who preach 'abstinence only,' he suggests that, done right, some kind of abstinence education might have real value.

We know that not all teens will choose to "just say no," but according to the most recent research, about half still do, and there's no reason to believe that gay and questioning youth aren't among those who abstain. . . . With all the peer pressure today on teenagers to experiment with sexuality, it would probably come as a welcome relief to most teens who are struggling with their sexuality that they can take their time in figuring out who they are and how to express their newfound feelings, for whichever gender. (p. 38)

Crain also calls our major advocacy groups on the carpet for remaining largely silent on the issue, and suggests they fear to tread into a discussion of teen sexuality "amid the Catholic Church scandal and its gay overtones." He calls that silence a "terrible mistake," and submits "their influence is needed in shaping abstinence education so that 'marriage' isn't the only green light for sex. A committed relationship, or at least adulthood, would seem just as reasonable" (p. 38).

"I FEEL LIKE CHICKEN TONIGHT"

There's a reason I call this chapter "The Untouchables." Not just because I'm talking about underage gay kids who are considered untouchable—if not totally unapproachable—by many gay men out of fear of legal or social backlash; it's also because some of the topics themselves—like sexually active gay youth—are things a lot of folks don't want to contemplate, let alone talk about.

The biggest taboo of all—one colleague of mine calls it "radioactive" and seems surprised I'm even going to try to address it—is the subject of adults over the age of eighteen who have sexual relations with anyone who is underage. A simple look at the headlines these days shows the firestorm that's erupted courtesy of Holy Mother Church and her abusive minions; it may be unfortunate that our gay rights groups don't want to enter the fray, but it's completely understandable. What group charged with advancing our equality in the eyes of civilized society, and seeking that vaunted place at the table, wouldn't run from guilt by association? No one in his right mind wants to be linked with some cabal of predatory priests and the bishops that have long looked the other way. "You're really going to bring that shit up?" another friend of mine asks me. "I wish you could just skip all that . . . it can make us all look bad."

But any attempt to document the lives and experiences of underage gay kids, without talking about the adults who cross the line and have sexual relationships with them, would be rather incomplete. More than that; it'd be a total cop-out. It happens a lot. It has always happened; most likely it always will. And—this is where we better fasten our seatbelts—to dismiss all such relationships as inherently evil and abusive wouldn't be completely honest.

Now please hold your calls, letters, and threatening e-mails; I am *not*—repeat, *not*—saying that abuse does not occur, that young people aren't frequently exploited and misused by older men who take them for "boy toys," then discard them in favor of the next pretty young thing who comes down the pike. In fact that may well be the nature of the overwhelming number of cases.

Take Rudy, for example. He's a thirty-seven-year-old carpenter in Venice, California, who was barely sixteen when he was approached by an older man who made it clear he found Rudy intensely, physically desirable. "He was actually a friend of my father, and it was like he saw something in me right away that I was just beginning to deal with. My dad never really talked to me much or paid much attention to me after I got to be a teenager. . . . I was a disappointment, I guess, because I wasn't stone butch like my two older brothers. This guy, Ray, was always very nice to me, always smiling when he saw me. One night my parents had a party, everybody got drunk, and I woke up to find this guy in my room, just standing there watching me. I was going to yell, then I saw his pants were open, and he was holding his dick. He smiled, and put his finger to his lips to tell me to be quiet, or maybe it was like, 'Keep this a secret.' Anyway, he sat down next to me, and the next thing I remember was I was blowing him. He wasn't bad looking at all. He was actually very hot . . . I didn't mind doing it at all . . . it was very exciting. But then from that time on he started being very mean to me, started making comments about me in front of my dad, and my father just joined in. They were calling me his 'daughter,' just being real assholes. One time I stood up to him . . . said something like, 'You used to be nicer before you told me to suck your dick,' and my dad got up and decked me. I didn't stay much longer . . . I think I ran away about a month later, as soon as I saved up some money." Rudy tells me the memory is as vivid as if it all happened last week. "I think it really fucked me up for awhile, made it hard for me to trust anyone older."

"John," now a thirty-five-year-old Army major, was fifteen when he was approached by an instructor at the military school his father shipped him off to, in order that he might "get butched up." Like Rudy's dad, John's father wasn't at all happy about the way his son was turning out. "So off I went, depressed as hell about leaving home, and was rather shocked to find out I totally got into the military lifestyle. I know it's a cliché, but the male bonding and discipline really helped my self-esteem, and I started kicking ass academically. Hell, I even loved wearing that uniform.

"I went out for the basketball team and made it. Wasn't all that good, but I was better at it than I ever thought I could be. Our coach was a retired Navy captain . . . he was always watching me, making me feel kind of strange. This is the part where it starts to sound like the setup to a bad porn flick: one night after practice I was the last guy in the shower, and I looked over and there he was, just staring at me with a big bulge in his shorts. He said, 'Come here.' If this *was* a porn flick I guess we'd have just started fucking right there . . . but I just grabbed my towel and ran like hell."

John says that shortly afterward the coach disappeared and nary an official word was given in explanation, but the campus was abuzz with rumors. "It was 'that old faggot' this and 'that old faggot' that. No one else ever knew about the shower episode, but it really tore me up inside, because I was beginning to realize I was a 'faggot' myself." John says even though the coach never touched him, the experience likely set him back years in believing that being gay could ever be something positive. "Whenever I thought about guys, or felt any kind of sexual desire for men, all I could think of was that old man leering at me and I never wanted to be like that."

I encountered several similar tales as I talked with gay men about their first brush with sex. That's why I would never minimize the trauma of such experiences. Many of the younger men I talked with told me similar tales. "I'm eighteen now, but the first time I had sex with another guy I was sixteen," says Jeremy, a high school senior in West Virginia. "I don't know how old he was, but he was at least ten or fifteen years older than me. I was working at a gas station and he would come in once in awhile, get gas, buy some cigarettes, whatever. One night it was just me in there, ready to close, and he comes in, strikes up a conversation. He tells me I look really good, like I could be a model or something, asks me if I have a girlfriend. He asks me if I want some of the beer he just bought. I say sure. . . . I'm not a dumb hick, I can see where this is going . . . we end up out back, and he had me go down on him, and I thought, 'Wow, cool, I'm finally doing it,' but then it got bad." I ask Jeremy what he means. "I mean I let him do it . . . but really it was like he raped me. I was too scared to try and stop him. It wasn't like I could tell anyone, was it?"

Even when the sex is completely consensual the situation can be extremely unhealthy for the emotions of the youth involved. "I was sixteen when I met Bob," says Gary, a nineteen-year-old in North Carolina. "He was about thirty or so and very handsome . . . tall, muscular, tan, you name it. We talked online for weeks, then I finally met him, and he was so sweet and gentle. He never rushed us into having sex. That was all my idea. That's what I told myself, but I realize now he was totally playing me. We were together about a month or so. I would go over to his house and we'd make love for hours. It was incredible." But then something changed. "He stopped answering my e-mails, and blocked me from his buddy list on AOL. He wouldn't answer the phone or call me back." Gary says after a week he went over to Bob's house to find out what was going on. "You can finish this sentence, I'm sure . . . he'd found some other boy to play with. I was devastated, almost suicidal about it. I didn't get over him for a long, long time."

I couldn't help but be moved reading stories such as those. But I also found men of all ages who told me very different tales. "I was probably fifteen or so and though we didn't call it that then, I was 'struggling with my sexuality,'" says Leonard, a fifty-five-year-old telephone lineman in Texas. "Summers I'd spend on my grandparents' ranch, and there were always these hired hands coming and going. My grandpa thought it would be good 'character building' to make me sleep with them in the bunkhouse, to see how the working-men lived. Well let me tell you, I found out! This one ranch hand, he was a very hot guy, probably like twenty-two or twenty-three, I never asked. He showed me everything two guys could do together. You can say after that summer I wasn't struggling anymore. I still dream about that boy. Bless you, Grandpa!"

"Although I had experiences with friends, my first *real* experience with an older man occurred when I was sixteen and traveling on a train between Minneapolis and Sioux City," remembers Richard, a sixty-seven-year-old retiree living in Nebraska. "He was totally awesome and appeared to be extremely well endowed. I was traveling with a cousin of the same age and when my cousin fell asleep after the lights went out, this person invited me to sit with him. He was gentle and kind and gave me memories that will be with me until my dying day."

"I was sixteen, and I hated being gay," says Howard, a thirty-five-year-old administrative assistant in southern California. "If I hadn't met 'John' I would have probably killed myself. He was out running on the high school track, saw me sitting alone in the bleachers, came up and asked me if I was OK. I told him no, I wasn't. We started talking, I just started crying, and he took me to his car. He didn't make any move on me, then . . . he just told me he was gay, too, and that life would get better." Howard says he started seeing John "once in awhile, not really like a boyfriend thing, just like a good friend thing. We didn't really have sex, not like full-on fucking or anything . . . but I let him blow me and he let me blow him, and I felt pretty good about it. He was such a nice guy and I needed a nice guy like that. He really opened up my eyes to the idea that being gay wasn't the worst thing in the world."

Howard and Leonard's stories were typical of about a third of those I talked with who said they'd had sex with older men before they were eighteen; they represent men who see such experiences as welcome "initiations" into the gay world or who view the older men they had sex with as "saviors" who rescued them from loneliness and isolation. Other men had completely different experiences, neither rescues nor initiations per se, but rather simple loving or lusty relationships between people on two sides of an invisible line. "I had somewhat regular sex while still underage with other kids my own age, and have slept with a couple of guys who were sixteen or seventeen while in my early to midtwenties," says Mousie, a twenty-nine-year-old software engineer in San Jose, California. "Each time it was after meeting them while they were visiting friends of mine that they had met online. It was just like any other casual sex I'd had, no added fear or excitement, precisely because it *was* just like any other casual sex I'd had. I considered them consenting adults and still do and the one I'm still in touch with would say the same if I asked him today. Being called a pedophile isn't a concern, since I don't happen to think what I did makes me a pedophile."

"I can't understand why so many gay people have such a problem with guys who have sex with guys underage," says Matt, a nineteen-year-old food store employee in Baton Rouge, Louisiana. "My boyfriend was twenty-three when I met him and I was seventeen. Now he's twenty-five and I'm nineteen, and it doesn't freak any of our friends out. I've actually been out longer than he has . . . he only came out last year and I was telling all my friends when I was sixteen."

"It's hard to explain to your older friends when you fall in love with someone who's so young," says Warren, a thirty-six-year-old insurance agent in the Midwest. "I met my lover when he was sixteen and I was thirty, and we're still together six years down the road. I don't think of myself as a user or an abuser, but I know we still raise eyebrows when we go out. I've had to endure being called a 'pedophile' and it hurts. I didn't fall in love with Joseph because he was sixteen. I had never even looked at a younger guy like that before, but he was charming, smart, and yes, very beautiful. He is still all of those things. He has opened up my heart like no one else. If I'd walked away because society said it was the 'right' thing to do, I would have missed out on something very special."

In my polling I asked respondents what they thought of such relationships; asked whether it's ever OK for someone "older" to be involved with someone who is underage, assuming that each is "in love" with the other, more than half of the youngest group—those thirteen to twenty-three—said "yes," as did a majority of the top two age groups, those forty to fifty-nine and those over sixty. The twenty-four- to thirty-year-olds, and the thirty- to thirty-nine-year-olds, were less approving; only 45 percent and 40 percent, respectively, sanctioned such relationships.

Not so approving, either, were the several psychologists I talked with on the topic. "It is true many guys will acknowledge having had what they think of as 'sex' with an older guy when they were younger and underage," says Howard Fradkin, a psychologist and counselor of gay men in Columbus, Ohio. "When I ask them if now as an adult, if a younger guy came on to them, would they have sex with them, even if they were turned on by the younger guy and even if the younger guy says he wants it, almost all of them say *no way*." Fradkin sees that as a double standard, and hastens to explain. "As we talk about it, they come to see that what they defined as their initiation into the gay sexual world was instead an abuse experience which they felt uncomfortable with in retrospect. And for many of them, they can see how this set themselves up to look at gay life as only about having a lot of sex and being valued solely as a sex object, which oftentimes felt discounting and hurtful because they wanted more than just sex. The older guys basically used them and then didn't want anything else to do with them. Could it ever be OK? I say no. If an older person today really wants to help a gay teen, then refer him to the gay teen group, encourage him to link up with others his own age, and refuse to objectify him in the name of helping him."

Richard Gartner, a New York–based psychologist, suggests that youngsters coming to terms with their sexuality may welcome the attention they get from older men, without being aware of the abusive aspects of the relationships. He admits there are times when sex between adults and older adolescents isn't traumatic, but he still counsels strongly against it. "The problem is that there is no way to know in advance which boys will or won't be traumatized," he says. "Even boys who feel they want the sexuality may feel overwhelmed by it and may not have the capacity to judge the implications of adult sex. They may treat the relationship as far less casual than the older man."

Other counselors have a slightly different take. "If the boy is fortunate enough to meet a man who is an 'out' gay man, and carries some pride in who he is as a gay man, this can make a tremendous difference on the gay boy's perception of how he feels about himself," says a counselor who works with survivors of sexual victimization in the greater Seattle area and who wishes to remain anonymous. "If this comes with the older man having sex with the boy, it doesn't necessarily take away that positive perception of being gay. In fact it can convey the message that really and truly, even down to the experience of sex, it is OK." Still, this counselor suggests few gay teens are equipped to handle all the emotions inherent in such a powerful relationship, and that older men should "err" on the side of caution. As for the boys themselves, he offers this advice: "There is plenty of time for sex. Don't fill it with needing to heal from sexual victimization."

Christian, a thirty-year-old club deejay in Virginia Beach, tells me about the wild night of his "first gay experience"; it happened with a twenty-eight-year-old serviceman in the Philippines, when Christian was a fifteen-year-old living with his U.S. Navy family on base. "I found out this dude was gay through my best friend, who was a few years older than me. My best friend had *no idea* I was like that, but once I heard about this guy, it was like I totally had an 'in' now." Christian says he made that classical arrangement, telling his mom he was staying over at a friend's place, while telling his friend he had to go home early, but instead of going home, he made a beeline for the older man's barracks room. "We watched some TV, some videos, drank a lot of Red Horse [a potent Filipino beer], and I caught a good buzz. I moved over to the bed and patted it so he'd come sit beside me. We got close and I started rubbing his thigh. And then it just went from there; it's sort of a blur, but I remember we rolled around and made out forever. There was one point where he stopped and said something like, 'Look, we should talk about this,' and I was like, 'Please, not now!' We got naked, started grinding, then blew each other. I remember we laid there for a long time afterward talking, but about what I have no clue. At that point I can't imagine I had much capacity for conversation. The next morning I bolted as fast as I could."

Christian says he and the serviceman remain friends to this day, but only recently did he tell his older friend what happened on the way home that hot morning after. "I was totally guilt-ridden and paranoid," he tells me. "I was totally scared. I thought I was going to hell. The cab had to pull over so I could puke. It was really bad. Of course, that's what I get for being raised Catholic. I felt like everyone that looked at me knew what I had done. It was a crazy-ass feeling. I'd been in big trouble before that point for stupid things, but I had never felt this kind of 'I'm in big trouble' feeling before. Haven't since then, either. It took a long time to calm down from it, but it was . . . what . . . only two weeks before I went back for more."

Christian says he's not exactly sure you could call him a "victim," especially since he went so far out of his way to instigate the situation. And it's not always the younger partner in such situations who may find himself victimized. "I doubt anyone is going to feel sorry for me," says "Donald," a fifty-five-year-old realtor in Charleston, South Carolina. (Donald isn't his real name; you'll see why he uses a pseudonym in about five seconds.) "I was arrested for having sex with a fifteen-year-old boy two years ago. I'll be honest—I figured he was a minor, but I didn't know he was *that* young." Donald describes himself as "rather fat, ungainly, and nothing you would call attractive," and says he really had no intention of doing anything untoward with the youth in question. "But my God, he was stunning, and I've been alone a long, long time. He spotted me walking downtown and just came on to me like gangbusters. He asked me for a ride, and before I knew it he was in my car, doing things to me no one had done for years."

Donald says that wasn't the night of the arrest. "Oh, no, I saw Josh on several occasions. I should have counted myself lucky I got away with it the first time, but once you've had attentions like that it's hard to walk away from them." Donald says he gave Josh money often, bought him nice things, and felt perversely blessed. "Of course I knew he was a hustler, and not the kind of person I'd ever pursue, but he fell into my lap—literally." After a few months Donald was beginning to get nervous, and was in fact giving Josh one last "ride" when the cops showed up. "I'm actually rather fortunate. The kid apparently had a reputation for preying on 'older gentlemen,' and it shocked me that I didn't end up doing hard time. But it's still been a living hell to live through. I'm an adult, and I should have known better."

Leaving aside such stories as Donald's—and dude, what were you *thinking?*—I'm not sure who's right or wrong here, or even if there is a right or wrong when such complex issues as age, love, sex, and sexual identity come into play at one time. As I mentioned earlier, it's clear that gay men, and society in general, have extremely inconsistent views on the topic. As I write this, a very popular movie is playing at a theater near my apartment; it's called *Tadpole* and it has to do with a sixteen-year-old boy who falls in love with his middle-aged stepmother and has a sexual tryst with her best friend, a middle-aged woman. From what I read the critics love it, and the viewer comments are similarly positive. What kind of reaction do you suppose there would be if that boy was in love with his stepfather, and in the course of the film had sex with his dad's best bud?

I'm certainly not the only one to take note of the double standard, or the presence of a new gay "morality police." Writing in the August 20, 2002, issue of *The Advocate,* Richard Goldstein, executive editor of *The Village Voice,* talked about how modern society has turned a rather natural desire for fit and handsome male adolescents into a pathology, even coining the term "ephebophilia" to describe it. "The ancient Athenians certainly didn't regard an attraction to such lads as a disease, but we do," he wrote.

> Just having the hots for teens is enough to make you an ephebophile, according to some therapists. They regard this attraction as the sign of a stunted sexual development—and so it is, if it becomes a fixation that retards intimacy or damages a child. The problem with this diagnosis is that it can be easily applied to any gay man who finds teenagers sexy. That's when a newly minted mental illness becomes an instrument of oppression. (Goldstein, 2002, p. 62)

Citing numerous cases of older heterosexual men, some of them celebrities, who've been caught in flagrante delicto with teenage girls, Goldstein mentioned the quality of media coverage that's more often nudge-nudge, wink-wink, a sort of way-to-go admiration that would be right at home in the locker room.

> It's the latest version of a forbidden game many men would like to play, whether they are willing to admit it or not—and as long as the object is a girl, no one considers it a disease. A straight guy with a jailbait jones might be known as a dirty old man, but no one would call him an ephebophile. (p. 64)

Goldstein quite rightly refused to minimize the long-lasting effects of actual child abuse; still he questioned the double standard implicit in a culture that "condemns men who have sex with teenage boys while savoring the fantasy" of men who have sex with girls the same age. "The underlying message is that homosexuality is more dangerous than heterosexuality and more diseased. . . . If we eroticize the nymphet, why not the lascivious lad?" As Goldstein sees it, it's a conversation too many gay men are afraid to have. "[It's] crucial to fight for candor about sex and young people. It's the best way to see that such feelings can be safely—and morally—expressed" (p. 67).

Even when those feelings are expressed, many gay men I talked with tell me they do their best to suppress them. Take Jack, a sixty-three-year-old retiree in west Texas. "A few years ago I met a handsome young man, small and very well-built and hung, at a hotel pool in Midland. He seemed to spend a lot of his time there—apparently he was staying at the place alone, with no family around—and he seemed to watch me closely every time I walked by. Finally we began to talk. I'd assumed he was a college student—he'd said he was a sophomore—and the conversation was about to move up to my room when I asked him what college he was attending. That's when he mentioned a large high school in the Texas Panhandle. Hell, that would make him sixteen, tops."

Jack says the boy went on to tell him that he was on the high school wrestling team. "He was in top shape, trust me. It wasn't like I was hitting on him—if anything he was hitting on me. He even said he liked his men 'mature.' This boy knew what he wanted and I suspected he'd had plenty of practice at it. I won't lie and tell you I wouldn't have loved to fuck that hot hard little butt of his, but I just smiled and said, 'I think I better go to my room by myself. I'd love to meet you in two years.'"

BIG BROTHER IS WATCHING YOU

"I knew when I took Chris 'under my wing' I was going to catch a lot of shit," says Steve, a thirty-three-year-old software salesman in San Francisco. "He's quite young (just turned seventeen) and to be honest, he's really cute. I knew all my friends would think he was just a 'boy toy,' and that I was probably fooling around with him. Trust me, I'm not." Steve tells me he met Chris outside a coffee shop; a runaway, Chris was living with friends and trying to get his bearings in a strange new city. "I know all about the shit so many gay kids have to face, especially if they're runaways. I know the shelters aren't necessarily the best places to be (I was thankful he wasn't in one!) and I know that his prospects for making something of himself as a high school dropout aren't the best."

Steve tells me he's started dropping around that coffee shop a little more regularly and Chris frequently comes by and joins him for a half hour or so. "I might buy him lunch on occasion, but I don't give him money or anything like that. I just want to show him that someone cares enough to listen to him, that he can ask me questions if he wants and get the 'straight' scoop. I make sure the conversation is always on the up and up, nothing sexual . . . though I guess sometimes I put on the 'mom' hat and tell him to be careful about who he's hanging out with, and that if he does get involved with someone to use protection. Just can't help myself there. I'd hate to see him hurt himself."

I ask Steve how he likes his role as "big brother." "Is that what I am? I've never really thought of it that way, but I guess, yeah, in some ways that's what I'm doing. It sounds kind of pompous to say I want to set a good example, but if that's what I'm doing, so be it."

Stories like Steve's weren't exactly common among the men I interviewed. We've already heard from several men who freely admit they forgo any kind of liaison with someone younger, especially someone underage, out of fear of what could happen or what others might think or say. In that piece in *The Advocate,* Richard Goldstein talked about the "child abuse panic" whose biggest casualty may well be such positive nonsexual relationships between gay youths and adults as Steve and Chris have forged.

> Now a teen must think twice before trusting such a friend, lest tongues start to wag. The teen could suffer social ostracism, and the man might risk arrest. Generations of young people have benefited from the great capacity for mentoring that many gay men have. Who knows how many boys will now be deprived of this nurturing in the name of safety. Talk about throwing the baby out with the bathwater. (Goldstein, 2002, p. 67)

I'm happy to tell you I did find a few more like Steve out there. "Arnie" won't tell me his real name or what city he lives in—he cites concerns about "getting the cops on his ass"—but he will say he's a retiree on the "high side of sixty" whose home is known locally as a place where young gays can gather in safety. "They know how to find me and they seem to know the rules before they get here: no drugs, no smoking, no alcohol, and definitely no sex of any kind on the premises, though I'm sure some of them have gotten it on once they meet here and leave. That's why I keep a generous portion of condoms and safe-sex pamphlets on hand." Arnie tells me he never intended to become a de facto gay youth organization, that "it just sort of evolved after I lost my partner of thirty years to heart disease. I didn't want to give up on life, and it became a wonderful distraction from my sorrows. I happened to meet a very charming young man and a few of his friends. . . . On a lark I invited them over, and was amazed when they showed up." Arnie admits he was a little fearful at first that "people would talk," then realized he didn't give a shit if they did. "They started coming back on a regular basis and it seems they're always bringing someone new over. We just sit around and chew the fat. I hear all the time that today's young people aren't interested in gleaning any wisdom from adults, especially old fossils like me. That has not been my experience. They constantly want to know what life was like in my day, pepper me with innumerable questions, and ask advice like the dickens. I have become the 'gay granddad' they turn to and it has been one of the most rewarding experiences of my life."

Marcus, a seventy-four-year-old retiree living in Kansas City, says he doesn't make contact with young gay people in person, but rather by computer. "I can't say I have much of an active gay life, except what exists on my Mac." But that hasn't stopped him from trying to make a difference in young people's lives. "I'm a regular in a chat room called 'Ask a Gay Guy Anything' on America Online, and I talk with dozens of youngsters every week. I find that, on this computer, I can talk like them and really communicate, probably more effectively than I could in person. Several young people will sign in to the room and ask advice, then later they send me instant messages to follow up on what the room was talking about, especially if they didn't feel comfortable talking out in the open. I have continued to hear from several of them and some still like to ask my advice. I enjoy the feeling that I might have helped someone."

"It is entirely possible for a gay male adult to have a strong bond with a gay teenager that is totally, 100 percent nonsexual and healthy," avows Jason Rich of *Growing Up Gay in America*. "This adult can act as a surrogate parent, big brother, role model, support system, mentor, and friend without the 'relationship' becoming perverse. . . . Due to the lack of support gay teens receive, I believe it is almost a responsibility of gay adults to support gay teens in a nonsexual and positive way by helping them to lead a happy, healthy, and productive lifestyle. This can be done through mentoring, friendship, and guidance. Obviously, there's always a chance a gay adult's actions in regard to helping a gay teen could be misconstrued by the outside world; however, if the adult's actions are truly legitimate, he should have nothing to fear."

"The myth of pedophilia is powerful," says NYAC's Craig Bowman. "It scares adults who have something positive to offer young people who lack role models and who could benefit from having someone help them navigate adolescence. I would encourage adults who want to support young people to identify the programs in their communities and get involved." SMYAL's Arthur Padilla notes that his organization has more than 100 volunteers, half of them adult gay men, who work one-on-one with gay youth under his organization's auspices. "I truly believe that these relationships are positive and that youth are able to get support, history, knowledge, and experience, as well as getting friends," he says.

"There's so much more all of us can do," says Sam, a forty-nine-year-old artist in South Carolina. "Especially if we live in places where being gay carries such a social stigma and young gay kids are bombarded with negativity at home, school, and just about everywhere else. If that young gay kid has a question, for God's sake answer it. If he wants to know what being gay is all about, tell him. I don't care if you meet him on the Internet, in a club, or shopping at Wal-Mart. These kids are the future, folks. They're the ones who'll be taking care of us, God willing. And if they need a friend, we better damn well step up and do what we can . . . otherwise we lose another generation to the same crap we all went through."

Chapter 5

Bridging the Gap

I didn't fall for my partner *because* of his age. I fell for him *despite* his age. I was looking at *him,* not his ID, and the world can just go screw off if they have a problem with us.

Josh, forty-four,
Atlanta lawyer

Jerry is a forty-two-year-old Florida man with a twenty-four-year-old lover. "He is everything I ever wanted in a guy, and more." Russ is a twenty-year-old college student in New Mexico whose "best friend" is a sixty-year-old retiree. "I don't know how I'd survive without his advice," he says. And Mark is a forty-five-year-old record shop owner in the Midwest whose junior partner is extremely junior. "Seth is eighteen, going on thirty-eight," he tells me. "I look on him like I would my son—if I had one—and I will leave him this business one day. We've become that close."

Three situations, one thing in common: a huge gulf in years that's either a nonfactor or the very basis of the relationship in question.

You may recall the inspiration and motivating factor of this work was my accidental confrontation with "ageism." Sure enough, as we've gone along I think it's clear that sort of confrontation is a fairly common experience for many gay men as they approach or reach middle age. It's also something many gay seniors confront on a near-daily basis. As we saw in other chapters, especially the last, a certain "underageism" is also afoot in the land, where older gay men either ignore or dismiss the plight of many younger gay men. And far too many men, young and old, find ways to exploit or abuse each other.

As I talked with hundreds of gay men over the past few years—and took a more objective look at my own life—I took note of an entirely different trend. It seems that more and more gay men of all ages are bridging that gap of years that exists between them and forging relationships that run the gamut from simple friendships or business partnerships to full-on flowering romances worthy of a Harlequin novel.

Of course I was already aware of such relationships. There are, and have always been, younger men who are quite friendly and receptive when it comes to older men, and vice versa. There are folks who will talk to anyone in a bar or online, even if they have no intention of pursuing a friendship that extends beyond last call or signoff. There are countless young men for whom a certain amount of "maturity" is an absolute prerequisite in a short- or long-term partner; there are innumerable older men who find themselves bored silly in the company of their contemporaries, they're only happy when they're coupled with someone who personifies the excitement and energy of the youth they still possess in large part, even if the fires burn a little less hotter as the years pile on.

Though such "age-disparate" relationships were often overshadowed by the hostility and apathy I encountered elsewhere, there was simply no way I could write about ageism in the gay community without talking about those couples for whom age differences are a complete nonissue, or those who see it as a key element in their mutual attraction. It's hard to quantify how many there are or how often they occur; some men tell me they had many older friends when they first came out, then lost those friendships as they made more and more friends their own age. Other men tell me they never had younger friends at all, until they grew older and suddenly made an unexpected connection. Some men pursue people in different age groups for little more than a brief, passionate fling; others were out there husband hunting, and whoomp, there it was. One young man told me once he didn't believe that older and younger men should date, that he simply didn't think "that sort of thing" would ever last very long; one week later he had a boyfriend more than twice his age and they stayed lovers for more than a year, which when it comes to relationships isn't exactly a miserable failure.

But there's another, self-indulgent aspect of all this as well. It would be extremely disingenuous for me to broach this topic and not talk about my own experiences; though we began this trip with my first brush with ageism, I have to admit that many—if not most—of my longest-lasting personal relationships have been with someone far younger than I. I'm not sure if that makes me completely biased or the perfect person to write about it. I'll let you be the judge; this is, of all the topics bandied about in this book, the subject that strikes closest to my heart, for reasons that will become clearer a bit later on.

Just thought I should let you know.

LEGENDS OF THE "FALL"

"I'll never forget the first time I saw my future boyfriend," says Jerry, a forty-two-year-old customer service representative in Fort Lauderdale. "It was at a club here in town, on one of those nights where they knock down the age limits so the younger crowd can get in." Jerry admits that finding a mate on that warm steamy night was the last thing on his mind. "Hell, no, I wasn't trying to find a boyfriend. I was just looking to get laid with a cute young hottie."

Cupid, as they say, had other thoughts. "I saw him with some friends of his, looking at me looking at him, kind of making fun of me. But Tommy wasn't laughing, he was just smiling a lot and looking down at the floor." Jerry says he waited for a chance, swooped in, and asked Tommy if he'd like to dance. "We were out there for like an hour, just bumping up against each other, obviously turning each other on. Sex with this kid looked to be a pretty good possibility; then something happened right as we got off the dance floor, I'm still not sure exactly what. The way he grabbed my elbow to make sure I didn't fall over the other drunks . . . the way he said he'd wait for me when I went to take a leak. I just saw this . . . sweetness, I guess you'd call it. I just saw him very differently."

Instead of sex, Jerry says they had coffee, then went for a long walk along the beach. "I knew he was a lot younger than me (though not as young as I thought he was when I first saw him) but the more we talked, the less I cared. He obviously didn't care how old I was (I made sure to tell him right away) so we decided to do the old-fashioned thing and actually date for awhile." Jerry says it was several weeks before they finally took the tumble. "My God . . . what a night. We just devoured each other." One year later they're still together.

I've always been curious about the dynamics of such age-disparate relationships, how they function, what makes each partner so drawn to the other. In 1999 I wrote an article on the topic for the now-defunct *HERO* magazine, a publication devoted to gay male couples caught in the throes of monogamy. (*HERO* was one of those mags you either loved or hated; it had a tagline, "the magazine for the rest of us," that tended to encourage or enrage many gay men, depending on where they stood on the "one man at a time" philosophy.) In that article—which, by an amazing coincidence, was also called "Bridging the Gap"—I spoke with a half-dozen or so couples, many with large age differences between the partners, to find out what was working and what wasn't, and how they got together in the first place.

Back then Shawn told me he was twenty-three when he looked "across the crowded room" in a Denver nightclub and met the man who would change his life. "There was definitely something different about him," he remembered. "He just stood out from all those boys. This was somebody like I'd never seen before. This was a man" (Bergling, 1999a, p. 24).

And an older man, at that. Quite a bit older. "Would you believe forty-three?" he asked me, recalling his own surprise when the two finally stopped circling each other and got to talking.

> I hardly believed it to look at him. He was trim and muscular, a little shorter than me but about twice as wide. When I got close I noticed he had a few gray hairs, and a couple of extra lines around his eyes. I almost took off. Then he smiled. That's all it took to keep me standing there. (p. 24)

By the time I wrote the *HERO* piece, Shawn and his "old man" Mike had just got finished celebrating their seventh anniversary, and Shawn's thirtieth birthday, in the house they were sharing just outside of Denver.

> All I can say is thank God he smiled like that, at just the right moment. That was a time when I was all about fooling around with young guys, guys who hadn't really lived yet. Mike has shown me so much, taught me so much. I feel like I owe him everything. (p. 24)

I was curious to find out what had transpired between the two in the years since the *HERO* article was published. They'd made it seven years, but was it possible they'd passed the decade-plus mark unscathed? As it turns out, of all the *HERO* couples I interviewed, Shawn and Mike were the only ones whose e-mail address still worked. "I'm happy to say yes, we're still together," Shawn, now thirty-four, writes me. "It's odd, because Mike is older [fifty-four], but I feel a lot closer to his age. We're growing closer all the time it seems, we're always getting better at knowing each other's moods and needs."

In Chapter 4 I mentioned the "double standard" that so often applies when gay life is matched up against the straight. In the heterosexual world, May to September romances hardly raise eyebrows anymore, so long as it's the older man with a younger woman in tow. (In my work in television I've often noted wryly how that particular relationship is echoed in the frequent pairing of older male news anchors with younger women on the news set. Throw in the wacky uncle, i.e., the weatherman, and the smartass kid in sports, and hey, ya got yourself a family!) You need only look as far as Hollywood to see what I mean, where any number of aging actors sport a "trophy" wife. Even on Capitol Hill the number of aging congressmen with vibrant young wives—usually not their first—seems to grow with every election cycle.

Older women paired with younger men are a bit more problematic. Though one sees more and more of such couplings all the time, they still inspire a lot of nasty chatter among the unenlightened. But that's nothing compared with the older man/younger man dynamic. It's a kind of relationship that has always existed in the same-sex world, but it's a liaison that brings with it a certain amount of historical baggage, not to mention much harsher criticism than that faced by older women. We touched on some of these already: the "sugar daddy" or "chicken hawk" on the prowl, the young hustler or "boy toy" looking for status or security, to name just a few of the phenomena most frowned upon. In and outside of the gay community there are many who would tell you that any sexual or romantic association between older man and younger man just reeks of exploitation or recruitment. The assumption automatically places the older partner in the power position, with the younger man relegated to a mere plaything or trophy. While such relationships certainly *do* exist, to a point where they've achieved accepted cliché status, they do not equal the sum total of all such situations. The cliché ignores the symbiotic union two people can create when they reach across a generation gap, so long as each brings with him something he can offer the other.

"Some men like that smooth skin and 'I'm young and I'm a beautiful man' attitude," suggests Doug Favero, a Washington, DC-based psychologist. "Maybe most of us do . . . it's what our culture puts on the highest rung of the ladder. We may be genetically programmed to idealize the young, thus—at least in hetero relationships—guaranteeing couplings which perpetuate the species. But I also see a lot of admiration in our community for the mature, successful, nurturing older male, too. Not as sexualized an admiration, maybe, but still an attachment ideal." Favero says extremely interesting things can happen when two people, each holding one of those ideals, happen to stumble on each other.

Adam tells me he wasn't looking for love when he met his last boyfriend. He was just hungry. For fast food. "I was late for work, and I wanted to grab a burger. The boy in the drive-through was all smiles and flashing blue eyes. He seemed to be flirting with me a little, so I flirted back. It was all so harmless and fun. I guess he spotted my rainbow stickers on the car, because the next time I walked into the place he flew out of the drive-though window and waited on me at the counter. He smiled a lot. I smiled back a lot."

Adam, who admits to "midthirties" when asked about his age, says the flirtation went on for three or four weeks, "every time I went into the place or pulled up at the window." Finally, Adam says, he slipped the kid his number. "I didn't know how old he was. I was afraid to ask. He called me that night. Thank God he'd just turned eighteen." Adam says he dated the burger boy for about six months, and it was one of the most passionate romances he'd ever had. "This was a beautiful, sweet boy who didn't know anything about gay life except what he'd heard on TV or read in the paper. He didn't know about gay bar attitude or being bitchy for the hell of it. He was totally unspoiled and innocent, and extremely curious about what guys do in bed. He wanted me to teach him what being gay was all about. I was happy to oblige. In a lot of ways he helped me, too, by reminding me that there could still be such a thing as a whirlwind romance that comes at you out of the blue, that I could still get swept off my feet. He really made me feel alive and probably a bit smarter than I really am."

Adam cooled things off after several months, but not because he was growing tired of such "fast" food. "Oh, I know this sounds so condescending, but I actually felt guilty about hogging his company. When I was young I had a chance to date lots of guys my own age, and I thought he deserved the same thing." And where is "happy meal" now? "He works in a law firm in Philly and he's living with a guy in his thirties. We're still good friends. In a lot of ways he's luckier than me. He knows what he wants."

Earl tells me his partner was a "take charge" kind of kid from the moment they met, a youngster who'd come out to his family at eighteen. (Earl says he didn't come out to his family until he was well past thirty.) Though not so far apart in age—only eight years—they were worlds apart in experience, and, as Earl puts it, "in the emotional strength he provides in our relationship. . . . We've been in a monogamous relationship since our first encounter in 1996 and our emotional foundation is still deeply rooted in the trust and security he bestowed upon me when we first met."

David is a seventy-one-year-old retired writer in Santa Rosa, California, who didn't come out until he was fifty-eight. "Because I came into this lifestyle later, my partners, mentors, and friends have all been younger. In fact the young man who introduced me to gay sex was only twenty-nine. My current partner is twenty-nine years younger than I am and we've been together now for nine years. I think the attentions of a younger man for one so much older is rather flattering. Older gay men seem to be so much more insecure and possessive to me than the younger ones, who've always been very respectful. The sex is pretty good, too."

"I purposefully seek out older, more mature men," says Chris, a twenty-seven-year-old retail manager from Hampton Roads, Virginia. "The reasons why I'd do that seem pretty obvious to me. Older guys have already done all their screwing around, while younger guys are often into screwing anything and everything. It's been my experience they're less inclined to cheat, and for some reason, I find they're usually more masculine, too. And while I'm not looking for a sugar daddy, the money factor is important. A guy who's forty is probably already settled into a career and has some direction in his life, while a twenty-five-year-old probably doesn't have it all together yet."

Leo is a thirty-seven-year-old business owner, originally from Costa Rica. While his relationship with Michael, a twenty-six-year-old from Spain, isn't what he'd call "serious" at this point, it's still something that gives him great joy. "I do sometimes wonder what he sees in me, why some other hot jock boy—like him—can't give him what I do. I get a little self-conscious that I may not be good enough, but he sure thinks I am." Leo says the two travel extensively, speak the same languages, and have similar education and interests. "We enjoy our bodies very much. . . . If the age difference manifests itself anywhere, it's in outside activities; he is more into active team sports like soccer and baseball, where I'm into more personal sports like biking and hiking. But really, that's about it. Sometimes he has more 'stamina' than I have, but I'm usually so turned on that I can go all night with him. We really haven't suffered from our age difference. If anything, we exist because of it."

In my surveys I found dozens of other couples, much farther apart in age than Leo and Michael—some as much as twenty years or more—and many do consider themselves "serious," even lifelong partners, with track records to prove it. Josh, a forty-four-year-old lawyer in Atlanta whose quote began this chapter, has been living with his "junior" partner Alan for more than ten years. Alan was barely nineteen when they met; Josh had just celebrated his thirty-second birthday. "Like a lot of couples with large age differences between them, we've had to put up with a lot of crap," he tells me, including the accusation that it was only Alan's "young and hunky" looks that brought them together. "I won't lie—he was really hot, and still is. I can't tell you that wasn't what made me sit up and take notice, or something that still doesn't give me tremendous pleasure," he explains. "But there's lots of hot boys in the south, and lots of hot men, too. Alan was something special. It only took a few dates with him to see that." That's not to say there weren't problems. "I'd had several relationships before I met him and he hadn't had many before he met me. We had some rocky times in the beginning, even broke up a few times. It was often very hard reconciling the differences in age and experiences, and not just relationship experiences. I'd had a pretty full life before I met him, but there was just something magical in the way we kept coming back to each other, and now I don't think either of us can picture being without the other."

WHEN TWO WORLDS COLLIDE

But "differences" in age and experience can't be minimized. Just ask Bill, a twenty-two-year-old college student in Connecticut. "I've always had a thing for older guys, since I first came out at nineteen. I still hope to have a long-term relationship with the 'right' older guy, since I just don't find myself attracted to guys my own age, but so far it's not working. . . . Every time I meet someone, it's like they want to be my teacher, or they have this 'been there, done that' attitude and they don't take me very seriously. I know an older guy is going to have a lot of life experience and sometimes I worry that's going to get in the way of me finding someone." Mark, a thirty-seven-year-old small business owner in Akron, Ohio, tells me he has the opposite problem. "I like younger guys and for some reason (which I'm thankful for!) they also find me attractive. Some of them I've dated for months at a time, but it always seems we end up breaking up over the most trivial fight or argument. My parents fought all the time. . . . I grew up in a loud house and a little argument here and there means nothing to me. The guys I've gone out with just can't seem to handle me. They put way too much meaning into every little disagreement, like they have this perfect image of a world that doesn't really exist. I'd date people my own age, just to have some stability, but guys my own age just don't do it for me. They never really have."

"When I was first exploring my sexuality I was always attracted to older men, those ten to fifteen years older," says Hudson, a fifty-four-year-old designer/consultant in Washington, DC. "I liked their style, oftentimes their look, their presence, what they thought, and how they expressed themselves. I find that as I get older those that are most attracted to me are younger, sometimes to a fault. . . . I was visiting Russia a few years ago and was introduced to a wonderfully attractive young man twenty years my junior. He was an American and within a few months he was living with me in Washington. Although he had much to offer, I found that my comfort level—after the sex—

was painfully minimal. Those twenty years make a big difference in some men's lives."

"There's a lot to be said for synchronicity in age," says thirty-nine-year-old Todd from Washington, DC. "In my early thirties I dated guys who were often more than ten years younger than me. One was eighteen. The sex was terrific . . . the conversation was woefully limited. It finally dawned on me that a man my age wasn't going to find much commonality with someone who still lived at home and couldn't see beyond college." Chris, a twenty-five-year-old from Portsmouth, Virginia, has an entirely different view of the sexual dynamic when it comes to his thirty-eight-year-old boyfriend. "I want sex four times a day. Sometimes I think he'd be happier if it was four times a month."

Then there's family to consider. Gordon, a thirty-seven-year-old grocery store manager from Long Island, tells me how he avoided meeting his young beau's parents for "nearly a year," so tied up inside was he, wondering what they'd think about their twenty-two-year-old son's "older" companion. "I could picture the family barbecue, and long awkward silences while his dad sat there, sipping a beer, just giving me the evil eye over the hot dogs and hamburgers," he says. "'So you're the guy who's doing my boy,' I always saw him saying to me. It didn't really turn out that way, but it was *still* a little strange meeting them. And they were ultraliberal, card-carrying PFLAGers."

Bruce, a thirty-nine-year-old restaurant manager in Passaic, New Jersey, points out what may be the single biggest challenge faced by couples years apart in age and worlds apart in experience. "I've been in a few of those 'ages apart' relationships and I don't know if I can ever stomach another one. In the beginning it can be magical, absolutely. I remember one young guy I met and I tried hard not to fall for him. Then I gave in; he was just too special and unique to let go. We had a few great months, then his feelings for me just changed, almost overnight. He was only about twenty or so, and sometimes your feelings at that age can change. I don't know if younger guys can really be monogamous, or even if they should be. But trouble is, I'd really fallen for him by then. I was deeply in love with him. It almost destroyed me."

Besides any internal difficulties and changes they encounter, many "age discordant" couples find themselves confronting external problems. Kyle, a nineteen-year-old college student in North Carolina, says that dating anyone older can be problematic in those backwater towns where gay relationships of any kind are still looked on with a jaundiced eye. "I'm part Asian, so I look pretty young to begin with. If I go out with anyone who's over twenty-five it's going to look funny, because straight guys of different ages rarely hang out with each other in public when they're not related, except in very specific situations like the gym or socializing after work. It's definitely going to look strange to some people."

Even within the safety of the gay ghettos, older/younger couples can face a bit of a backlash. Or at least, some fangs and claws. "My young lover and I get it all the time," says David, a fifty-eight-year-old writer in Manhattan. "The snide comments, the back-of-the-hand whispers; darling, we hear it all the time. My dear, if I was going to let it bother me, I'd say something, but I simply smile and move on. Jealousy is a very ugly thing. Yes, that's all it is. And they have every reason to feel so, for I am in heaven with my young love."

Johnnie, a thirty-five-year-old nightclub owner who also hails from the Big Apple, isn't involved in such a relationship but he hears the comments "all the time, almost every single day . . . they range from 'Hey kid, why did you bring your dad out with you tonight?' to 'Sir, is your son old enough to be in this bar?'" Rick, a thirty-one-year-old operations director for a Seattle ad agency, tells me he's had three boyfriends who were at least ten years younger. "I'm always called a pedophile, since I tend to like guys in the nineteen to twenty-two range, and I find that quite a few guys in that age range are attracted to guys who are older and more stable." Rick laughs off the negative comments he hears—he seems to be having too much fun to care very much—but other men tell me the comments have a real sting to them, whether they come from jealous friends or "bitchy queens" camping out in bars.

Terry, a forty-seven-year-old food service manager in Fort Lauderdale who says he's often approached by younger men—"I guess it's that middle-age attraction thing"—tells me he often hears the social tongues wagging overtime. "The couples I have known, some decades apart in age, are not allowed to be seen as a couple. They're perceived as 'Sugar Daddy/Boy Toy.' I have known lots of couples like that, genuinely in love with each other, and all they get is people being jealous and judgmental, who criticize them for their age differences, instead of just being happy for what they've found together."

"I can see the hurt in my lover's eyes when he hears that kind of shit," says Ronnie, a twenty-year-old office worker/intern in Los Angeles who's dating a forty-three-year-old. "He laughs it off, but I know it hurts him when they call him 'cradle robber.' Then the other night we were out in West Hollywood and someone said something about me being a 'tomb raider.' Can't tell you how pissed I was about that. I almost wanted to deck the guy."

That "tomb raider" comment also grates on Jason's ears. He's a thirty-four-year-old community service worker in Mississippi who's been living with his older lover for almost a decade. "Lou and I met about nine and a half years ago, when he'd just turned fifty. So many of my friends disapproved of us. They just thought it was creepy that a guy twice my age would come after me so strong. But I thank God he did, because he's been everything to me. Do I worry about what's up ahead, when he's a lot older, and he may need me to take care of him? Of course not! That's what you do when you love somebody." (Jason and others I met like him introduced me to a term I'd never heard before—gerontophile—as in one who's specifically attracted to, as Jason put it, "men of age." That's a theme I'll be talking about in Chapter 6.)

"In general, people my own age bore the hell out of me," says Alan, a sixty-year-old brokerage analyst in San Francisco. "They've become so stuck in their rut and just can't seem to get out. I try to keep up with the changing scene, and so I enjoy the company of younger people who have fresh and interesting ideas and perceptions." But Alan says dating someone younger can make him feel "out of place" on occasion. "I had a ten-year, on-and-off-again relationship with a much younger man. When we spent time together alone, we were nearly unaware of the difference in our ages, but out in a crowd of young people, I stuck out like the 800-pound gorilla. I just can't see myself in such a relationship again."

Still other men tell me it's not the comments of others that bother them so much; they have their own internal critics working overtime. "I used to hit on young guys all the time, with abandon," says Charlie, a forty-three-year-old office manager at a firm in Charlotte, North Carolina. "Especially in the gym, where I find myself often surrounded by younger guys. Many of them end up being straight, and that's fine with me . . . sometimes it's fun to have younger people around in a nonsexual way. But some have been gay, and I've dated several I met that way. Lately, though, I see other guys my age doing the same thing, not just in the gym. I see them doing it at clubs, and it just looks so sad and pathetic. I've begun to wonder if *I* look that sad and pathetic, too, and I find myself thinking I don't want to ever look that way."

For all the criticism they get, the catty comments they may hear—or overhear—and the second guessing they go through, the "bridge gappers" do get at least theoretical support from most of the men I surveyed and polled. "True romance and love are just so rare in the gay world, or at least, that's how it seems sometimes," says Nathan, a thirty-year-old accountant in Phoenix. "I say if two people make that connection, fucking go for it, man, and to hell with what anyone else thinks." Glenn, a twenty-three-year-old postgraduate student from Rockford, Illinois, says he hasn't been attracted to anyone much older than he is, at least not yet; but he refuses to dismiss the possibility. "If I did fall for an older guy, then that would mean he's the one who's got what I'm looking for, so I wouldn't give a shit how old he was. The fact that I fell is all that matters."

In Chapter 4 we talked about my poll question on underage/over-age relationships; three out of the five age groups polled showed clear majorities tilting in favor of such couplings, as long as "true love" was present. When I asked the same groups what they thought of age-disparate relationships where each of the partners was "legal," the favorable numbers grew tremendously; overwhelming majorities in every age group said they approved, as long as the couples were "truly in love." Most of the psychologists I talked to were also supportive. "One of the major difficulties that a male couple has is competitiveness," says Michael Shernoff, the New York-based psychotherapist we heard from back in Chapter 2, who suggests that an age difference of at least fifteen years between partners can actually be beneficial. "This age difference mitigates a lot of the competitiveness, since each of the men are in different phases of the life cycle." Doug Favero, a DC-based psychologist, agrees. "It's undeniable that in many situations the older partner can bring some emotional stability and maturity into the relationship, while the younger partner can bring with him an energy and enthusiasm that can bring out the older partner's own inner youthfulness. As long as each partner is willing to be open and sharing of his feelings, even a large age difference doesn't have to be an obstacle to their contentment with each other." In the October 12, 2002, edition of her PlanetOut advice column, noted author and Los Angeles-based psychotherapist Betty Berzon addressed a question from a fifty-one-year-old gay man who'd fallen head over heels for a thirty-three-year-old. The older man, who signed himself "A Generation Apart," said his new love had him "acting like a teenager," but he confessed his younger love had extreme reservations about the implications of dating an older man, especially about what might "lie ahead" in the future. In response, Berzon explained that while age differences do show up in both trivial and substantive ways, everybody ages at different rates. "Some people are old at fifty, some are young at seventy." She writes, "No one knows really what his or her future will be, but one thing is fairly certain—it will be easier to age than it has ever been. It already is." As for offering long-term hope:

> I can only offer that relationships with more of an age difference than yours have worked well. . . . I've found that life works out best when it is lived not in the past and not in the future, but in the present. You both seem to be enjoying one another now. Why not leave it that way for a while?

Others aren't so sure. Paul Smith, a clinical social worker who's also based in Washington, says he believes that older men who seek out those much younger than themselves may well be acting out some neurosis surrounding sex, aging, or emotional immaturity. "Most men relish the opportunity to pursue and mate with others who share common ground relative to their own stage in life," he says. "The wider the age gap, the less able men are to find commonality and levels of social, emotional, and age-appropriate compatibility that most men seek. . . . Often couples with wide age differences result in parent-child or mentor-mentee dynamics that can create a one up–one down imbalance. These dynamics tend to undermine the equality and reciprocity that give balance and equity to male coupling."

Red, a thirty-nine-year-old artist in the southeast, seems to agree. "I've met many men my age who behave like teenagers. I think gay men, to a greater degree than the general American public, have a delayed adolescence." He says, "Often closeted as a true teenager, they experience the infatuations and emotions of teenage years later in life. Coupled with America's obsession and worship of youth in general, many men extend being an adolescent into their thirties and sometimes their forties. Partnering with a younger man closer to actual adolescence just reinforces the trend."

One man I surveyed says he long ago gave up trying to find that perfect young partner after years of trying. "It didn't matter how mature I thought they were originally, or how much they seemed able to deal with me on a man-to-man level," says Don, a thirty-seven-year-old engineer in Augusta, Maine. "In the end it was like most of them were looking for Daddy, someone to direct them in life. I have enough trouble directing my own life. I can't be responsible for helping them find their way, too."

"I guess some guys look for someone out of their age group out of some kind of 'needy' motivation, but that hasn't been my experience at all," says Bryan, a thirty-one-year-old banker in Walla Walla, Washington (has to be one of my favorite city names, anywhere). Bryan says he's always liked younger men, for one simple reason. "I think I'm a good looking, in-shape guy, and I like other good looking, in-shape guys. The older I get, the more I see people my age kind of falling apart. Call me superficial, fine, I don't care. I'm not really looking for a serious relationship right now, just nice, casual flings. The younger guys, the college dudes, just do it for me. I get along with them, they get along with me, we have fun. I don't think that makes me needy or anything. I'm just honest enough to tell you what I'm after, and that's pure physical attraction."

THE "TWINKIE DEFENSE"

What began as a "physical attraction" for Matt, a thirty-four-year-old federal worker in northern Virginia, has now just passed its one-year mark. He first saw his nineteen-year-old boyfriend, Fred, at a dance club and naturally assumed he was twenty-one. "By the time I found out how old he was I was smitten, but the age difference did make me a little uncomfortable." The two have pursued a sometimes rocky but ultimately satisfying relationship. "Do I ever have to hold my temper because he's still too young yet to know how to act in certain situations? Yes, I do. I don't want this to become a father/son relationship. That's not at all what I'm looking for . . . but I understand in a lot of ways he's still growing up."

Matt calls to mind something a lot of older men who "date younger" have pointed out to me, what I've come to call the "twinkie defense": your young lover may walk and talk like a thirty-year-old, but he's still a kid inside. Knowing that, a lot of older men tell me that they often feel responsible for anything that goes wrong within the relationship, whether they're actually at fault or not. "It's probably the biggest obstacle we face," says Ted, a forty-one-year-old account manager in northern California. "Aaron is twenty-three and we've been dating for almost two years. He'd had boyfriends before at school, but nothing this serious. Being in a relationship where you're expected to behave with a certain amount of responsibility and maturity was totally new to him. After the first few months' afterglow wore off, we started having the little squabbles and exchanges any couple has and Aaron would just go over the top . . . every fight was like, 'So, are we breaking up?' and just overdramatic stuff like that." Like Bruce, Ted says he realizes that sometimes younger people can fall "out" of love almost as fast as they fall into it and it's given him some sleepless nights. "He's really settled down now, in fact I'd say he's way more grown up than I was at his age, but occasionally we still have blowups and they're often based on his inexperience. I have to remember he's still young, and it's difficult for me to muster all the patience he probably deserves."

Wayne, a thirty-six-year-old sports promoter in Philadelphia, says he sometimes resents the fact that he does most of the "heavy lifting" in his three-year relationship with his twenty-three-year-old boyfriend. "We were friends first before we got serious—he was actually my intern while he was in college—so that's made it easier for us to avoid those 'couple problems' a lot of guys have. But yeah . . . it's hard sometimes to remember this is his first real go-round with another guy, and I find myself holding back when I really want to knock some sense into him." Wayne assures me that's not meant literally. "I just mean it can be *so* frustrating dealing with someone who's convinced he knows everything and makes those assumptions we all make when we're young."

Wayne suggests one problem with dating younger guys—those in their late teens or early twenties—is the fact that they often see the world idealistically, in shades of black and white, with little in between. "You have to get some years on you before you realize that black and white don't exist very often, that everything is a lot more gray. But I love my guy so much, it's worth the trouble."

Andrew, a thirty-six-year-old pharmacist in St. Paul, Minnesota, tells me a thing or two about guys who see only in such "black and white" terms. "I was dating this young guy named Jimmy, about nineteen or so . . . he was totally convinced that he'd gotten to the pinnacle of his intellectual and emotional development. I would point out from time to time, quite gently, that perhaps he might see the world a little differently once he'd gotten to, oh, twenty-two or twenty-three. That would piss him off so much, he'd call me condescending and arrogant, and we'd just get into these stupid fights. Attractive as he was otherwise (and not just physically, the kid had a really sweet soul), I just couldn't put up with him for very long. It was too exhausting, and I wasn't going to stick around waiting for him to grow up."

Which brings us back to Matt, who scoffs at the idea that his beau Fred needs him to "wait around" while he matures into a more fully realized person. "Is anyone a full person yet? I think life's an adventure, a road, not a destination. It's fun to be part of someone's life when he's just started off on his journey. Hell, I have my faults, too. I don't know if I could ever find anyone else—of any age—who I'm so compatible with in so many important ways. You have to remember, in any worthwhile relationship it's love that's the bottom line."

FRIENDS, INDEED

Mike is a thirty-five-year-old photographer in Worcester, Massachusetts, who met his best friend Ty at the gym. "We mainly just worked out together at first. He was a college kid, just starting to get serious about training, and I'd been lifting on and off for years." Mike says they were just workout partners at first, spotting each other and engaging in a "friendly competition" to see who could "get more ripped." Mike says Ty was a real breath of fresh air. "I guess he's part of this new generation of gay kids who aren't really hiding their sexuality, but they're not exactly flaunting it either . . . we sort of figured each other out, gay-wise, pretty fast. He's a good-looking guy, but I never really hit on him. I'm sure he wasn't 'into' me. It was nice to make a nonsexual connection for once."

That friendship soon moved off the gym floor to include grabbing a postworkout bite at a nearby sandwich shop, and now the two spend quite a bit of time together, taking in films, hitting the clubs, and going on joint vacations. "It's funny, 'cause all my older friends are just convinced I'm banging him and I'm somehow ashamed to admit it, but that's really not what's going on. I think of him a lot more like a kid brother, except I like him a lot more than I do any of my real siblings. He's just a fun guy to hang out with, and obviously since I can't get rid of him, he must like me, too."

Russ, a twenty-year-old art student in Albuquerque, New Mexico, tells me he "wishes" he could spend that kind of quality time with his best friend. Trouble is, they're almost 2,000 miles apart. "His name is Frank and he turned sixty last month," he tells me. Russ and Frank have known each other for almost five years, but they've never actually "met" in person. "People will probably laugh at me for calling someone I met on the Internet my 'best friend,' but that's really what he's been for me." Russ says he met Frank during a very troubled time, when he was fifteen and convinced he was the "only" gay person in the entire world. "You know how lonely it can be, growing up gay in a pretty remote area. I met Frank when I was going into chat rooms a lot, trying to find anyone to make me feel a little less lonely." Russ says Frank was one of the few "honest" people he ever met in cyberspace. "He told me exactly how old he was, which was something very few older guys ever did. Most would lie, tell me they were teens, too, then try and get me to send them a dirty picture. Frank was never like that. He was just a very nice guy to talk to."

After they'd talked for several months, Russ asked Frank if he could call him and hear his voice. "He got a little worried about that, since I was still so young. But after awhile he let me call him—collect—and we've been talking pretty steadily since then." Russ says Frank was like the older brother he never had, someone to vent to after a particularly shitty day at school or a fight with his parents. "It wasn't just a one-way thing, though. . . . He was going through a tough time with his divorce, and kids who didn't want to see him. I guess having a young guy to talk to was something kind of good for him, too."

I ask Russ if Frank ever wanted to have him come for "a little visit" and he gets perturbed by the question. "If you're asking me if he wanted to have me come out so he could 'play' with me, the answer is no!" Russ explains that Frank has actually turned *him* down on several occasions when Russ proposed a visit. "I think he wants me to get a lot older, have a life of my own and get on my feet, before he meets me for real." Until then, Russ says the two are content to instant message each other and talk on the phone a few times a week. "He's given me so many pep talks and gotten me out of the dumps more times than I can tell you. He also gave me a lot of good advice about staying in school and about where to go to college. Mostly he's just there when I need him. If that's not a best friend, what is?"

Russ was one of several young men who told me they'd found mentors online, people they could talk to freely without fear of being viewed merely as sexual playthings. "I guess some of my older Net friends may have the hots for me," says Brandon, a nineteen-year-old college student in Alabama, "but they keep it pretty clean and they show some class. Sure they flirt with me a little, and sometimes I flirt back, but more often it's about, 'How was your day?' and 'You seeing anybody new?', that kind of thing. I don't have any gay friends here at school, or any real gay friends at home, either. My Net friends are my lifeline and a lot of them are older guys. Which is just cool with me. It's nice to talk to people who've actually had a life!"

Of course it's not just about the Net. Some younger guys find good friends among the older crowd right here in the real world. David, a nineteen-year-old college student in Pennsylvania, tells me he's had "older gay friends" as long as he can remember. "They've taught me everything I know and helped me figure out how to figure things out for myself. Who else was I going to learn about the world from, a bunch of ignorant kids my own age? That's the blind leading the blind." Mike, a seventeen-year-old high school student in New Hampshire, tells me about the "forty-two-year-old gay guy" that he works with. "Sometimes we'll grab a bite together after we get off work. We can talk about guys and make fun of Republicans. I cherish those conversations."

"Intergenerational gay male friendships are invaluable," says Michael Shernoff. "There is a wisdom and wealth of life experience to be gained by having access to older men who have lived and struggled with many issues that younger men are experiencing for the first time. The advice of an older and beloved friend regarding romances, relationship difficulties, life changes, health . . . it's too often simply not available to younger gay men due to the terrible age segregation within so much of the gay men's community. Personally, I have been blessed to always have had older gay men friends who enriched my life with the oral history of bygone eras and decades through which they lived. . . . It feels as if my life is more integrated having these older men as wiser and emotionally supportive family members of our tribe."

Daved—yes, he uses that iconoclastic spelling—couldn't agree more. He's a tremendously witty thirty-year-old friend of mine who just came back to the DC area after a few years' exile on the Left Coast. "I've been mentored by my friend Michael, who's a large, hairy bear of a man who's now fifty-three," Daved says. "He's helped me along through life for the past eight or so years. I'd be largely a dimwit without him." Daved says Michael, more than anyone else, has helped him to better understand the oft-bizarre rituals of male-on-male dating, something that his "goddamned Midwestern upbringing" just never prepared him for. "Over the phone last week, Michael explained to me the concept I still hadn't grasped at thirty about how to give attention to men. How to feed their needs, then withdraw a bit to keep them wanting more, how not to think 'being nice' was always the key. He taught me how to react around men I might run into who've not been receptive of me in the past. He taught me how not to offer the obvious compliments—'You have pretty eyes'—but instead to shoot for something that will really strike the person, like their creativity, or the way they sang a song." Daved says it all seems so painfully obvious now and that he "scolded" Michael for not clueing him in before. "He explained that I had to reach a certain stage in my life before I'd be able to use any of his knowledge. He was absolutely right."

Daved says he'd enjoy the opportunity to "give back" by offering a younger person the same kind of guidance, within the context of a friendship, or maybe something deeper. "Right now, I have my attention directed at a nineteen-year-old intern who works with me. He's certainly gay, though he may be like I was at nineteen, and not know what to do with it yet. I still regret that the thirty-year-old in *my* life at *my* job when I was nineteen didn't just *take* me, though it's what we both wanted! I could not yet make the move; he *should* have."

Another interesting situation I stumbled upon involves two men—one middle aged, the other in his early twenties—who work together in the same office. Peter tells me when he decided it was time to come out, he turned to the only gay person he knew, Ben, his co-worker at a company in Cleveland. "We hadn't really been friends before that . . . I was actually a little afraid to approach him because he was 'out' at work, and I wasn't sure if I was all that comfortable having people see us together." Then Peter ran into Ben at a gay bar—one of the very first gay bars Peter ever walked into—and the jig was up. "We just smiled at each other, then started talking. We ended up getting very, very drunk. I had a ball."

Since then Peter says Ben has "really taken me under his wing, really helped me get comfortable with the idea that I'm gay." What makes this situation so unique? *Peter* is the "newbie" at forty-seven, while Ben, at twenty-two, is the gay veteran. He's been out since he was seventeen. "I'm just amazed that someone so young is so confident and together when he walks into a club and I feel like I'm wearing two left-footed shoes. I could sit here and regret the fact that I wasted half my life (maybe more than half) pretending to be someone or something I'm not, but Ben won't hear about it. He just keeps me going in a really positive direction."

Considering the polarity that can exist in so many gay social situations, it's probably not so amazing that many of the intergenerational friendships I found first blossomed in the workplace. In many ways, work is the great equalizer; no one really cares if you're "hot or not," as long as you get your job done by 5 p.m. Many men who wouldn't think of approaching each other socially find they actually have a lot in common, or at least, commonly held ideals or a sense of humor.

Some older men who run businesses that cater to younger crowds tell me that youthful workers are a must, and occasionally they discover that in hiring an employee they found something much more valuable. Mark, the forty-five-year-old record shop owner in Missouri, tells me he hired Seth at sixteen "because he really seemed to have an innate maturity, and a good sense of the business. . . . He's working on starting his own deejay following, and he brings a lot of extra traffic into the store." Already an extremely devoted worker, Seth turned out to be an unexpected shoulder to cry on when Mark's partner abruptly left him for another guy. "I just can't say enough good things about him." Now Mark says he's made Seth a partner, but he's a lot more than that. "I don't know if he'll want this store when I'm ready to retire—or in this economy if I'll even have a store for long—but if it's here, and he wants it, it's his."

For some older men I interviewed, it wasn't a case of having one good friend among the younger set, but rather a whole crowd. "It seems like every few years I fall into a new group of guys in their twenties, sometimes even their late teens," says Randy, a "fortyish" realtor currently living near Memphis, Tennessee. "Either that, or this group of young guys just kind of forms around me, like I bring them together by having a great party or a night out on the town." That's not to say Randy doesn't have friends in his own age group—"I do, and always will"—but for most social occasions he tells me he prefers to run with his "youth posse," for a variety of reasons. "As I say, they're just a lot of fun to be around. I guess in some ways it's the same thing that leads people to be teachers or coaches (I do a lot of that!) because you just absorb their energy and new ways of looking at the world. A lot of guys in my age group just turn into boring old farts, all consumed with their businesses, with getting rich, with buying this or that. I don't mind dealing with guys like that professionally, but for party time I like my boys, because they keep me feeling young. So far I haven't had any trouble keeping up with them."

I ask Randy if he purposefully seeks out young guys, and edges out his old friends in favor of "fresh meat." "Oh, hell no, this isn't a boy-band I'm running here," he exclaims, and the Menudo allusion makes me laugh. "There's an old saying that some people are collectors and some are selectors. I'm a collector. I like having this big family around me, since I'm never going to have one of my own, at least not in the traditional sense. I try to keep in touch with everyone who's ever come into my life, pulled up a chair, and stayed awhile. Some of the guys look up to me and I like that."

David, a thirty-six-year-old in St. Petersburg, Florida, says he too has run with a younger crowd from time to time, and he's always found it energizing. "Part of it is getting looked up to, yeah . . . but more it's like I can learn a little something from them, too. Like that life doesn't have to be so serious and humdrum, that I don't have to leave my youth behind me just because I'm staring at forty in a few years." David says he's heard the same kind of criticism and comments that older/younger couples hear. "I get that 'Why don't you act your age' comment all the time. Even my mother made a comment once, that I should hang out with a more mature crowd. But I've always believed that being gay is such a liberating thing, that we're free of so many of society's conventions, I don't know why 'age appropriate' friendships shouldn't be tossed out the window with the rest of the garbage."

Randy from Memphis says he's also come under fire from his contemporaries occasionally. "They think I'm some kind of chicken hawk or tell me I've got some kind of Peter Pan complex and can't deal with getting older. I just shrug that crap off, and say, 'Whatever.' I know a lot of what they say comes from jealousy or because their thinking is so limited that they can't fathom how a forty-year-old and twenty-year-old can ever be real friends. Trust me, you can."

THE EYES OF A BOY

Like so many people do these days, and like so many of the couples interviewed for this book, they met first on the computer: one was a forty-year-old journalist, recently cut loose from a failing Internet start-up; the other an eighteen-year-old high school graduate working as a Web designer before starting college. From the start it was pretty clear this wasn't going to be any mere "hookup," or liaison that would exist solely in cyberspace. Though they were separated by such a huge gulf in years and a life's worth of experience—not to mention 600 miles across four states—it took only a week of instant messages, e-mails, exchanged photos, phone calls, and conversations via Webcam for each to become convinced that the other might be "the one."

You might have guessed it by now, that that's not some tale pulled from a survey or interview. That's from *my* life, the story of how I met my former boyfriend, Andy. So convinced were we that we'd found someone special in each other—and so impetuous with my emotions was I that I never thought deeply about what I might be getting into— that less than a week after we met online I packed up my SLN (Shitty Little Neon) and drove all night, down to Hilton Head, South Carolina. That's where Andy lived, and that's where he'd reserved a room for us in a near-deserted hotel, hard by the sandy shores of Port Royal Sound.

The moments of our first meeting in the "real" world are fresh as yesterday in my mind, a collection of vivid images I can see now as plainly as if I'm watching a videotape or DVD: his green Jeep Chero- kee peels into the parking lot in some anonymous strip mall I'd parked at, so that he might guide me through the maze of parkways that led to the hotel. . . . he climbs out of the Jeep and walks toward me boldly . . . how goddamned beautiful he is, short brown hair tousled by the breeze, eyes flashing behind his sunglasses, face all smiles in the hazy December sun. . . . he ignores my outstretched hand, laughs a hearty "come here," and pulls me into a bear hug. . . . I can still feel the wool of his sweater against my face. . . . I can still smell his young-man smell.

We would spend two days together, walking on the beach, driving around aimlessly, hanging out in the hotel hot tub, eating out on the town . . . and making mad, passionate love. A more idyllic start to a relationship few couples have been fortunate to have, and there would be many more of those to come, until a little more than a year later— on a much colder December day—when we would part company as lovers.

A sadder ending I have not yet lived through, nor do I ever wish to.

Andy wasn't my first serious relationship with someone far youn- ger; I am, in fact, more than ten years older than either of my two pre- vious "exes." I also have a significant number of long-standing friendships with guys in the same age group as he, along with friends now in their late twenties and early thirties whom I'd met first when *they* were adolescents. Like Randy and David, I've often found good friends among the younger set; I've also encountered the same kind of criticism and disapproval they have, heard the accusations that I'm living in some kind of never-never land where I'm in a perpetual state of denial about my advancing years. And I've been called a chicken hawk more times than I can count. As Randy puts it, "Whatever." (Actually my response to such criticism usually isn't quite that polite; usually I tell the individual advancing the critique, "Go pound sand up your ass.")

Certainly I don't *avoid* people my own age; far from it. I've always had contemporaries I've called friends, as well as people in my inner circle who are far older than I. I value their company and their counsel. But like anyone else, there are certain qualities I find myself drawn to, and, quite naturally, I find them in nearly all who become my friends and lovers: a youthful enthusiasm, an open and wide-eyed view of life, a total lack of jadedness (the "been there, done that" attitude that seems to plague the gay community) along with the energy, daring, and willingness to try new things I like to believe I still have. And sad to say, those are things I find more often among guys *not* of my generation. (Ironically enough, the few times I *have* found someone my age who had those attributes, they weren't remotely interested in *me;* they were hanging with the younger guys, too.)

Andy was the pure embodiment of all those qualities, with an IQ of 160, the face of an angel, and the body of a young god besides. It surprised few of my older friends and acquaintances in DC that I should be having sex with him—many of them have no problem seeing young gay guys as appropriate playthings for someone older, a worldview I find rather sour and demeaning—but many were shocked to find out he was my *boyfriend,* and not my boy toy. "You're *dating* an eighteen-year old?" they'd ask incredulously. "Are you out of your mind?"

Yes, I was. Quite mad—madly in love. Trust me when I say I did try to fight the feeling, even telling Andy in those first few crazy weeks that I wasn't at all comfortable with the concept, that he might do better to find someone closer to his age, that perhaps he, a young gay guy just coming out, might enjoy "playing the field" a bit before settling down. And even if we forgot all that, we had geography to deal with; at best he could make it up to DC a few times a month, and several months down the line we'd have to face the fact that he was going to school in California. That's when he looked me squarely in the eye, put his hands on my shoulders, and asked me to give him a little credit for knowing what he wanted; what he wanted was me and fuck the future. I melted.

I won't bore you—not too much, anyway—with the minutiae of our day-to-day triumphs and challenges; you've already heard a lot of the same stuff reflected in other couples' stories. We had moments when we were so totally in sync that we simply felt like older and younger versions of the same person, a closeness I cannot say I've shared with anyone else. We had a year of incredible romantic highs: walks on other beaches from Rehoboth in Delaware to Provincetown on Cape Cod, long bike rides, workouts, movies, and so many warm nights and hot morning showers that it all feels like one long joyful interlude. After viewing the Web site we used to share, and the hundreds of pictures of us we posted there, hundreds of folks used to write me, amazed and encouraged by the obvious love Andy and I felt for each other.

But we also had the flip side, moments when that gulf of years and experience between us seemed so vast that we just couldn't get across it, no matter how much we wanted to. I recall one melancholy night when I caught him staring at me while I worked at this computer, a look of supreme sadness on his face. Sudden mood changes and unformed angst weren't exactly strangers to either one of our personalities, so I simply asked him what was wrong, what was he thinking about; it took awhile to get him to explain, but finally he admitted that he'd found himself wishing he could have somehow met me "out of time," in a parallel world where we were both the same age.

I told him I'd often thought the same thing myself.

Then there was the night, at the end of an argument over something long forgotten, when he confessed that any fight with me was something so painful and stress inducing that he wasn't sure how to deal with it all. I remember telling him that a squabble or two among couples was perfectly normal, sometimes even beneficial. Only grudgingly did he seem to accept that, moving me to express how much I hated to be the one who got to shatter all of his illusions about love; he looked back at me, telling me matter-of-factly that "if they're illusions, they need to be shattered." Easy enough for you to say, I told him, since you're not the one who always has the hammer in his hand.

All things considered, I don't know if it ever would have worked out with Andy over the long term, despite his exceptional intellect, personality, and maturity (I used to tell him—sometimes only half jokingly—that he was the adult in our relationship). Though many of the couples I've interviewed had great age differences between the partners therein, very few started out as middle-aged men involved with postadolescents just coming into their own. Andy was, after all, just a six-month-old babe in arms when I was a new recruit slogging my way through the mud at Marine Corps boot camp on Parris Island—which happens to be located, by a curious coincidence, just across the sound from Hilton Head; you can actually see the taller towers of the base from the beach where we took our first long walk together. (Maybe the Powers That Be were trying to send me a not-so-subtle message.) Although Andy used to implore me to share all my randy stories of youthful sexual conquest—honestly, it was like he never tired of them, he always wanted to hear *more*—maybe on some level he began to agree with my initial contention that, as I had lived a full life before I met him, perhaps he deserved the same thing.

I used to wonder if it was distance, not differences, that defeated us; I don't know of many couples, of any age, who could easily deal with the 3,000-mile separation we had to endure once he packed off to college. Whatever disagreements or rough patches we encountered when we spent our precious time together, we could usually resolve them with a warm touch or smile; that's hard to re-create over the coldness of unreliable telephone connections, or with e-mails and instant messages that can easily be misinterpreted. We did spend one last weekend here in DC, a three-day period when we celebrated our one-year anniversary, and nary a cross word occurred between us. I suppose that's why I was so shocked when he called me the Friday after Christmas, and in halting fashion, started to explain that his feelings had changed. (Ironic that he would cite the very same reasons I once gave him for my hesitation about getting so deeply involved in the first place. As the saying goes, sometimes it really sucks to be right.) I guess it's vaguely amusing that Andy would, to the very end, give truth to my assertion that he always made me feel like a kid again. When it was finally clear that we were over, trust me, I felt every bit the teenager; I have managed to survive—and thrive—after more romantic disses and breakups in my life than I can recall, but when Andy left me I was simply devastated. It was like feeling heart-break for the very first time. All those trite little pop songs on the radio, the ones about broken hearts and dreams that die, they felt all too real again, and moved me to tears I thought I no longer possessed.

Like a lot of ex-lovers, we've tried to remain friends, but it's been a spotty effort at best. There's just too much raw emotion to get through before we can settle into a less-intense relationship. I have no doubt that one day we'll be the best of friends, maybe even by the time you read this. In the meantime, against all the best advice I get, I tend to chew over what went wrong, what I might have done differently, like an accident investigator looking for clues in the wreckage. Thinking back, I have no idea on earth why I didn't get in my car and drive down to Hilton Head immediately to make my case in person. Pride I suppose it was, the idea that it was somehow unseemly that this middle-aged man should be forced to throw himself on the mercies of a child.

It's often occurred to me how it may not have been the fact that Andy was young or inexperienced, or all those miles between us, that broke us apart at all. It may well be that I'm just not very good at all this relationship business, at least not yet. Like a lot of men—not just *gay* men—I think a part of me has always yearned to be single, a free agent, able to be fruitful, so to speak, with a multitude of choices. I may be one of those guys whose needs can best be met by "friends with benefits," one who prefers the sweet intimacy presented by a series of familiar faces on his pillow, and a half-dozen or so well-known bodies to snuggle with, without the more constraining ties a more traditional relationship presents. Inside those, my moods tend to the mercurial, my anger sudden and fierce, my tolerance nonexistent. Even with the most perfect of partners I can be far too demanding, and not giving enough. And though with Andy my body and heart remained faithful, I cannot say that my eyes wouldn't sometimes wander elsewhere, if only for a millisecond.

The reflection isn't on him. It's on me. All the couples I've interviewed amaze me with their anecdotes of caring, sharing, and the joy of discovering themselves within the context of a true partnership; whatever their ages, they've figured out secrets to long-lasting relationships that I've never been able to uncover.

But there's still time, I suppose. Heck, I'm only forty-two.

Chapter 6

After the Fire

Youth, large, lusty, loving—Youth, full of grace, force, fascination. Do you know that Old Age may come after you with equal grace, force, fascination?

Walt Whitman

A few years ago I was working out at my gym, finishing up on the treadmill, psyching myself up to hit some weights, and that's when I saw him come in: a petite, almost elfin older gentleman, with a shock of shining silver hair atop a ruddy face, fitted with workout togs that looked a little out of place, and probably more appropriate on someone much younger. He glanced at me as he passed the row of running machines, a small secret smile on his face. I smiled too, but more to myself than in return; I just thought it was a little amusing to get cruised by a guy who was, in all likelihood, older than my late father.

Two thirtyish muscle boys working out side by side on the elliptical trainers laid out in front of me caught the whole scene—one actually elbowed the other—and they shared a laugh. I doubt the older gent saw it, as he was well inside the locker room at that point, but it still pissed me off. (I've always hated "attitude," the "popular kid in high school vibe" that so many gay men carry with them into gyms and bars. At least in my younger days such attitude was earned, by virtue of money or good looks or fashion sense. These days it's simply assumed.) And the muscle boys' laughter at the old guy's expense didn't just make me angry . . . it also made me feel a little guilty at my own reaction to what was, in reality, nothing but a nice compliment.

A half hour later the ebb and flow of my workout routine brought me within speaking distance of the older man; he was replacing some dumbbells on the rack after doing some arm curls and I noticed he'd been working out with some fairly respectable weight. I took a fresher, more appraising look at him; though the signs of age were more than evident—we all surrender to gravity in the end—I have to say he had remarkable muscle tone and a lack of excess body fat. Clearly this was someone who'd taken care of himself over the years, and that's something anyone can admire.

We struck up a conversation. His name was Roger, he said. He was a retired federal worker and still an active writer about aviation history. I asked him if he'd been a pilot and he told me yes, though he hadn't actually flown in several years, since his sight wasn't what it used to be. He spotted my Marine Corps tattoo, asked me when and where I'd served, and if I'd ever been overseas; I told him I'd been stationed at Subic Bay in the Philippines. He smiled a little and asked me what it was like "on the ground there." I thought that was an odd way to pose the question, but I told him I'd loved it; with all those great beaches, palm trees, lush jungles, tropical weather, incredibly friendly people, what's not to like?

I asked him if he'd ever been in that part of the world and that small smile came again. I spent some time there, he said, explaining he'd flown over those beaches and jungles I'd just described a "hundred times or so." When was that, I asked him, and why didn't he ever land and check the place out? He was too occupied at the time, he said. "With what?" I asked. His answer was short, but carried a wallop. "Bombing the Japanese," was his reply.

Turns out Roger—who had just celebrated his eighty-fourth birthday; my father was eighty-three when he passed away—was a combat bomber pilot who'd seen considerable action during World War II, and that knowledge made it impossible for me not to see him in a whole new light. I'm one of those nerds who loves the History Channel, probably because my father was also stationed in the Pacific during the war; never one to pass up the chance to tell a war story, he used to keep me enthralled for hours as we'd go through the voluminous stacks of photos he'd taken while serving aboard various battleships, cruisers, and aircraft carriers. Roger, it seemed likely, had the same warehouse of tales, except his were told from a different vantage point: the cockpit of a B-29.

We stepped over to the water fountain as we spoke and I tried to picture him as he might have been more than half a century ago;

perched in his pilot's seat, silver hair replaced by thick brown/black strands under his cap, headphones on his ears, the leather bomber jacket thrown over khakis. Walking across the airstrip on some distant tropical island, casting an eye on his waiting plane, then looking up at the deep blue sky above, I'll bet his stride was confident, maybe a little arrogant, instead of his current slow and careful gait as we made our way across the gym floor. I looked over and saw the two muscle boys watching us from the free weight area, stupid smiles still plastered on their faces, and I just wanted to smack them silly. What possible right did they have to find my conversation with this man a subject for their amusement, I wondered. Were they laughing because they thought I might be on the prowl for a sugar daddy? Did Roger's interest in me seem odd or inappropriate? Or did they just think that someone his age didn't belong on the same gym floor as they . . . someone who, by the way, had seen and done more by the time he'd hit his midtwenties than they would in their entire lifetimes?

I found myself thinking about that day at the gym with Roger as I was getting ready to write this book because it's a perfect example of the way so many younger and middle-aged folks look at our senior citizens, if ever we look at them at all. It matters not whether they're military veterans like Roger, veterans of the ongoing struggle for gay civil rights, or simply veterans of a long life on the planet Earth; we often treat them all with equal measures of apathy or derision. Small and shuffling, gray-haired shadows of their former selves, they move around at the edges of our vision, most of them irrelevant to our hustling, bustling lives, other slow-moving obstacles we have to get past so we can get where we're going.

But they were once as we are now, and they are what we will one day be, if we're fortunate enough to live that long. That's probably what scares us so much about them, why so many young people eschew the company of the aging and the elderly if they're not directly related to them. Senior citizens are the signpost up ahead: next stop, the Twilight Zone, except this isn't that TV land of the eerie or fantastic. This is reality, baby. This is twilight, as in the end of a long golden day of sunshine, warmth fading, a chill in the air, and night coming on fast.

"HOPE I DIE BEFORE I GET OLD"

Earlier in this book I talked about those segments of gay society that idolize young people and their youthful attributes above all else. Though I don't believe that phenomenon is nearly as widespread or universal as generally assumed, it's still undeniably out there. From what I hear the larger problem isn't that we deify youth, it's the fact that we have learned to demonize age, to fear and loathe it. Indeed, there weren't many among the younger men I interviewed or surveyed who had anything very good to say about the prospects of aging, especially aging as it applies to being a gay senior citizen. "I know the alternative to getting older is not being around for your next birthday," says Toby, a thirty-five-year-old telecommunications worker in Omaha, Nebraska. "Obviously, living to a ripe old age is probably better than dying young, but I have to admit the idea of actually *being* old is rather frightening to me." Note Toby's interesting qualification there, that living to be old is "*probably* better than dying young," as though he's really not all that certain about the choice. Steve, a twenty-two-year old maintenance man in Syracuse, New York, doesn't even bother to make the qualification. "Odds are I'll take myself out somehow before I ever get old and decrepit," he avows. "I can't see living like the old people I see. . . . Wasn't it the Rolling Stones that sang, 'Hope I die before I get old?' That's gonna be me." (Actually, Steve, that was The Who, but thanks for the memories.)

"My God, the idea of getting old is just so depressing," says David, a twenty-four-year-old student in Orlando, Florida. "There are older gay people down here, all over the place, and I just can't imagine what it will be like for me when I'm that age. I can't see myself or my friends that way, not when we're young and our lives are all about dancing and singing and having mad sex. One day we'll be them . . . all stooped over, walking slow, wrinkled and bald and gray. It's too weird to contemplate."

Paul Smith, the Arlington, Virginia, clinical social worker we heard from in Chapter 5, says attitudes like David's are common. "Gay men have, in the past, viewed aging as a loss: loss of sex appeal, loss of hair, loss of libido, loss of social appeal, loss of physicality. The list gets long. It has been challenging to try to reframe that deep sense of loss for aging men so that they can begin to see aging in a more positive light, for instance, to expand their thinking to embrace aging as something they have always done, done well, and is nothing new. To see it as just another stage in a life filled with many stages, which, like all the others, can offer something useful and fulfilling. To see it as another door opening to new opportunity as a previous door closes."

Many of the younger gay men I spoke with aren't quite there yet. "I used to think 'old' was thirty," says Ian, a twenty-nine-year-old consultant in Savannah, Georgia. "Now I've moved the goalposts up to forty on that one . . . and I imagine I'll have to move them again at some point. I guess there'll come a time when I can't move them anymore, but it's not something I like to think about."

In my polling I asked each of my five age groups if they feared "growing old"; more than half of my youngest group, and just under half of my second youngest group, replied in the affirmative, but from there the numbers sank rather precipitously. By the time the seniors logged in, less than a quarter of their number had any real fear about aging. It's probably a predictable trend, but no less instructive in its embrace of reality; once you're actually old, you find a lot of the demons you once feared just aren't as bad as you thought they'd be. Either that or you make your peace with them.

"When I was younger, the idea of ever being my father's age was totally repellent to me," says Adam, a seventy-year-old retiree in Palm Springs, California. "For me, watching him as I grew from a child to a young adult, old age meant being set in your ways, having a generally ill disposition, a closed mind, and a variety of ailments. Now that I'm about ten years older than he was when he died, I'm quite relieved to say none of that applies. I don't claim to be anyone's spring chicken and if I could trade this sore back and stiff knees for some punk kid's I'd be happy to. Other than that . . . well, the sky is just as blue, food is still delicious, and I have a wealth of friends and a tidy nest egg to live off of. Truthfully, I can say I am quite content."

Indeed, the young people reading this might be intrigued that of the seniors I polled, those folks sixty and above, a full 79 percent said they were "happy with their age." That's not too much of a drop-off from the 90 percent of thirteen- to twenty-three-year-olds who answered "yes" to the same question. "I'm never going to claim that being old is a picnic," says Dan, a sixty-four-year-old technical writer in

Boston. "Being old *and* gay also presents its own sets of problems, but it's what I have to deal with and I deal with it like everything else, one day at a time, one foot in front of the other."

Hal Kooden is a New York–based psychotherapist and the co-author of *Golden Men: The Power of Gay Midlife* (Avon Books, 2000), a book many have called a virtual "how to" manual on surviving and thriving through middle age and beyond. He tells me he was moved to write about older gay men after seeing so many of his counterparts succumb to HIV/AIDS in the 1980s and 1990s. "They were more afraid of getting older than they were of dying. I lost most of my political cohort, men who would now be public role models of successfully aging men." As Kooden sees it, among the biggest challenges for gay men at or approaching midlife is learning to see themselves through different eyes, to see themselves as "viable, attractive, exciting, sexual, vibrant, and risk taking." And they often have to do all that, he says, without cultural or community support. But that's not to say many gay men aren't up to the challenge. "In fact, because of the coming-out process, we have developed skills that actually help us to grow old successfully," he says.

Back in Chapter 1, I mentioned another book, Raymond Berger's groundbreaking 1982 work *Gay and Gray: The Older Homosexual Man.* Berger's research goes a long way toward deflating the popular stereotypes about older gay men that have long existed and might well contribute to the fear of aging so prevalent in many younger gay men. In the prologue to the 1996 second edition of *Gay and Gray,* Berger cites numerous works already published long before the original *Gay and Gray* appeared, research well known in psychiatric circles but largely unknown to the general public, that was already swimming against the tide of conventional wisdom: older gay men, it turns out, often "mitigate" the negative effects of aging with a network of faithful friends. And while many older gay men were less sexually active and less involved in the gay community, they didn't show any higher levels of depression, loneliness, or general unhappiness. "Contrary to popular stereotypes, these men had come into their own as they aged," the author contends (p. 1).

By any measure, *Gay and Gray* helped to debunk some of the long-held beliefs regarding gay seniors, and presented them as a hugely diverse, vital population; it also promoted the novel idea that being gay may actually be an advantage in helping men get a handle on those advancing years. But Berger himself notes that the book's publication was met with some criticism, that in his zeal to dispel the lonely old gay men stereotype, he may have painted "too rosy a picture" of gay aging. And sure enough, though many of the older men I surveyed and interviewed were just as "well adjusted" and happy as many of Berger's subjects, the challenges and problems that older gay men face *can* be harrowing.

OUTING AGE

According to the best estimates of the U.S. Department of Health and Human Services' Administration on Aging (AOA), there are somewhere between 1.75 and 3.5 million Americans age sixty and over who are gay, lesbian, bisexual, or transgendered. Only in the last several years have government officials—prodded along by gay advocacy groups—begun to take a serious look at the quality of life issues faced by gay seniors and how those issues might differ—for good and for ill—from their heterosexual counterparts.

The AOA fact sheet—available on the organization's Web site at <www.aoa.gov>—suggests older gay seniors may face the double whammy of dual discrimination, ageism *and* homophobia, and may therefore feel out of place seeking assistance from groups that cater to older people in general. The AOA suggests that many gay seniors came of age in a time before society had even begun to accept gays within its mainstream; a generation after Stonewall, many are still deeply closeted, or truly out to only a handful of close confidants.

I encountered many men like that in my interviews and surveys. "Maybe it's a Southern thing, or maybe I'm just kind of an 'old fogey' in that respect," says Bob, a sixty-one-year-old banker in Huntsville, Alabama. "I'm just not the kind of guy who feels like he has to lead the Pride parade. I'm not at all ashamed to be gay, and I've been out for years to the people I think need to know or should know. I'm certain there are whispers about me, but no one ever asks, so I don't feel inclined to tell." Edward, a sixty-year-old technical writer in Ohio, says he's still "far back in the closet" when it comes to his everyday life. "The only people who know about me are the people I chat with on my computer. For now that suits me fine. It would be far too complicated for me to come out at this point."

According to *Outing Age,* a first-of-its-kind, comprehensive report issued in 2000 by the National Gay and Lesbian Task Force's Aging Initiative, there's often good reason for that reticence, besides the considerations noted by Bob and Edward. Some older gay men considering retirement communities may find themselves victims of homophobic attitudes on the part of other residents, or the facilities themselves, if they make themselves known. Their health care providers, schooled as they might be in treating age-related conditions, may not possess the necessary sensitivity or expertise in treating senior gay men; they don't know which questions to ask or how to handle the answers they may get. And just like any teen or twenty-something, older gay men often face rejection from their families when they come out; the fear of that rejection by itself can keep many gay seniors hiding in the closet.

Even when senior gays *are* out, it's no guarantee they'll have smooth sailing. As *Outing Age* points out, should one member of a senior couple fall ill, the other may find himself excluded by his partner's family when it comes to making decisions regarding treatment. Without advance planning and documentation, unmarried partners usually find themselves locked out of inheritance, and they're currently ineligible for spousal or survivor benefits readily available to married heterosexual couples.

Kurt is a seventy-year-old retired accountant living in the Northeast. "Considering my former line of work, you'd have thought I'd be better prepared, but my late lover's illness emptied both of our accounts. I have a small pension and Social Security, but it's barely enough to get by on. Lord help me if I get ill." Bob, a seventy-two-year-old retired professor living in "the West," tells me proudly that he's "old and have lived longer and better than I ever suspected would be possible." But he has worries. "I have wondered about that day coming when I could no longer live by myself, and would be thrust into an environment where I might have to go back into the closet or receive care and treatment that discriminated against gays." John, a sixty-three-year-old retiree living with his partner of twenty years in Las Cruces, New Mexico, tells me his family "will fight like the devil" any attempt he might make to provide for his partner after his death. "I have a substantial nest egg, and I will leave it all to [my partner] Barney. It's all in the will . . . along with some extra cash he may need for lawyers to fight off their inevitable assault. They have never accepted the fact that I am gay or that I've been living with a gay man as a lover for all these years."

Bruno, a sixty-seven-year-old retiree in Cleveland, doesn't have any kind of nest egg at all; still, he says he's "probably more fortunate" than many other senior gay men since he lives in an "informal" group home with a handful of others like himself. "We all found ourselves in similar situations, no families to depend on, with only modest means to draw on for our living situations. Unlike most straight men we didn't have that natural support structure to lean on so we have to lean on each other. I imagine many other aging queers have to live such a lifestyle."

Outing Age addressed some of those specific "lifestyle" situations it found among gay seniors, and many, as Bruno suggests, don't find themselves in "fortunate" circumstances; the report cites a New York City study that showed more than two-thirds of older gay men lived alone, as opposed to a little more than a third of their heterosexual counterparts. (In Los Angeles that number of gay seniors living alone is closer to 75 percent.) The report suggests that living alone equates with poverty and says senior gay men may be more likely to face economic insecurity than elder straight men. Precious little is being done to change that status quo.

Urvashi Vaid, director of the NGLTF's Policy Institute, lays out the dilemma in the report's preface. "This country's aging policies assume heterosexuality and close relationships with children and extended families to provide basic needs as we age," she writes. "Yet what of those people without such family ties or those who are not parents? Should the ability to access good care in old age be dependent on one's parental status or one's relationship to one's family of origin?" (NGLTF, 2000, p. v). The problems aren't merely the product of a hostile or ignorant straight society; Vaid also takes the gay community to task for fostering "devastating race, class, and age bias." She acknowledges the fact that such biases are broad-based within the larger society we live in; nevertheless, she holds the gay community's feet to the fire for what she calls a "persistent youth bias" within the gay subculture.

"Age is a dirty word to many people in America," she writes.

> People lie about it. Others avoid or ignore those who are old.
> Youth is a virtue, but old age is just plain sad, so we are told. Pol-
> iticians pander to the senior vote each election cycle, but fail to
> authorize urgently needed funds for social service programs. . . .
> And with the notable exceptions of some extraordinary individ-
> uals and organizations, the [gay] movement has followed this
> overall cultural pattern. (NGLTE, 2000, p. iv)

AWAKENINGS

Rick says he knew he was "different" at an early age, eight, maybe
nine years old. He didn't know exactly what the difference was, exactly . . . well, that's not quite true. He was pretty sure his playmates
didn't like to dress up in their mothers' clothes when no one else was
around.

There were other things, as well. Like the time his mother caught
him going down on the fifteen-year-old kid next door when he was
thirteen. "I went into total repression," he recalls now, as a seventy-
one-year-old retiree living in Palm Springs, California. "Although I
was continually attracted to boys and men forever after, I attempted to
lead a straight life." On to college he went, where he met a woman;
later he would marry and have four children. Still, none of that kept
him from haunting the occasional truck stop or peep show. He was in
his late thirties when the "gay revolution," as he calls it, arrived in full
flower. "I began to call myself bisexual at that point. I finally came
out to myself as a gay man in 1990, and to my wife in 1991. I can't
believe it took so long."

Rick's story—and the scores more like it I found in my surveys and
interviews—came as something of a revelation for me. Call me naive,
but I suppose I just had no idea that so many gay men at midlife and
beyond were still so deeply closeted, or so deeply conflicted about
their sexual orientation. It calls to mind the "gay outreach" gatherings
I used to volunteer at in the late 1970s; these were parties held at various bars or private homes in the DC area, usually attended by fifty or
so middle-aged or senior gay men. I use the term "parties" advisedly,

since the outreach gatherings rarely resembled lighthearted or joyous celebrations; more often they were like wakes or funerals, except all the corpses were sitting alone at tables or on sofas, or standing in the shadows looking at their watches, talking to no one, and leaving alone. Neither I nor my fellow teen volunteers, all members of the gay youth group sponsored by the same organization, could ever quite figure out why all these older men were so morose. We always had a blast at *our* group meetings; it was absolutely liberating to hang out with other gay kids, go for pizza, just shoot the shit, and laugh. (Those meetings were memorable for so many reasons, such as the time I walked into the place and saw two guys kissing in public for the first time. I can still recall those two adorable sixteen-year-olds, so firmly linked by a lip lock that our gay youth counselor was forced to separate them. Good times!)

Nothing like that ever happened at gay outreach, at least not on the nights all us teens were mingling with the crowd, trying to get them to lighten up. And from my polls and surveys, I find there are still a surprising number of gay seniors—surprising to me, anyway—who would have fit right in with that crowd in the summer of 1979. How many men are we talking about? Here's what my polls say: I asked folks in my five age groups how "out" they were, whether their sexual orientation was just a secret between them and a few friends, if their families were clued in, or if they were "totally out," meaning *everyone* knew they were singing show tunes in the shower: friends, family, people at work or school, the cable repair guy, the kid who mowed the lawn, etc. Although a little more than half of the twenty-four- to twenty-nine-year-olds, and a little under half of the thirty- to thirty-nine-year-olds, said they'd qualify for "totally out" status, less than a third of the over-sixty set were flying their freak flag proudly. Most were only out to a few select friends and family members.

We've already touched on some of the reasons many senior gays stay partially or completely closeted; they share many of the same concerns as any gay teen or twenty-something. We've heard what the coming-out experience is like for young people today, how they break the news to parents and friends, what it's like to deal with schools and schoolyard bullies. But what's it like to come out when it's no longer your boomer-era parents or bullies you have to worry about? How do you tell your elderly mom or dad, or your middle-aged or senior siblings? What about your wife of half a century, your kids, or your grandchildren? And how do you handle their reactions?

Gerard is a sixty-seven-year-old retiree in southern California who tells me he finally made the plunge and came out about the time he hit sixty. "I suppose you can say I'm the poster child of denial, since I always knew I liked the boys instead of the girls. It wasn't something I just suspected, since I 'fooled around' with a lot of my playmates growing up. Some of us still fooled around in high school after we got girlfriends and on into college. I think most of us told ourselves it was mostly just an embarrassing part of being a kid, akin to picking your nose. It was something you didn't talk about and you expected you'd grow out of it. Of course I was very wrong about that and I expect you can imagine the hellish life I had trying to pretend I was something I wasn't."

Gerard says he watched the gay rights movement grow "from afar," and that it felt a little like a party he wished he could join but hadn't been invited to. "By the time you started seeing the parades and this explosion of homosexuality in the public consciousness, I was already a married man with small children. It wasn't like I didn't love my wife, either. I loved her very much, and our kids. After she passed away, I even considered getting remarried a few years down the line, since a straight life was all I knew. I caught myself in time before making that big mistake." Gerard says he started talking to other gay men online, and eventually that led to social contacts. "I've never been to a dance club (I wouldn't know the first thing about how to behave!) but there are bars here that cater to the older crowd. I've made some good friends. Who knows? One day I may even start dating."

I ask him if his children know. "That's the funny thing. After I decided to come out I called them together, ready to drop this bomb on them. My daughter never even blinked. She said, 'good for you, Daddy, it's about time.' It seemed like they always knew, which makes me wonder what my wife thought."

Ike, a seventy-two-year-old retired ironworker in Pittsburgh, says he doesn't have to wonder what his wife thought after he broke the news to her when he was sixty-four. "Basically she wanted to kick me out of the house. I can't really explain why it took me so long, since not only did I always know I was gay, I had a number of sexual experiences with other men after I turned forty or so. I was always very discreet and she never knew anything about them, but just finding out I was gay was too much for her. She called me a liar, a cheater, a scoundrel, you name it. We still live together, but it's a pretty unhappy home. It's no longer a marriage—it's more like having an ill-tempered roommate. Thank God we never had kids."

Don, a sixty-year-old professor in Ann Arbor, Michigan, only came out to his wife after he underwent court-ordered therapy, the aftermath of his arrest for indecent exposure in a public rest room sting. "She doesn't know about the arrest, thank God, but she accepts my orientation. Since then I've come out to my best friend and he totally accepted me. I'm also out to selected colleagues at work. It makes me feel free and full of life." For the past couple of years Don says he's been seeing a younger man, Dave, whom he considers his "lover," but as yet he hasn't gotten a divorce. "After forty years of marriage this is a pretty difficult issue. Other than my sexual orientation, our marriage has been good. Sometimes when I'm in a restaurant and I see an older couple—mid-seventies and eighties, our concept of 'older' evolves—I worry that will be us. I wonder if I can ever have total fulfillment and I wonder how long Dave will be patient with me."

Ron, a sixty-three-year-old retiree in Fort Lauderdale, says he's been "totally out" for a "few years" now, but that only happened after he left the Midwestern city where he lived for most of his life and took up "this new genteel existence" of a happy retiree in Florida. "I spent most of my adult life in hiding and focused my energies on making enough money to retire. Now that I've done that and moved to this marvelous community where I find so many gay men my age, I'm much more comfortable being me with no apologies." That includes his children from a marriage that broke up years before his coming out.

"They wanted to know if I divorced their mother because I was gay and I can truthfully say no," he tells me. "I think we thought we loved each other, but that flame died fairly quickly. We were one of those couples who stayed together until our kids were on their own, then we split. It was several years later before I came out. I think my son and daughters handled the 'gay news' better than they dealt with the divorce. They're much more mature now and it's nice they want their old man to be happy. I was very much afraid they wouldn't want to associate with me anymore."

Psychologist Doug Favero says that sort of trepidation is just as common among older men considering coming out as it is among the younger, queer and questioning crowd. "We often fear ruining the image which our family has of us, usually an idealized image which helps our family see us as normal, successful, and protected," he suggests. And that can happen, "even if we have come to know that gay life is relatively safe and good for us. Coming out means breaking through that 'projection' which the family has placed on us." Other mental health professionals say the sheer emotional intensity of familial relationships also comes to bear. David Bissette is a psychologist in Alexandria, Virginia, who tells me about half of his patient base is made up of gay men, many of whom are struggling with identity issues. "The reasons for not coming out may vary drastically from situation to situation," he says, "but it is the intensity of feelings between family members that can make it hard to share something controversial about yourself."

It can be extremely challenging when you're sharing that information with someone whose entire conception of you is based on a lifetime of evasion, disinformation, or outright lies, however well-intentioned. So challenging, in fact, that some men choose not to. Richard, a seventy-two-year-old retired federal executive in California, first admitted to himself that he enjoyed sex with other men when he was thirty-two, after his first marriage failed. But that didn't stop him from marrying a second time, to a woman he still calls his wife. "I am not out. Rather, I am out to only two gay male friends who know my true identity and the fact I enjoy gay sex. To everyone else, including my wife, I am definitely in the closet. I hate the deceit of cheating on her, because I do love her and want to keep her, but I fear she'll leave me if I tell her the truth about acting on my gay side. She's not homophobic, but I know she wouldn't understand my betrayal of our wedding vows. If I were to lose her I'm sure I'd want to look for a gay partner, preferably someone younger, but that would raise a lot of eyebrows, and involve coming out to my children and grandchildren, so it's probably not going to happen."

"I thought I was actually doing the right thing by concealing who I really was inside," says Jeffrey, a sixty-five-year-old retired physician in Oklahoma. "I hadn't really dealt with being a homosexual growing up and I married my 'college sweetheart.' I did very much care for her, but I was never in love with her quite in 'that way.' I had always had fantasies about men. I even saw a shrink for several years to try and 'change.' After so many years of therapy I finally faced the fact that I was in fact queer, but I didn't tell my wife or children for years after that. My children were very supportive, but my wife was extremely angry. *Not* because I was gay (she told me she'd often wondered if I was!) but because I had kept so much of myself hidden. We split up soon afterward, and now I live alone, trying to get my bearings on a whole new life. It hasn't been easy."

Coming out to family wasn't exactly easy for Ernie either, a sixty-three-year-old attorney currently living in New Hampshire, and preparing for retirement to "someplace warm, preferably with palm trees." In his case, divorce wasn't an issue, since he says "the bloom fell off that rose a long time ago anyway," and he hasn't seen his ex-wife in years. But he's got children he's always stayed close to and several grandchildren that he loves to dote on. "They all moved south a long time ago, and I'm finally ready to join them full-time, instead of every other holiday season." I ask Ernie how and why he chose to come out. "I never really let the gay part of me take hold. I married early, had the kids, then buried myself in my career. It was only after my divorce that it finally dawned on me I'd be free to explore my sexuality, which I did in small, incremental steps." Ernie says he was surprised to discover how many like-minded men of similar age and experience he's found since; he's had a number of short- and long-term relationships over the past decade and a half. "But I hadn't told my kids, and it was beginning to get to me. My daughter, our first, was always very close to me, and I grew very tired of being evasive. If I had a new beau when she came to visit she could always tell (apparently I've grown very transparent) but I couldn't tell her why my moods were so elevated. So a few Christmases ago, when she and her husband and their children came for the holidays, we went on a long walk in the woods, and I broke the news to her."

Her reaction? "Stunned silence for a mile or so, then she took my hand and just leaned into me. I guess I raised her right." Ernie says he asked her to clue in the rest of her small clan. "It might have been more wise to wait until after Christmas dinner. We were all sitting there around the table, enjoying our meal with Christmas carols on the stereo, a fire in the fireplace, very much like a scene from a greeting card. Then her youngest—she was about five at the time—piped up with 'Mommy, does Grampa have a boyfriend?' I must've gone several shades of red before the entire table simply erupted in laughter. It was truly priceless."

Within a few months Ernie says he'd told his two younger children, both sons, and though noting the experiences weren't quite as memorable as his granddaughter's holiday ad-lib, Ernie says they were "priceless" in their own ways. "I can't say I love them any more than I already did—that affection was already boundless—but there's a real closeness now that simply wasn't there before. Thinking about it, I wish I hadn't waited so long."

Ernie didn't wait nearly as long as Carlos, an eighty-four-year-old retired physician living in Austin, Texas. "I was stupid not to realize I was gay when I was a child. All the signs were there. I was a bit of a sissy, the last to be chosen at a ball game, hated recess except for the chance to take a pee. I was unable to catch or throw a ball. I preferred serious reading or listening to music. I did have one fantastic experience when I was ten with another boy the same age, but we were caught by my parents and that was that." Carlos says he got married, had a family, all the while keeping his secret. "I had a lot of gay patients in my medical practice. They seemed to enjoy telling me their experiences, and I thoroughly enjoyed listening, but I was in denial." After his wife passed from the scene he finally came out to himself, but had every intention of "leading two lives" until he slipped up with two of his daughters. "They accepted it and accepted me. So I told the other two children, one at a time. They also accepted the news with varying degrees of joy. I tell my friends selectively. I have intentionally not told my brother. I figure he'll have trouble with it. Someday I probably will tell him, though."

LEFT BEHIND

While older and younger gay men face many of the same challenges—from all my research, far more than they ever suspect—there is one challenge that regularly confronts senior gay men that's simply part and parcel of being human: surviving the death of a longtime partner. Certainly gay men of all ages have had to deal with the sudden tragic loss of a loved one; life can be magnificently cruel that way. Through the 1980s and early 1990s the AIDS epidemic made such premature bereavement a prominent feature on the gay landscape; gay men in their thirties and forties had to learn, long before it should ever have been a necessity, how to say good-bye and pick up the pieces of a shattered life and heart.

For senior gay partners, moving past their sixties and into their seventies and beyond, facing the end of days is simply, well, a fact of life. "When you're a young man you feel like you will live forever and that's how it should be," says Harry, a seventy-eight-year-old retired broker in Manhattan. "That sense of immortality makes one bold and adventurous. But you do begin to contemplate death—remember I said contemplate, not fixate on—when you grow old, never more so than when treasured loves and lovers begin to pass away." Harry says he lost his "life's love" almost ten years ago; his name was Max and they'd been together nearly twenty years. "He was nine years older than I. . . . We had a wonderful life, which was remarkable since we met about the time each had given up on ever finding someone." Harry says that over time he and Max grew so close they were "like different halves of the same person," which made letting go after Max's long illness that much harder. "I was quite the mess, and often considered suicide. I'd heard all my life how some elderly men die within a few months of their wife's death, but I never really internalized that concept until I was in the same boat. Unlike some men I know, each of us was well provided for should the other die suddenly, so that, thank God, was never an issue. But it was very, very hard, I will not lie to you. Just getting out of bed was hard sometimes. It seemed so futile to go on." Harry says his family—"both those related by blood and those related by choice"—helped get him through the dark times. "I am blessed that way, and there's no way to tell you how much it helped to simply have someone to keep me company in this big, suddenly empty apartment we shared."

Stephan, a sixty-three-year-old retired city worker in Baltimore, hasn't lost his partner of more than fifteen years, but it's something he admits to thinking about . . . and fearing. "He's had one heart attack already and the doctors say he might not survive another one. I was never afraid of growing old. Now that I am old, my biggest fear is being alone after being part of a couple for so long. He's the love of my life, every day I wake up with him is a blessing, but I have worried myself sleepless sometimes just thinking about how I'll live without him."

For Jerry, a sixty-year-old manager of a chain of food stores in central New York, it's not worries about getting left behind that keep him up at night; it's worrying about his partner of the past ten years. "Bobby is only forty, with a good forty-plus years in front of him. Right now I'm in excellent health . . . my doctor says I'm the youngest sixty-year-old he knows, but I've had a few sleepless nights, yeah, thinking about what will happen to Bobby later on in life."

Dozens of the men I surveyed voiced similar issues to those just discussed. Some are grieving over the loss of someone long loved and now greatly missed, while others are deeply concerned about their aging partner's health, or the welfare of those they might leave behind. Many tell me they're looking to their friends and family for support; others admit that since they've forged a more isolated existence with their partners and spent most of their time exclusively with each other, they cannot conceive of going on alone. Putting myself in their places, I can only imagine the heartaches they deal with or may soon have to face. It's not hard at all for me to envision the gaping hole you find inside you when the other side of the bed, once so warmly occupied, is suddenly empty and very, very cold. I've felt that pain, though the idea that I may one day meet up with Andy again, somewhere down the road, is a small consolation. But to think of him as gone forever? That's just too painful to contemplate, yet that's a pain thousands of gay men face each year.

The kind attention of good friends, reestablishing some neglected family links, and keeping myself as busy as possible helped me work through my own loss—it's still helping—and counselors I talk with tell me that strategy can work as well for longtime companions severed by death. "I always try to tell my clients to focus on the love and life they shared, and the good memories they still have, not so much what they lost," says Kris, a grief counselor in Washington, DC. "I advise them not to bury themselves in too many activities, because that can simply delay the pain, not eliminate it. You do have to give yourself time to grieve, to cry, to feel the pain, but not to dwell on it. It's going to hurt like hell and you have to get through it, but I remind them that they *will* get through it, they'll survive, even be happy again. And they better not feel guilty about it, because no loved one would ever want them to feel guilty about going on. You have to go on."

As for those who haven't lost their partners yet, but find themselves worrying about the future, Kris has a message. "It's vital to treasure what you have now. No one can know how long we have here. To spend your days in dread of what may happen tomorrow, or what may happen next week or next year, is a profound waste of time and energy. Enjoy your lives now—now is all we really have anyway."

Scott is a forty-five-year-old volunteer bereavement counselor at a gay men's health clinic in San Francisco. He's been helping gay men work through their grief since the mid-1990s, and he says he's noticed a change in who comes through the door, and who calls on the phone. "Before the [HIV and AIDS] meds got better I talked with lots of younger people, and lots of middle-aged folks," he says. "Not just people who'd lost their partners, but people who'd lost friends and were having trouble dealing with that loss. We saw some older people in those days, but not nearly as many as we see now. This is the generation of men who came out in their late twenties and early thirties right after Stonewall, and as this generation of men who've lived as couples for several years ages, we'll see and hear more from them."

Scott says his clinic has its own staff of counselors on hand, as well as referrals for outside professionals. "It's really amazing how strong a lot of older gay men are. They've already been through so much in their lives and I think they're a lot tougher inside than they get any credit for. Probably tougher than a lot of straight people are in the same circumstances, but for those who do need that extra helping hand, having places like this is an invaluable resource, especially if they don't happen to have friends or family to lean on or talk to."

"Strac," a sixty-year-old special projects officer in Dayton, Ohio, has been forced to find his own way since the death of his partner from kidney failure two years ago. "I would like to find another mature man to share my life and in the meantime I've cultivated sexual partners whom I see frequently." Strac says he opted for early retirement so he could care for his ailing partner, and has since reentered the workplace to build his finances so he can retire again. He's keeping a positive attitude, working out, and keeping any relationship options open, "but I have no fear of being alone, if that's what happens."

As for Jerry, who worries about Bobby facing a future alone, talking about that unknown future day isn't something he and his partner do very often. "Do straight couples ever talk about such things? I guess they don't have to as much because all the social mechanisms are in place for them to get benefits and such. It's funny, because we've actually been thinking about moving to Vermont [where gay unions are, at this writing, legally recognized and protected] but it was more of a romantic idea. Now I realize there could be real financial reasons, too."

Jerry says it's really not the money issues that trouble him when he thinks about his partner. "Don't get me wrong, I love Bobby like I've never loved anyone else, but I think, for whatever reasons, he's come to love me even more and he really depends on me. The idea of getting older, then sick, having to have him take care of me, then just dying on him . . . it fills me with a pain like no other. I guess all I can do—all any of us can really do—is learn to simply make the most of the time we have."

"WE ALWAYS HAD EACH OTHER"

Scores of senior gay men shared their stories and opinions with me as I researched this book, but the most charming tale I've encountered so far actually came to me a few years back, when I was writing for *HERO* magazine (Bergling, 1999b). It was the story of "Dusty" and Jim, who lived together as a committed couple for nearly half a century. Virtually from the moment they met until the night that Jim lost his battle with lung cancer ten years ago, they lived and loved with a quiet intensity that's hard to fathom in this more jaded, cynical age. Little wonder that they were among the star attractions at the 1993 March on Washington, where they took center stage at a mass, symbolic wedding of gay and lesbian couples.

Their life together speaks to the experience of so many gay men of their era—and so many of the themes I've talked about in this book— that it'd be a shame not to share the conversation I had with Dusty, then seventy-two, in his northern Virginia apartment; I'll present it here as it was published in the second issue of *HERO* in early 1999, with my questions and Dusty's answers printed verbatim.

Dusty met me at the door that September day with a wide smile and a firm handshake; there was a noticeable spring in his step as he guided me toward the dining room where we sat down and chatted over coffee and my tape recorder. I noticed he kept using "we," not "I," when he talked about his apartment; I looked around for a room-mate until I realized he was speaking of his late partner, as if he was about to enter from another room. Dusty smiled when I made mention of that. For Dusty, Jim will always be present, not past tense.

So how did you two meet?
I came down to Washington after the war, in October of 1946. I was 20 years old, going to work at the Veteran's Administration. They set me up in a rooming house. I was all alone in this room with two beds in it, already having trepidations about the move. Then Jim came home, and all of a sudden I was very happy to be there.

There was an instant attraction?
For me there was. Jim never really admitted it, but I always felt we sort of fell for each other at that moment.

It had to be difficult to express those kinds of emotions in 1946.
Of course it was. In those days all you had to do was pick up a phone and call the police. You could get arrested for that sort of thing.

So how did you finally get your feelings for him out in the open?
It was a few months later, on a very cold night in January 1947. We'd been out to dinner, and I asked Jim if we could push the beds together, just so we could double up on the covers. He said he'd been thinking about the same thing. We sat up awhile, drinking shots of bourbon. I swear I didn't have anything in mind, and I don't know what could have possessed me. He was lying on his back near the edge of my bed. I was just so much in love with him by then, and I thought "What the hell . . . the worst thing he can do is get up and punch me in the mouth." So I bent over and kissed him. I was going to pull away and his arms went around me. That's as far as it went that night, just kiss-ing. Two months later, we went further.

Weren't you worried about what might happen the next morning?
Actually I slept like a log. Jim woke up first, he bent over and kissed
me and I threw my arms around him. I remember asking him if we
really had to go to work that day.

What made him so special?
Oh, just everything. His smile. He was just the most mild mannered,
steady guy. He could be tough when he had to be, he wasn't a
milquetoast or anything. He liked to joke and tease. I wanted to be
with him all the time. I used to run home from work just so we could
spend more time together, have dinner. Jim was the pretty one, as far
as I'm concerned. I was the jealous one. Friends of ours would hit on
him, but they learned not to. I used to take them aside and threaten the
shit out of them.

So you guys made gay friends at the time?
Actually, not for quite awhile. We knew there were other gay people—we didn't say gay yet in those days—but you had to be careful.
There was this place, not exactly what you'd call a gay bar, but a restaurant and bar where it was generally known that men like us hung
out. We got all dressed up one night and walked down, paused outside
the entrance, then went in. All we saw was this mass of men and they
all turned to look at us. It scared the shit out of us, and we just turned
around and went back out. I guess we just didn't have the nerve
enough yet.

Did you ever go back?
We never did. A few days later there was a front page story in *The
Washington Post,* telling how the place got raided. When that happened the police would take you in and you'd get fined. The paper
would print your name and address, and where you worked. If you
worked for the government like I did, you could get fired. They
wouldn't even let you come back in, they'd just pack up your stuff
and send it to you. It was just a tragedy, really horrible. I remember
the DC Police used to send their most handsome cop out to Lafayette
Park across from The White House. He was arresting guys right and
left.

It's hard for most people nowadays to even imagine a time like that.
It could be a pretty sterile existence. There were a lot of guys in the 50's who committed suicide. These days when I see two young, pretty boys kissing outside in the broad daylight I just feel marvelous inside. They don't have to go through what lots of folks back then did.

Did your families ever find out about your relationship?
The greatest thing that ever happened to me was about two years after Jim and I got together. My family loved Jim, my parents used to introduce him as their third son. One day my father was down to visit, we went for a walk and he said "I'm going to talk and you're going to listen." When my Irish-Yankee father said that I was too terrified to speak. Anyway, my father said, "You and Jim seem to get along real well. Don't mess it up. Stay with him." I knew then that he knew. Then he said, "You know your mother and I love you." And it was my father who took my mother aside and told her about us. She used to pester me every damned time I was home, asking when I was going to get married. Then she stopped, and I figured my father had broken the news to her.

Now you know how fortunate you were.
I only heard the horror stories later, from friends who told their parents and were then told never to come home again. Yes, I knew how lucky we were. Jim's parents were dead; one time his brother invited us over for drinks, and tried to fix him up with this woman right in front of me. We just left.

These days lots of gay couples make their lives in gay neighborhoods with lots of gay friends. But you and Jim didn't have that.
We started making gay friends in 1969. That was sort of our magical year.

The same year as Stonewall.
Just a coincidence. We didn't even know what Stonewall was. It just felt like the time to get out and finally meet people. But for all the years before, and all the years after, we really just made our life to-

gether, from the time we met to the time Jim got sick. We always had each other.

I can't imagine how hard it is to go on after you lose somebody who was part of your life for so long.
It was very hard. My gay retirement group and my friends helped me get through it. I'm not over him. I wouldn't want to be over him. I don't look at other people, I'm not remotely interested in another relationship. Nobody could come up to his standards. I've always been religious—I'm not suicidal or anything—but I'm not afraid to die. You want to know the truth? I can't wait to see him again!

You told me your Oath of Commitment ceremony was the highlight of your life.
I'm so proud of that. I had it framed and hanging out at our place.

Any thoughts on the gay marriage debate?
I don't really believe in all that stuff. I think gays should be allowed to make their commitments legal down at city hall, and have all the same rights and benefits as straight people. Just don't call it marriage, that's where the problem is. We could get a lot more support from straight society that way.

I say 47 years together gives you the right to offer some advice on how to keep a commitment going for the long haul.
We never cheated on each other, not once. We could look, if we wanted, but never ever touch. If you've got something good, why risk losing it for a cheap thrill? Lovers *always* know when someone's stepped out on them with someone else. If you've got someone who loves you, worries about you when you're sick, takes care of you, why would you ever give that up? You might be holding in your hand your only chance ever for true happiness. And sometimes there's no going back. (Bergling, 1999b , pp. 74-75)

RAINBOW'S END

"You'll feel right at home, in your new home away from home," the brochure fairly screams at you off the screen. Actually, it *does* scream at you; there's a loud voice and music track accompanying the flawless 3-D picture on your high-definition kitchen com unit. There are also intoxicating visions of sunlit expanses, spacious comfy-looking condos and cottages, but your mind's drifting a little (it does that a little more often these days than it used to). What's that tune in the background, you keep wondering; sounds like Erasure, maybe Pet Shop Boys. *Wow, does that bring some memories back.* Hardly seems possible your dance hall days are almost forty years gone . . .

"And there's so much more," that cloying and annoying voice-over continues, obliterating Andy's or Neil's or whoever-the-hell-else-it-might-be's singing and snapping you back with a jolt to the year 2025. "All the comforts and conveniences you've come to expect—and deserve—can be found in gay abundance. And we do mean *gay.*" Now the picture has drawn back to include swimming pools, clubs, and restaurants; there's a montage of service personnel so ridiculously and completely exquisite that you're beginning to believe that all those tabloid tales of cloning camps for young studs may not be some writer's overworked imagination after all.

"Yes, Pride Village is waiting for you. To find out more, well, just say so." The announcer pauses, but you're not about to make a sound, not a peep; with all this damn newfangled technology, even an errant cough might register on your com unit, therefore summoning one of those damned virtual salesmen, ready to make a more personal pitch at you, before you've even had time to pour your morning coffee. (Life was *so* much easier before all media were interactive.) You press the mute button discreetly, still savoring the image of scantily clad cabana boys ready to service your needs, even if your "needs" aren't everything they once were.

It's not like retirement hasn't been on your mind lately. You're just wondering whether you feel like leaving your home here, in favor of these hot gay retirement spots in Arizona, Nevada, California, and Florida. You've grown to love this small condo, perched on the edge of your hometown's thriving, growing gay community, but you also have to admit the powerful pull of a town custom-created for people your age, with your interests in mind. There's just so much to do in those places; so many of your friends are moving down the coast or out west, away from the cold winters, and away from the cold shoulder of a popular gay culture perpetually youth-obsessed. They're lining up to join a community ready to welcome them with open arms. As long as they can pay the gate, of course. That goes without saying. For as you've come to learn, they don't call these the "golden years" for nothing. More than ever before, in the twenty-first century you need lots of gold to live well. (Bergling, 1998, p. 82)

I wrote those words back in 1997, for an article that would be published in the April 1998 issue of *Genre* magazine. I called it "The Rainbow and the Pot of Gold," and it dealt with a number of financial issues, among them, what's waiting for today's middle-aged and younger gay men when *we* start down that road to retirement. (The article was inspired by a minicrash on Wall Street when the Dow took a 300-point tumble, just before the late-1990s economic boom sent stocks into the stratosphere; looking back now at how the economy tanked post-September 11, 2001, it's almost amusing how all that seemed like a big deal at the time.)

I'll revisit some of the other themes of the article later on, but for now I want to focus on that futuristic setup that started the piece, the idea of a gay retirement village. I purposefully set my scene far in the future, since no such place existed at the time, and no one I knew or contacted was aware of any plans for one, though many found the concept intriguing. (Hell, if I'd only had the venture capital, *I* might have considered finding a developer.) In 1997 it seemed—like my kitchen com unit and virtual salesman—it might well be several decades before any such community would come to pass. Well, color me embarrassed. Turns out that three years *before* I wrote that piece, a fellow by the name of Bill Laing already had a blueprint in place for a sprawling development in Florida called The Palms of Manasota.

Located in a rural area about fifteen minutes from St. Petersburg, The Palms currently features twenty-one single-story detached condominiums, with about forty more single-story duplex and triplex villas under construction at this writing; plans are underway to build a pool, a community center, an assisted living facility, and fourteen independent living apartments. According to Lisa Childress, The Palms' vice president of marketing and development, the first phase of the development, which she calls "the nation's first gay and lesbian adult living community," is already sold out, and the new duplexes and triplexes are going fast.

Sadly, Bill Laing didn't live long enough to see his vision come to full fruition; he died of prostate cancer in May 2000. But he did live long enough to see seventeen homes completed, and the living trust he created helped move the project along. "This community is a dream come true," says Childress, talking about some of the challenges that gay seniors face when they try to be "out" in traditional retirement settings. "The fear of isolation, depression, abuse and discrimination is real and the dream is for those baby boomers who have been out most of their lives to have a home *and* a community in which they can age gracefully and as an out and proud gay and lesbian." She's troubled by the prospect of gay and lesbian life partners, many of whom have been living together openly for many decades, who find they need the care that an assisted living facility can provide, only to find they have to conceal that relationship, or find they're denied the visitation privileges of married spouses. "Photos and mementos go back in the drawers, and they go back in the closet. Here senior gays and lesbians will be free to age in an environment where their personal care needs are met. You will get the care you need. Those who do not have adult children to care for them in their old age, and after the loss of a partner, do not have to fear that their health care will be compromised."

Childress says there are other similar communities in the works in places such as New Mexico, San Francisco, and elsewhere in Florida, but The Palms is the only one that's moved so far so fast. "We don't consider any other community that is in development direct competition," she says. "We talk to and support each other." But she's not afraid to point out what she sees as a major advantage. "This is an affordable community. Many gay and lesbian communities being developed across the country are upscale communities, whereas The Palms of Manasota is designed to target middle-class America. Affordable housing is a concern in this country but not a concern in this community."

Childress sent me testimonials from several residents and they were all rave reviews. "Charlotte" talked about how "it's nice to live in a place where you can walk outside and hold hands and nobody asks you any questions." "Bruce" says he was so intrigued by local media reports about the place that he flew down to check it out; he was so impressed by Laing and his vision that he "immediately purchased an available home. Three months later I moved in and have enjoyed seeing the community grow ever since." And "Judy" says The Palms has surpassed all her expectations. "We came here to enjoy life, to make new friends, to enjoy the weather and water. We accomplished all of that and more. We never imagined we would have this playground to live in and a true gay community to live in as well."

"The idea of the gay retirement village, regardless of how it evolves, is definitely a wave of the future," suggests clinical social worker Paul Smith. "I am certain that as gay men become comfortable with being gay identified, out and visible in the larger community, there will be more and more enclaves emerging. With the combination of growing affluence and longevity, and a stronger sense of survival beyond the threat of HIV/AIDS, it is reasonable to envision enclaves of gay resort and retirement communities that go beyond the seasonal concentrations found on Fire Island or Provincetown." Author Hal Kooden concurs. "I like the idea of retirement communities. If in the city, I favor a coed one with part of the facility for homeless LGBT teens—an intergenerational community where extended families can be created."

In my polling and surveys I asked my respondents what they thought of such a retirement home setup; a solid majority of every age group said they'd enjoy living around other gay people once they hit retirement age, in either formal or informal settings. Some were absolutely bullish on the prospect of planned communities such as The Palms. "If the price was right I'd move in right now!" says Jim, a forty-eight-year-old salesman in west Florida. "I'd definitely consider it." Keith, a sixty-three-year-old marriage and family therapist in Iowa, is also intrigued. "My parents have lived in a denominationally affiliated retirement community for years and it's a wonderful place for them." Sam, a fifty-one-year-old business owner in Virginia, says he thinks "a gay retirement community would be great—think of all those older gay men around!" And though retirement is a long way away for Curtis, a thirty-four-year-old telephone lineman in San Diego, the idea seems to grab him. "Would I live in a gay-themed retirement home? Hell, yeah! I think it would be like a bathhouse for toothless old farts. Seems like it could be a lot of fun."

Other men suggest to me that—absent their assisted living facilities—such communities might not be all that necessary if you're simply looking for comfort and company, because so many cities across the country already have large gay neighborhoods. "If you want to live with a lot of older gay men, just get a condo near Dupont Circle," says Barry, a thirty-five-year-old lawyer in Washington, DC. "It's getting gayer and grayer all the time around here."

Fred, a hotel owner/manager in Fort Lauderdale, tells me he sees more and more older gay men, many of them couples, moving into town all the time. "It's really exploding down here, and it's a very, very gay-friendly place to live. It really caters to older gay men." Paul Smith also points to Fort Lauderdale, as well as Palm Springs and Rehoboth Beach, Delaware. "They have emerging gay communities with thriving social, economic, and political infrastructures that are supporting viable sustaining communities year round."

Rod, a fifty-two-year-old land surveyor/mapper in San Francisco, says such retirement issues and living arrangements come up a lot among his friends, who are also in their fifties; he's not looking for a gay-themed retirement area, but rather plans to get a condo in Palm Springs as soon as possible, "while the prices are more affordable. In another ten years when I'm retiring it could be way too expensive."

Interestingly, a significant number of men I surveyed and interviewed were actually rather hostile to the concept of such places as The Palms, and likewise critical of gay men who'll only consider gay neighborhoods, or older men who only seek the company of others their age. "Think younger, stay younger," avows Jim, a sixty-year-old educator in the Great Plains. "I never could understand why older people wanted to live around other older people. What a waste! All you do is get old. Stay around younger people and see the world from their perspective." Jack, a sixty-eight-year-old retired librarian in San Francisco, says he'd never consider it either. "I never like living in any homogenous community. Variety in one's experience is very stimulating. I think something such as a gay-themed retirement home or community would be somewhat stultifying." And Don, a fifty-nine-year-old retiree in Palm Springs, admits he'd consider such a place if necessary—he sees elder health care to be of supreme concern, especially if it's tailored to gay men—but beyond that he's skeptical. "Being in a home of 'Mary this' and 'Louise that' does not appeal to me."

"THE LIFE IN YOUR YEARS"

A few years back my late father overheard my complaints to a friend about my "old aching knees," a small gift left over from my Marine Corps days of running, running some more, then a little more running. At the time I was in my late thirties, and confided that I thought I was a little young yet to be dealing with what my pop liked to call "old pain." Pop just laughed and shared a nugget of fatherly wisdom. "Just remember, it's not like you wake up one day and you're seventy. You have years of deterioration to look forward to."

Sure enough, as one gay and gray gent told me recently over a beer at a bar in DC, "Life may be a bitch, but getting old is a real bastard." For older gay men who still make the occasional trip out to gay watering holes frequented by younger men, the physical and emotional experience can be taxing. "I was at a 'retro' night at Cobalt, a bar here in Washington, and I had a few unsettling moments," says Ed, a fifty-seven-year-old government worker. "They were playing 'I Will Survive' and 'Dancing Queen' and so many other songs I remember dancing to for hours back when I was younger. My friends pulled me on the floor and all around us were these kids who hadn't even been born yet when those songs came out. They were just throwing themselves around; all I could manage was this little foot shuffle and even that was tiring. I do miss the energy I used to have."

Ed says that wasn't the only melancholy experience of the evening. "I probably had one too many cocktails and the songs were bringing back memories of so many friends I had who aren't around anymore. I got a little misty thinking about them. Don't get me wrong, I've had a pretty good life, all in all, and I can still have fun on those rare nights I go out to bars and clubs, but it's a little sad sometimes contemplating how much of life has gone by."

I found a number of similar "misty" reflections akin to Ed's in my surveys, especially among men who came out in those giddy days of the early and mid-1970s; having come out myself in 1977, I've had several of my own on occasion. Jim, a fifty-one-year-old home inspector in northern Virginia, tells me a number of his friends died of AIDS and others he knows are living with the disease. "I don't think a lot of them will live to a ripe old age," he says sadly. But though healthy himself, he still admits he's not looking forward to life as a senior gay man. "I really try not to think about it. A friend of mine said it best: 'Golden years my ass . . . I can't hear very well, can't see too good, and I ache all over. What's so goddamned golden about that?'"

Lest you begin to believe that *all* older gay men aren't doing much more than sitting around crying in their Metamucil, bemoaning their aches and pains and pining over days gone by, think again; dozens I've met and interviewed are rather happy living in the now and still looking forward to the future.

I encountered several such men one Sunday afternoon in northern Virginia at a Memorial Day barbecue held by a group of Primetimers, an international group that caters to "mature" men and the younger men who admire them. There are dozens of local chapters scattered throughout the globe and members come from all walks of life. Some have been out for years and find they prefer such gatherings to a gay social scene they no longer find accepting; others are men who've only recently come out and lean on their fellow members to help them get a handle on their new gay life.

"The newer members, the ones who've just come out, can be so amusing," one older gent told me in confidence by the buffet table. "They like to talk about gay sex so boldly and openly. . . . I guess it's because it's a new thing for them and they do that to get used to the idea. It can sound strange." I have to second that. It was a little odd to hear such folks "talking dirty" and then giggling about it; they sounded like junior high school kids on a playground. It was also a little unsettling to see the way they looked at Andy, who'd come with me to the party to help me spread my surveys and poll sheets around; he was wearing shorts and a tank top that showed off his nice physique and a lot of the older men were eyeing him with a near-palpable desire, the way a hungry dog might become fixated on a pork chop fresh off the grill.

But those men were a minority. Most were of the friendly and dignified sort, clearly enjoying one another's company. Their conversations did touch on sex from time to time—these *are* gay men, after all—but just as often the talk would shift to family, politics, literature, film, or outings and events the group was involved in. One younger man—I guessed him to be in his thirties—was there in the company of his late-fiftyish partner, a man he'd met at a Primetimers gathering the year before. For personal and professional reasons neither wanted his real name or age used—I'll call the younger one Bob and the older one John—but they weren't shy at all about their enthusiasm for the group. "These meetings are like a big family reunion for us," said John, whose real family doesn't keep in contact since his coming out a few years ago. "I always hated bars and clubs and there wasn't any kind of social venue I found palatable. Then I found Primetimers, and I met Bob." For his part, Bob said he'd always found people in his age group "largely shallow," and it was only after he stumbled on the organization's Web site that he realized there was a place he could go to find "the man I've always been looking for."

Dozens of the older men I met and interviewed were also members of Primetimers chapters all across the country; you can find them anywhere from Atlanta to Boston, Austin, Texas to Chicago, San Diego to Seattle, and many, many points in between. Their very existence, and the existence of numerous other formal and informal gatherings of late middle-aged and senior gay men, give proof to the assertion that a social life doesn't always need bright lights and throbbing music in order to thrive. Dick is a sixty-one-year-old retired federal worker living in Palm Springs, California, where he estimates the average age to be "in the high fifties." He keeps himself busy; he's a Primetimers member, and a member of a gay men's nudist group called the Jackrabbits. Apparently no one told him you're supposed to slow down when you get "up there." Or maybe he just doesn't slow down enough to listen. "We generate lots of social activities among ourselves, barbecues and cocktail parties and the like. I'm a crisis line volunteer, and a volunteer with Caballeros, the Gay Men's Chorus of Palm Springs. There are dozens of entertainment, theatrical, and musical venues to participate in, and lots of older folks to attend them with. We go out to bars occasionally, but very little of our social life revolves around bars or nightclubs."

Robb, a sixty-three-year-old realtor in Kentucky, says he believes "too much" of gay life revolves around those bars and nightclubs, along with alcohol and drug use. "My primary options include the local gay chorus and a church that is very gay friendly. In both settings people from their late teens to their late sixties interact according to interest, activity, time, financial ability, and age is never a determining factor." Richard, a sixty-six-year-old retiree in Arizona, doesn't diss the bars and clubs, since he believes "they are important to those who want them, they meant something to me once, and they're still valuable to the community today," but his own social life has moved outside the nightclub district. "We're into our friends, dinner parties, Primetimers [again!], hiking, fishing, and so many other activities they're just too numerous to mention."

Darrell, a fifty-eight-year-old retired federal worker in Washington, DC, says a big part of his social life is a retirement club made up of older gay men and lesbians. "I know that bars and nightclubs are the usual manifestations of gay culture, but I go out very little. I've been in a monogamous relationship for thirty years, and there are lots of gay men in DC my age so I never feel left out. Just walking around the Dupont Circle area gives me a good sense of what's happening in gay life. I saved money and have a good government pension, so I have to say I love my retirement here."

"I'm on the cusp of being one of those 'senior gays' you're talking about," says Larry, a fifty-seven-year-old retiree in eastern Tennessee. "I live in my own home with no mortgage payments, in an area with a low cost of living. I'm not a hermit, but I do enjoy my solitude. I have friends in the area that I visit with and who in turn visit me. We share dinners, movies, lunches, recipes, seeds ads cuttings, and jump into the fray whenever one or the other of us needs help. I think it's people who don't know how to entertain themselves who lead the most unsatisfactory lives."

Visiting my seventy-five-year-old mother at her home in West Virginia—as I too rarely do these days—I was struck by how she keeps herself occupied, very much along the lines described by Larry. I suppose widows and some aging gay men have a lot in common; perhaps I should introduce them. They could trade those seed thingies. Plopped down on her couch while she made dinner for me—I wasn't hungry, but you know how it goes—I started flipping through her imposing stack of magazines; the woman gets more reading material each month than she could ever possibly read, a genetic trait she's apparently passed down to me. I was thumbing through the pile and found one that had a back page of famous or noteworthy quotes. With this book already in progress, its composition perpetually weighing on my mind, perhaps it's no surprise that one age-related quote would jump out at me, attributed to a certain Abraham Lincoln: "And in the end, it's not the years in your life that count. It's the life in your years." I have no idea if Lincoln ever really said that, but when I think back on all I've been told by the senior gay men I've encountered, the truth of the phrase is undeniable.

I wasn't done with the magazines quite yet (hey, Mom's meatloaf is a masterpiece and such things cannot be rushed). The December 2001 issue of *Blue Ridge Country* caught my eye; I'm a city/suburbs boy at heart, so all those vistas of two-lane highways winding through autumn-colored mountains, of log cabins in deep woods topped with smoky blue fog, beckon me hither. I started flipping the pages and had barely started to dig in when my eyes fell on the most charming essay by a writer named Elizabeth Hunter. It was called "So Many Seasons in a Season, So Many Lives in a Life," and though she said nothing about the aging process that hasn't been said before—and nothing specific about gay men—I defy you to find a word in the following paragraph that doesn't speak to everyone, be they straight or gay.

> I passed the midpoint of my 50's on my last birthday. If I gave the mass culture the time of day, which I try not to, I'd be depressed at being so over the hill. It amazes me how willingly we acquiesce to being graded according to our ability to remain forever young. It has us always aiming backwards, twisting around to fix what we're inevitably leaving behind. Naturally our backs hurt. No way we're going to retain or regain the gloss of youth. So why not marvel at the young skin of a seven or 17-year old, then turn our attention to where we are now in life? What's here and now for us isn't just decline and death, but days of discovery, of surprise, of opening doors that can be unlocked only with accumulations of experience and understanding—the keys we hold. (Hunter, 2001, p. 8)

Like I said earlier, you never know when or where life's little epiphanies are going to find you. Like when you're sitting on a couch in West Virginia, your mom's in the kitchen, and you're waiting for her meatloaf.

1999 2000 2001 2002 2003 2004 2005 2006 2007 20 10 2011

Chapter 7

Yesterday, Today, and Tomorrow

Whatever tomorrow brings I'll be there, with open arms, and open eyes.

Incubus
"Drive"

Brian was sixteen years old when he came out to his parents. He'd known he was gay since the age of fourteen, but just didn't want to think about it, instead occupying his time with schoolwork and family life. He wasn't afraid to be different, but he didn't want to be *that* different. He'd always been taught that being gay was simply, irrevocably, morally wrong. Finally, after "stressing" about it for about a month, he sat down and wrote his parents a "very, very long" note. He admitted that he "thought" he was "probably" gay, that he was confused, and that he wanted them to accept him and whatever decisions he was going to be making over the next several months and years.

Brian's story—at least this part of it—doesn't come from my surveys or interviews, but rather from the April 16, 1998, issue of *Metro Weekly,* a local Washington, DC, publication that was previewing that weekend's upcoming Youth Pride Day. Brian was one of several out gay youth involved in the festival, only the second in what has since proved to be an enduring and ever-larger affair. I saved the issue—not knowing at the time that I'd eventually meet him, and that I would count him among my friends today—because what happened to Brian next, and how he overcame it, was pretty engrossing stuff.

It was nighttime. I went into their room. Gave them the note. Sat downstairs in the living room and thought, "Oh my God, what did I do?" It was the longest 15 minutes of my life. I had my bags packed. I was pretty sure they were going to kick me out. (Schulman, 1998, p. 22)

Brian's parents didn't kick him out; not on that night, at any rate. His father met the news with tears, his mother was disturbed—Brian says he knew this was hard for them and tried hard not to hold their reactions against them—they told him they still loved him, but wanted him to change. He stayed at home another year, but things grew ever more uncomfortable. "I wanted to bring my boyfriends home, just like my sister was able to bring *her* boyfriends home. My parents didn't like that idea" (p. 23).

Brian and his parents came to a mutual decision that he should move out when he was seventeen, which led to a long odyssey of hopping from friend's house to friend's house and sometimes sleeping in his car. "I was never sure where I was going to stay on any particular night," Brian told *Metro Weekly.* "I didn't have a job. I had no money. I had very few clothes. I didn't know what was going to happen. I didn't know" (p. 23).

What *might* have happened to Brian is sadly predictable. He could have ended up hustling to stay alive. He could have turned to drugs or alcohol; he might have been killed, or killed himself out of depression or despair. So what happened? He turned eighteen, and went back to school. "They didn't want to accept me, but they didn't have much of a choice. They asked me why I didn't have parents and I told them 'Because I left home because I am a gay male'" (p. 25).

Through it all Brian told *Metro Weekly* that, though "angry and bitter," he never stopped loving his parents. But he couldn't stop thinking—during all those "scary" times drifting on the streets, watching friends kill themselves with drugs and prostitution, never knowing for sure what fate might befall him—he just never could figure out what was going on. "I kept thinking, 'Why is this happening to me?'" (p. 23).

Flash forward four years. Now Brian is a twenty-two-year-old college student—he graduated high school over that summer of 1998, and landed a job that made him enough money so that he could put himself through school—and instead of being just another sad statistic like so many other gay kids in his situation, he's studying information technology, with an eye on landing an IT job one day. Life has turned around.

What's more, that rift with his parents has long since been mended. Brian says he moved in with his father, after his father's job sent him out of town; he then returned to the DC area and lived with his mother for several months until she joined his dad on the West Coast. "I've developed an awesome relationship with my parents. I allowed myself to put a lot of things behind me." As for their feelings about his sexual orientation, Brian says he hasn't had a serious enough relationship to "test" their reactions. "It's kind of hard to say. But I've definitely had some 'potentials,' and some friends that I have brought home, and I have to say my parents have come a long way. I really don't think that they are too 'weirded out' anymore. They treat me pretty much how I think they would treat my siblings and that's all I can ask. They might still be slightly weirded out if I was on the couch lying with a guy, but they would get used to it. I know they would."

I bring up Brian's story for a couple of reasons. First, it's just one more reminder to the post-thirty gay crowd, many of them quite comfy in their sense of "we have overcomeism," that today's gay kids are still going through some tough times. Even when their parents love them—as Brian never doubted despite his time on the mean streets—it's no guarantee they'll be able to handle the revelation of their son's sexual orientation. That Brian never lost faith that his parents would come around, and that he never gave in to bitterness or anger, is a testament to the upbringing they gave him.

Mainly I offer Brian's tale as a lesson, not just in hope and perseverance, but also in the wondrous change in situations *and* perspective that just a few years' passage can bring. "Four years ago I think I was still really confused about a lot of issues," Brian tells me. "Some issues I probably didn't even know I was confused about! Today, I am definitely a lot more at peace with myself. When I was younger I was constantly playing mental mind games with myself, always asking myself if I was making the right decisions and doing the right thing. Today, I'm more from the mind-set that it's not entirely what you do, but the confidence that you do it with that allows you to enjoy what you're doing, as well as enjoying your life."

Obviously it's not *just* the passage of time that turned Brian's situation around; he was incredibly lucky nothing bad happened to him.

For one thing, he'd be the first to tell you that. Still, for a kid in his late teens he was also amazingly proactive and gutsy when it came to the choices he made, and still makes. He does not smoke or drink alcohol, nor does he do drugs of any kind. He's also possessed of an amazingly mellow disposition that's obviously allowed him to roll with the punches, and, just in case you're curious, he's a rather attractive young man as well. Clearly, Brian is a standout. But remarkable as he is, he really hasn't done anything beyond the power of the average individual, so long as that individual refuses to give in, or give up.

So many of the men interviewed and surveyed in this book tell me about being "stuck in ruts," about being "victims of circumstances," or bad upbringing, or abuse, or addiction; some have been through such harrowing ordeals that it's stunning to think they're functional at all. I'd certainly never get up on my high horse and tell them to suck it up and get over it, whatever "it" is. All of us have surrendered from time to time, thrown up our hands and said to hell with it when the going got tough, even when gritting our teeth and slogging on might have served us better. I know I have. But I will offer Brian's story to anyone thinking about giving up on the future just because the past or present pretty much sucks. "Four years ago I had no clue where I would be today, but now I can honestly say I am OK and happy with where I am," he says. "I can only hope I will be as happy in four years as I am today. That's the same for the rest of my life. I very much look forward to getting older."

"STUCK IN THE MIDDLE"

"Twinks want twinks or daddies, daddies want twinks or other daddies," laments "CS," a thirty-two-year-old office worker who e-mails me from the United Kingdom. "Those of us in between have our age range limited . . . it would be a lot easier if we could just skip the years between twenty-five and forty-five, if you could go to bed on your twenty-fifth birthday and wake up as a sexy older man, and not have to deal with all those intervening years. I find myself stuck in this posttwink, predaddy time warp!"

I found a lot of sentiment like that among men in CS's age group, as I queried them about the things that concern them most as they pass out of their youthful stages, and contemplate their lives as they head toward their middle years. Many seem to feel that a happy gay life is best enjoyed by those just entering the scene or by those who've mastered it after years of struggle. "I really do envy both groups," says Cameron, a thirty-year-old writer in Dallas. "It's like the world is your oyster when you first come out, since everything is sort of catered to you. Then you go through this really odd, awkward time, when it's like you're kind of uncategorized. You don't really feel young, but you're too young to think of yourself as older, and sometimes it's hard to know how you're supposed to act. Are you too old for that shirt, that hairstyle, or are you too young for that club? Then when you hit your forties, it's like, OK, now I'm too old to care what people think, so why not have fun again? I see a lot of older gay guys and it's like they're having a second childhood. I guess it's something to look forward to, but it seems like it's going to be a long wait."

Others look to the future with different concerns, not all of them age related, of course. Brian, a twenty-four-year-old Secret Service agent in DC, was among those who told me their biggest fear as they get older remains the chance of contracting STDs such as HIV. "Unfortunately, it seems that no matter how safe you are, you can never be 100 percent protected from the transmission of sexually transmitted diseases," he says. "I worry that HIV or any other STD may take the lives of some of my best friends." Kent, a twenty-eight-year-old waiter/bartender in Orlando, says he thinks about terrorism and the possibilities of chemical, biological, or nuclear catastrophe. "Those are my big-ticket items, worry-wise. It never ceases to amaze me how gay men can be so focused on the trivial things in life, or dwell on the shit we all go through like aging, as if we're the first people who had to look at forty. With everything that's been going on in the world of late, I can only hope I have the *chance* to grow old." Still other men spoke of worrying about losing their parents, friends, and siblings to mishaps, old age, or disease. "I don't really worry about myself that much. It's just my nature," says Mike, a twenty-six-year-old photographer in Indiana. "I tend to worry more about those around me. Right now my parents aren't all that old—they're in their late fifties—and they seem pretty healthy. But you know that day will come, at some point in the future, when they won't be around anymore, and it really makes me sad to think about it, and I wonder how I'll handle it."

When I asked gay men about their biggest fears or concerns about the future, most talked about how they'll handle getting older as gay men, and how they'll navigate the uncharted straits beyond twinkdom. "I know I'm still too young to be considered 'out of it,' but I can definitely hear the clock ticking," says Tyler, a twenty-nine-year-old computer software specialist in Arizona. "I've enjoyed the gay scene as a young man, but I worry what it will be like when I get older, if I'll still feel welcome." Johnny, a self-described twenty-seven-year-old "klub kid" in Philadelphia, says he feels like the "party is going to be over" soon, and sooner than he wants it to be. "I never wanted to be one of those pathetic, over-thirty guys still going out all the time, still having casual flings and never really being serious about anything, but now I'm right on the brink of that and it scares the shit out of me." (We'll address some more of those "klub kid" crises, and some possible solutions, a bit later on.)

As we've seen, one popular contention among the middle-aged and senior set I spoke with held that once today's young people *are* out, they face a relatively carefree existence, whatever traumatic experiences they might have encountered along the way. Many older men seem to believe that along with today's relative prosperity, the mass culture, gay and otherwise, is so expressly tailored for youthful tastes and consumption that it should be virtually impossible *not* to be happy. That old phrase, "Youth is wasted on the young," popped up more times than I can count. "One hates to overgeneralize, but they don't seem to realize everything they have," says Arthur, a sixty-eight-year-old retiree living in New Mexico. "Perhaps it's because they never had to struggle against the long odds, never had to fight for much because so much was given to them. There seems to be so much dissatisfaction and disaffection among young people today."

I think Arthur, and many of the senior set who express the same thought, are "overgeneralizing" just a bit; every generation faces its own set of unique challenges, and you can't hold it against young people today that they were fortunate enough to miss out on all the fun of the Depression, World War II, or Vietnam. This post–September 11 world of ours may yet present hurdles we cannot even imagine, and God only knows how modern youth may be tested in the near future. But truthfully, I know what Arthur's saying, and sometimes it's enough to make any post-forty-something shake his head in wonder. For instance, I know that when I hit the grand old age of twenty-five, I thought about the prospect of being a quarter of a century old—for all of about thirty seconds or so—then went back to whatever it was I was doing. I certainly didn't sit down and do a major reevaluation of my great life goals, ponder all the things still left undone (I'm saving that for fifty). These days I've started to hear people refer to something called a "midtwenties malaise," some sort of amorphous angst that can stalk those who really, *really* wanted to be millionaires before their thirtieth birthday, but life, in its capricious way, hasn't afforded them the opportunity. At a television station where I used to work my boss used to lament how hard it was finding decent young employees actually willing to work their way up the ladder. "They expect instant advancement. Kids these days have a ridiculous sense of entitlement, and they're disappointed when their high expectations don't pan out," he told me. In my brief career working at a dot-com startup—which I'll tell you more about later—I found myself in a roomful of would-be youthful entrepreneurs, people who had not yet been anywhere, done much of anything, but remained utterly convinced they were ready to be masters of the universe, because, well, that's the way it was *supposed* to be.

It seems like quite a few gay men in that age group, at least the ones I surveyed and interviewed, second that emotion. One young man tells me how he regularly turns down "any full-time job that can't pay me what I'm worth," even if it means he has to wait tables or work retail in the interim, with his parents spotting him the cash he needs to help make ends meet. "I know that perfect job is just waiting for me somewhere," he says.

That "sense of entitlement" also leaches into some people's personal lives. Many young people I spoke with wonder why they haven't found that "perfect guy" yet, or why they're just not yet quite as fabulous as they hoped they'd be. "I really did think by the time I hit my mid or late twenties I would have settled down with an awesome guy, have a house, two labs, and take vacations to South Beach," says Robbie, a twenty-seven-year-old office worker in Manhattan. "But instead I'm living in a three-story walkup with two other guys, barely making ends meet, and there's no long-term relationship in sight. I keep wondering what I am doing wrong." Ben, a twenty-nine-year-old geologist in Washington State, says he's "vaguely dissatisfied" with his life so far, despite the fact he's got a steady job and makes a decent salary. "I got to where I thought I'd want to be, but now I'm finding out it's not enough. Sometimes I think I need to find a relationship to make life complete; other times I'm convinced I don't really want a relationship at all and that living single is best for me. I just don't know where I am or where I'm supposed to be right now."

In the July 5, 2001, issue of *Metro Weekly*—that DC periodical where we first met my bud Brian—editor Sean Bugg had an amusing take on all this. His essay was called "Stuck in the Middle," and in it he mused at length about the "three segments of life, each thirty years long," that comprise our human existence.

> In the early segment, you spend a lot of time growing and learning and, if you're lucky, surviving the first few years of having a driver's license. In the late segment, you get to retire and, if you're lucky, survive the last few years of driving. (p. 27)

The problem years, Bugg contended, come "in the middle," the part where one looks around to see what one has accomplished.

> My life has become a weird conglomeration of trying to accomplish all those great things that were expected of me while at the same time fighting off any indication that I might actually be getting older. These are not compatible impulses. . . . You may be thinking that thirty-three is too early for a midlife crisis. But if I start now I may be able to get over it by thirty-six or so, obviating the need to buy an impractical metaphorical penis like a Corvette. Instead I bought a Jeep, which is far more practical as metaphorical penises go. (p. 27)

Bugg's humor aside, that "vague dissatisfaction" that Ben talks about was a noticeable theme among the twenty- and thirty-something set. Not a universal theme, mind you; scores of men seem rather pleased with their professional and personal lives, and their visions of the immediate or long-term future. "I'm farther ahead in every way than I ever thought I'd be at this point," avows Lucas, a twenty-six-year-old technical writer in Rockville, Maryland. "I landed a great job, and a great guy, and it's like all systems go for me. No complaints or worries at all, really." Jeff, a thirty-year-old freelance designer in New Jersey, tells me he revels in his work and his single life. "Right now I feel like it's my boat, I'm the captain, and I can steer anywhere I want. Work is great, and I don't want or need a relationship to make me happy."

But many *are* troubled by their relationships or lack thereof. Many are worried about their careers or their dicey employment prospects. Or, despite having a job, even one they always thought they wanted, they're strangely fitful, thinking there has to be something better for them. Although I'm sure plenty of straight guys go through much the same thing, I'm beginning to think there must be something about gay men that helps breed such unease; my theory is that, absent any exterior reasons for concern, that nagging angst is fired by a kind of low or damaged self-esteem.

I put forth that idea in an article published in the February 1998 issue of *Genre* magazine. Called "The Greatest Love of All," the article talked about how self-esteem issues are often at the heart of nearly every major problem that gay men face. Whether it's bad or abusive relationships with lovers, friends, or family, serious problems with body image, involvement with drugs, excessive consumption of alcohol, practicing unsafe sex, lack of commitment to any kind of career or vocation, it doesn't matter; I think much of all that can be traced back to a basic lack of self-worth and self-respect, based on a sense of rejection—real or self-imposed—because we happen to be gay.

I'm not saying that self-esteem issues are the source of *every* sort of angst or dissatisfaction that gay men experience, or that every gay man is walking around doubting his true value, for that matter. A lot of us *like* us, very much, thank you. And I'm certainly not claiming that gay men have a monopoly on such things; seen Oprah, Doctor Phil, or any of those other daytime freak fests lately? I'm only saying that we *do* absorb a lot of negative information about our orientations throughout our entire lives: we're not manly enough, we're not normal, we're nasty, diseased, depraved, not fit for military service, we don't deserve our fair share of society's services. Sooner or later a lot of that is going to start eating around the edges of our self-perceptions and it takes some pretty strong inner stuff not to let it get to us. As I've discovered, gay men from their midtwenties to their early thirties seem to be prime candidates, since that's the age these days when a lot of them start taking a long look at where they are and where they feel they should be.

Just about everyone compensates for their perceived shortcomings in some manner—think of Sean Bugg and his metaphorical penis—and we've already heard from men who buff themselves silly in the gym to help beef up that sagging body image. When not taken to extremes, I think those sorts of endeavors are pretty harmless, and they can make people happy in many ways—you should see me driving around in *my* new car, stupid grin on my face—so long as they're mere accessories on a package that's already complete. Where the water gets murkier is when that dream job, that fab vacation plan, that new outfit, or the wonderful new boy on your arm are attempts at finding some kind of joy to fill an inner void.

I talked with psychologist Doug Favero about all this; a large number of his clients, most of them gay men, wrestle constantly with self-esteem issues. "Until we learn to accept ourselves and like ourselves, we're probably not going to find too much happiness," he says. "Most of us suffer from some kind of low self-esteem issues. We have this culture that tells us constantly who we should be, and that is, of course, heterosexual. It also tells us what we should earn and what we should look like. And there's just not many of us who can live up to that standard."

It's not that having a low or threatened sense of self-esteem is necessarily bad, but rather it's how we learn to deal with those feelings and what actions we take or don't take to overcome them that can affect all the threads of our lives. Coming out can certainly help, and can start to instill a new and confident identity after years of living in denial. But for many gay men it's not that easy; their issues of low self-worth can continue to haunt them, unexorcised by their honesty. "Some people almost seem to live under a cloud of low self-esteem that simply darkens everything they do," says Favero. "Such people may need therapy or counseling to help them see the brighter edges just around the corner of those clouds." Others, he tells me, can take their own steps to light the darkness.

Taking a cue from the likes of Oprah and Doctor Phil, I asked Doug Favero if he'd jot down some of those steps, and he was only too happy to oblige. Let's call them "How to Be Your Own Best Friend: A Step-by-Step Guide."

> *Step One: Take the Hero's Journey*—Formulate ongoing challenges which focus you on testing your strengths in daily life. Feel the power to influence your own life and the world around you.
> *Step Two: Become an Involved Member of the Human Family*—Spend time reaching out to someone in need or to a good cause greater than yourself. Feel yourself to be part of the whole of humanity.
> *Step Three: Revel in Something Beautiful*—Become acquainted with some good poetry, music, or art, and set aside quiet time to experience it. Feel involved in the deepest expressions of the human self.
> *Step Four: Take the Inner Journey*—Use your own imagination and dreams or get involved in a stint of growth-oriented therapy to bring your hidden depths to consciousness. Feel both the light and the dark inside of you and experience your bigness.
> *Step Five: Be a Creator*—Express your ongoing discoveries about yourself in writing, art, dance, or ritual, and experience, right up front, your "once in the history of the universe" uniqueness.

Favero points out that all of this is mere advice to take along with you on a journey toward better self-esteem, and he reminds me that the journey lasts a lifetime. "We all know the stories of the good-looking, wealthy people who are still possessed of that vague unease, that feeling that they're not as happy as they should be," says Favero. "Well, nobody gets complete, total happiness all the time. It's more like moments of contentment." In a way, he says that's really exactly how it should be. "Remember, we are all programmed to keep growing, to make new goals, and strive for them," he asserts. "Call me an optimist, but I've never seen anyone who I didn't believe had the capacity for positive change. Sure there's fear, and sometimes it's hard to get off the dime and get moving, but no matter what happens, our deepest selves want to grow."

And if that doesn't work, well . . . there's always a penis. Meta-phorical, of course.

"THE TRUTH ABOUT MONEY"

"I'm only twenty-four, but I've started to think about what life will be like for me when I'm an older gay man," says Jay, a graduate student and researcher in New York City. "My biggest worries are financial; I hope I'll be able to use the stock market, CDs, and money markets to fund my retirement."

Theo, a twenty-eight-year-old office worker in Berkeley, California, says right now, "investing in the future just isn't really an option" for him. "I have a lot of loans I have to pay off, and a lot of credit card bills, and the money coming in is barely keeping pace. I hope I'll be making good money one day and everything will start to take care of itself."

In Chapter 6 I mentioned an article I wrote for the April 1998 issue of *Genre* magazine ("The Rainbow and the Pot of Gold") that talked about how gay men were looking to the future, finance-wise, and what if any provisions they were making. The general consensus of the piece found that, while most gay men know intuitively that they'll have to make more financial provisions than their straight counterparts if they're going to be self-sufficient, few of us are doing all that we should, or could, to make that a reality. Tossing that extra change into a coffee can doesn't count.

"My relationship with money is one that says 'spend me,'" one young man in his midtwenties told me back then. "I haven't thought much about retirement. In fact, I can't think of anything worse than retirement. I'd rather stay busy until I drop dead" (p. 82). He told me he'd found great contentment in "eating out all the time, going to movies on opening night, and generally enjoying life." His comments were typical of many gay men his age that I spoke to for that article, a sort of "What, me worry?" attitude that was common among gay men in the midtwenties to late-thirties set. "I'm having so much fun now. I can always save later" pretty much sums it up.

Soon after the article came out, the stock market exploded, the economy skyrocketed, and lots of folks I know, many of them gay, started making cash hand over fist. On the national scene, the federal deficit vanished, unemployment dropped to historically low levels, and worrying about the future almost seemed passé. Clearly, happy days were here again. We could all enjoy life now and watch the millennium celebrations on our big-screen televisions.

But we know what's happened since. We saw that unprecedented economic boom go bust; overnight millionaires got snapped back to reality—if not the unemployment line—and the huge government surplus vanished, to be replaced by forecasts of deficit as far as the eye can see clearly. Corporate scandals and mismanagement wiped out or severely depleted countless retirement accounts and that sent thousands of folks already retired, or about to retire, back into the workforce. Happy days, my ass.

My own experience reflects a lot of this in microcosm. I was among those wooed away from a steady—if low-paying—job to take up residence at a dot-com firm that really, *really* seemed like a good idea at the time. I can't be too specific about the makeup or whereabouts of the firm—I don't want to get sued, and there are lawyers everywhere, you know—but suffice to say all was not as it appeared to be. What I'd been told was a solid company cash flow was in actuality nothing more than smoke and mirrors; after only a few months we all got our walking papers. So much for the stock options.

I was lucky, at first; I found another job soon after the Internet gig tanked—one that paid almost as well—at a national television network, but that job also went by the boards about the same time the national economy started free-falling. "Cost cutting and consolidation" is what the suits like to call it up in the executive suite; "I have to find another fucking job" is what it meant to me. Since then I've survived by freelancing at various places where I've worked before; I send out a lot of resumés, go on a lot of job interviews, with no success to speak of as I put these words down (pardon me if I sound bitter; it's only because I am). And my situation, pathetic as it sounds, isn't at all unique. Seems like most people I know these days—and many that I've interviewed—are just scraping by. In such a climate it may seem a little crazy to encourage people to save for some distant day when they have to think about how they'll make ends meet this week.

But much of what I wrote back in 1998 remains just as true today. Though my polls indicate a hefty majority of every age group does at least *think* about saving and investing for their futures—and how could we not, with all the dire forecasts—my interviews show that few are taking the solid steps they'll need to in order to actually *have* some gold in their golden years.

Some gay men, many of them just coming out, simply have no idea what it takes to keep an eye on finances. Jon, a twenty-one-year-old retail worker in Pennsylvania, tells me he "never bothers" to write down the amounts of the checks he writes; "I always know pretty much what I have in there," he tells me. I ask him how many checks he's bounced and how much money he's wasted in overdraft fees. "It's happened a few times," he admits. "Maybe I'll try online banking. You can buy a lot of stuff online too, you know." (The mind shudders.) Though not nearly as inexperienced in money matters as Jon, Dean, a twenty-eight-year-old marketing executive in Philadelphia, says he probably "pisses away" thousands of dollars each year "on totally stupid shit, like going out all the time, eating out a lot, buying these silly new toys and gadgets from the Sharper Image that I really don't need. Right now I'm pretty set financially, but I do wonder what the future will look like, if I'll have enough to retire well."

Here's what we know about the future: 77 million baby boomers heading toward retirement age over the next few decades, and Social Security as it's currently configured isn't likely to help much. Back in 1998 my experts talked about how gay men seemed particularly apt to put off saving and investing for old age—as I've shown previously, most of us don't really want to think about ever getting old—and a lot of us have lifestyles that don't steer us toward responsible fiscal management. We don't have to follow the same rules our straight counterparts do; we're not marrying, buying the house, having the kids, thinking about the kids' college. All that domestic Sturm und Drang isn't for us, so in reality we *should* have more money to set aside; trouble is, many of us didn't in 1998, and we sure as hell don't now. Though I *did* talk with a number of fiscally responsible gay men, sensible fellows that were looking ahead and tucking some ducats aside, just about as many weren't. Well into their late thirties and forties, they're still living pretty much the same way they did in their twenties; they party a lot, buy a lot of clothes, drive nice—and expensive—new cars. Nothing wrong at all with that sort of thing if you can afford it—it keeps the economy going—but if you're living close to the edge of solvency already, down the road that lack of thriftiness can come back to bite you in the ass.

"I wish someone had sat me down and taken away all my credit cards when I was in my thirties," says Chet, a forty-seven-year-old store manager in Oregon. "It took me ten years to get rid of all my debt. I am only now beginning to put cash aside for the future. I was having so much fun, but now it's time to pay the piper. You ask me if I've ever thought about retirement . . . who knows how long I'll have to work before I'm *able* to retire!"

I know a lot of people's eyes just glaze over when you start talking about finances; I know mine frequently have. But the simple fact that nearly every list of best-sellers includes books on winning financial strategies, and that most major gay publications these days include regular or occasional financial advice features, should tell you something: straight or gay, young or middle-aged, not many of us are doing all we could be to provide for our futures.

Ric Edelman is chairman of Edelman Financial Services and author of several popular books about finances and investing, including *The Truth About Money* (HarperCollins, 1998) and *Discover the Wealth Within You* (HarperCollins, 2002). What many single gays and straights often share, he says, at least until they arrive at middle age, is a feeling of immortality. "Not only do we think we're going to live forever, we think we're going to want to work forever. There are people who are totally focused on their careers and can't imagine retiring."

Then right about the age of forty, Edelman explains, something happens. "Suddenly work isn't as much fun as it used to be. You start looking ahead to the day you can retire, and you realize how much money you're going to need." And something else happens as you get into your fifties and sixties. "You start to see your peers dying, your college friends, your colleagues . . . and you realize you're really *not* going to live forever." That realization has come even earlier in a gay community still working through the AIDS crisis; the attendant health costs and legal concerns about those who might get left behind bedevil countless gay couples.

Although no one can be reasonably expected to be completely insulated when disease or disaster strikes, experts say the sad fact is that woefully few are adequately preparing for the clearly foreseeable future, that day they'll no longer take home a paycheck. According to Edelman, there's something waiting for those who don't prepare for the end of their working days and it's not a home in the Sunshine State. "It's called poverty."

So let's say that, up until now, your life has been a virtual blur of self-indulgence. Let's say you've been more concerned with setting up housekeeping in the here and now and haven't given a rat's ass about your retirement needs. Let's say you're only now waking up to some of the challenges ahead. Should you start stocking up on canned goods for the cold life ahead of you? In other words, is it too late?

"It's never too late," declares Edelman. "Everyone can say, 'I should have started twenty years ago, or ten years ago.' The past is irrelevant. Let's start today and move on. I like to tell people about my grandmother. Several years before she passed away at [the age of] 101, she had to visit the doctor. Turned out that she had worn out her pacemaker. Believe me, none of us has any idea how long we're going to live or how much money we'll need."

How do you go about making that money? Edelman has four basic steps he uses to advise his clients and readers to set them on the right path. "First, I tell them to get involved in whatever retirement plan their company offers and try to make sure you're invested in a diversified basket of stocks. Then I tell them to pay off all their debts. I'm not talking about manageable, long-term payments on things like mortgages, cars, or student loans. I'm talking credit cards. It's ridiculous to try and save money in some bank at 1 or 2 percent while you're paying off credit bills or personal loans at 18 percent. Get rid of those debts.

"Next, you want to start building your cash reserve. Ideally you should have twelve months' worth of spending in an emergency fund. Put the money anywhere it will be safe and earn some interest, in a CD, or a checking/savings account. Just someplace where you can get to it quickly without having to pay a penalty." Edelman says that once you have those pieces in place, you're ready to sit down with an investment professional or a financial planner. "That's the person who is going to help you look at your finances and help you plan your retirement."

That advice holds true for everyone, whether they're sitting fat and happy with a long-established firm or working two jobs trying to make ends meet in an uncertain economy. "Just make the decision to save and then do it," says Edelman. "Do whatever it takes."

I hope you'll forgive me if any of the preceding passages sounded preachy or scolding. You, my dear reader, may be among the dozens I've spoken with who have their financial house very much in order; you may be among those making that good living at a solid company, with a vested share of your company's retirement plan in place and investments in a wide portfolio of funds. If that's the case, bravo! You're doing well. But many, many more of you out there *haven't* begun to think yet about such alien concepts as saving or investing. And if these meager paragraphs have made you stop and think you could be doing more—or even just doing *something*—to provide for a little financial security decades down the road, it's been well worth my time to set them down.

A friend of mine once told me that we're all only two or three setbacks away from living in a box on the street. I don't know if I believed him then, but I damn sure see the wisdom of his words now. Whatever setbacks I've had—like the ones so many of my friends have had—they've been manageable so far. We're all still young and healthy enough to rally. But down the road? I look to my own family and I can see the difference between the lives of my six siblings and my own. They've all got spouses, and they all have kids. Some of their *kids* have kids. They have support structures in place for the years when they get old and gray—actually older and grayer—if their own provisions should fall short. As for my mother, well, she's doing just fine right now, but even if some unforeseen disaster did happen to befall her, with all of us pitching in there's a virtual cavalry ready to ride to *her* financial rescue.

There may yet be a long-term relationship in my future, or any of our futures, that helps provide some of the same sort of support structure my brothers and sisters share. (I can't see having kids, though. *Dating* kids, maybe, just not having them.) But it's just as likely we'll be heading down the road solo, with no one to lean on, except us. The choice is ours how we'll get there. And now is the best time to start.

"OVER" THE RAINBOW

Seth is a twenty-four-year-old college student in Providence, who tells me he's a regular club goer—he splits his time between New York City to the south, and Boston to the north, when he isn't hitting the local hotspots—but sometimes he wonders if that's all there is. "I've really enjoyed going out, and I guess I still do, but it does get old sometimes. But other than a few groups on campus (I don't really like hanging out with people I know from school), there doesn't seem to be many places to meet guys, other than online, and that always feels sketchy to me."

Nick is a thirty-year-old customer service representative for a manufacturing firm in New Jersey. "I came out when I was a wet-behind-the-ears kid and really dove into the gay scene. Had a great time, really, met lots of great guys, had some boyfriends, went to every Pride parade from Boston to DC, a couple of circuit parties. Now I think I started way too early, because I'm honestly just bored with gay life now. . . . It's not like I wouldn't want to find a great guy at some point, but all the rest of the stuff, the clubbing, the parades, it's just sort of tedious now. Mostly I hang out with my straight friends or just stay home. Haven't been inside a gay bar in maybe a year."

"I'm at the point where I don't trust gay guys anymore, unless I meet them in 'straight' situations," says Eric, a twenty-seven-year-old receptionist in Oakland, California. "The guys I meet in clubs are always too fucked up or slutty, and the people I talk to on the computer are just looking to hook up. The only guy I've dated in the last year or so went to my gym and he turned out to be kind of psycho. Now some women I know from work want to get me to go on a blind date with a friend of theirs. . . . Hell, I'm thinking of taking them up on it. I'm not doing so hot on the gay scene. I hate the gay scene!"

Meet some of what I've come to call the "over" the rainbow crowd, a small but clearly present group of gay men turned off by—or simply tired of—what they call the "scene": the clubs where gay men go to drink or dance, the festivals thrown each year to celebrate gay pride, the circuit parties held in various venues in the United States and Canada, the gay chat rooms or other online communities, and virtually any other place where gay men gather because they're gay. In *Sissyphobia* I interviewed a number of men who refuse to acknowl-

edge their homosexuality publicly—sometimes, even to themselves—
and wouldn't be caught dead at a parade or club filled with "those
fags and queers and whatnot." This group is different. Few have any
problem with being gay; in fact many seem to have come out as teens
or in their early twenties. But these days they seem to long for a gay
life that doesn't include spinning disco balls or overrated deejays;
many would just as soon do an Ironman than an AIDS Ride or play
ball rather than parade down Main Street.

I'm not necessarily talking about men who question the essential
nature of what being gay really means. "I'm one of those guys whose
sense of identity isn't all about what's between his legs or some other
guy's legs," says Leo, a twenty-five-year-old medical student in New
England. "Do I like having sex with men? Of course I do, but I think
there's a lot of guys my age who find all the rainbow/pride crap to be a
limiting view of gay life, if one can even use that term. I mean, what
does 'gay life' represent?" That's a pretty meaty debate, and it's not
one I have adequate room for here; for the purposes of this section,
I'm talking about men who look at the menu they find presented to
them, and find themselves hungering for something different.

In the May 2001 issue of *OUT* magazine, writer Kevin Arnovitz
put some of these thoughts down in a piece called "Gay Scene Dropout": "There is a growing group of gay guys, generally in the 18-34
age range, completely comfortable with their sexuality, but detached
from gay life" (p. 50). Arnovitz admits he belongs within their number; he skewers everything from the "stand and model bars" prominent in most gay neighborhoods, the music they play—"When did
the gay parliament meet and decree any song with a shrieking diva
and a bassy two-beat an anthem?" he asks—and the uniform du jour
worn by clones trying to fit within the mold. For him, gay life these
days has become like "the 24-hour Chinese restaurant around the corner—it's good to know that it exists if we need it, but how often do we
actually go there?" (p. 50).

It's not that he has started intentionally avoiding "gay spaces"—
the gay dance bar, the megaclub, the gay summer spots—but rather
that they've become irrelevant.

After an initial sexual exploration period during which I needed
these places as distribution centers for potential sexual con-

quests, I now find myself gravitating toward the mixed bar that plays down-tempo sounds . . . and the culture hounds whose pop interests extend beyond divas, low camp, and E! (p. 50)

Arnovitz notes that he sounds like something perilously close to a homophobe, but insists he is only "kvetching" because he cares.

What he wrote reminded me very much of my own "kvetches" about the gay scene, except mine were circa 1981/1982. Only out at that point for four or five years, I'd already experienced much of what Arnovitz wrote about and I really had only myself to blame; I'd taken to going out more nights than I stayed home and even the most sumptuous banquet is going to get old if one never allows oneself to grow hungry. Life took care of my situation for me; my enlistment at twenty-two in the Marine Corps—where I had to play straight boy (mostly) for at least five days a week—and my after-discharge exile to my parents' home in West Virginia—don't even want to talk about *that*—made getting inside those gay bar walls and hanging out at Pride festivals a rare thing of joy again, at least for the several years before I moved back to the DC area. Now I go out once a week or so, and it suits me fine; since I don't live anywhere near a gay ghetto, I have to be among "my people" at some point so I don't lose touch.

Arnovitz concedes as much, writing that "traditional gay spaces occupy an important place, especially for those just coming out. [They] continue to be the only truly safe space for unbridled expression, and their dissolution would be a tragedy" (p. 51). And his self-imposed separation has one other major drawback: it's a lot harder for gay men to get laid hanging out in straight clubs.

Finding someone is a numbers game; I don't hang out in gay spaces or participate in traditionally gay activities, ergo, I don't meet all that many gay men worth seeing, ergo, I haven't really built any sort of dating life over the past three years. (p. 51)

In that concern he sounds a lot like many other men I've talked with. If you're hunting, you have to go where your prey hangs out; but what happens when the regular hunting grounds and watering holes don't suit your tastes? You can sit around and bitch about it, I suppose. Gay men in their twenties seem exquisitely equipped for that pursuit. Or you can do what a handful of my interviewees are doing:

finding others like themselves, and making their own spaces and pursuits.

Ryan is a twenty-three-year-old operations manager in Chicago, who tells me he doesn't like the club scene because it's "full of drugs and piano bars are filled with snotty people." But that hasn't stopped him from finding people to hang out with. "I found a gay swim team and a running club, which is cool because I dig physical fitness. . . . I just don't get into what a lot of gay people do, like going out four nights a week and watching drag shows and shower contests." Jon, a twenty-four-year-old "working intern" in northern Virginia, tells me the gay scene paled for him "within a few months" of his arrival in the DC area. "I guess I'm just not that much of a bar lover. I was lucky that I met some other guys who felt the same way. You won't find us out much on Saturday nights, because we get up early on Sundays and play rugby, then grab a beer together afterward. It seems like someone is always having a party at his house or apartment, someone is always planning a rock climbing or a camping trip. I don't have anything against people who go to clubs, I just find more life outside of them, and I've met some great guys this way." Terry, a thirty-four-year-old sales executive in Denver, doesn't have anything against bars, either, but says he's found a group of gay men like himself that prefer hiking boots to dancing shoes, and sportswear to club clothes. "We go out once in a blue moon—that's not what we're about. People who think you can't meet gay men in the 'real' world aren't looking hard enough, or they're not looking in the right places, or with the right frame of mind." Terry says his group is more likely to be found watching a Bronco game on Sundays, as opposed to *Queer As Folk*. "I guess we're just more integrated into the mainstream."

My friend Dylan, a twenty-nine-year-old photographer—and the owner of a Web design company in Seattle—seems to have found a way to combine several of his interests, while moving with ease between the gay and not-so-gay worlds. He's one of a "very large" group of friends who range in age from late teens to pushing forty, a hugely varied and informal clan whose members seem equally at home climbing up the face of a rocky ridge or closing down a dance club at dawn. "We have students, professionals, blue-collar workers, even a motorcycle cop who was just put on the SWAT team," he tells me. "There are people who like to go out to the bars and enjoy dancing and partying, but we also love to hike, ski, mountain bike, you name it. For a while a large group of us were playing ultimate Frisbee every Sunday. It's all about variety."

With Dylan and other photographers in its midst, the group—they started calling themselves the Seaboys—began to document its exploits and travels. Dylan locked down the domain name, Seaboys. com, and before long there were hundreds of pictures posted online, with Dylan posting listings of upcoming events to keep the rest of the group in the loop. "Our most recent redesign allows users to control their own e-mail lists—putting the control of the site into the hands of the individuals," he says. "I've always looked at the site as a way for people to communicate, meet, and share photos and experiences."

Dylan says the original purpose of the site—just an easier way for the Seaboys to share photos, without all those tedious e-mails and attachments—has evolved so that now it's become a sort of online community with its feet in the real world, whether that's clubbing in Cancun and Gay Days at Disney, or pounding up some steep trail deep in the woods, ready to make camp by a roaring fire. "Seaboys. com definitely helps people connect and interact outside of the typical bar scene," he says, clearly proud at how far his site has come. "I think the Internet in general helps provide alternative activities and lets people connect in new ways. Everyone who might consider themselves a part of the Seaboys group is gay, but that's just one facet of our lives—not the only thing that defines us."

Back on the East Coast, there's New York City's Urban Outings, <www.urbanoutings.com>, which describes itself as "an innovative activity service that plans and organizes casual get-togethers for groups of outgoing professional gay men and women." Those activities run the gamut from such staid pursuits as board games, restaurant dinners, and Broadway shows, to fencing, kayaking, and horseback riding. The group's membership director told the May 2002 issue of *Instinct* magazine that UO organizes about 360 activities a year, for members who range in age from the late twenties to fifties (Liberman, 2002); many of them are in the same boat as others who've grown tired of the normal rituals of the gay scene.

I've heard from other men, in different parts of the country, who've formed their own groups like UO and Seaboys. Sometimes they're almost as organized and publicized, and they coordinate their activities via Web sites; others are much more loose and free-formed, and use newspaper ads or old-fashioned bulletin boards to spread the word. However they're constituted and whatever methods they employ, they help to create new places—often far away from the well-trod gay scene trails—that make it easier for some gay men to meet, mix, and mingle.

Even those happily ensconced in the gay scene aren't afraid to prod the denizens of club culture into opening up their minds to new ways of thinking; they'd also encourage some of those gay scene dropouts to drop back in from time to time. Moody Mustafa, the DC-based physician/fund-raiser/photographer we heard from back in Chapter 3, is one such individual. "I urge my gay friends who are stuck in clubs and bars to explore the more cultural side of gay life, and likewise I urge the other side to let loose and hit the clubs every now and then," he tells me. "Too many of these people sit around waiting for people to hand them invitations on a silver platter. There is a lot to do in this town or any other, but you have to be proactive and participate. By the same token, if you don't like any of the activities, create your own. Thinking 'inside the box' is not just a trait of some gay men; it is a human trait. . . . There's a lot of general laziness and apathy, and that type of thinking spreads easily in a group of impressionable people such as young gay men. It's hard to motivate people and you end up with a lot of disgruntled and dissatisfied people in the gay community. Many of those people in the over-thirty set, as well as the under-thirty set, just bitch all the time. However, they—and their apathy—are their own worst enemy."

"I think a lot of my peers enjoy the 'club rut,'" says Brian, the twenty-two-year-old college student whose story started this chapter. "And personally I don't think there's really anything wrong with that. It's when the scene controls *you,* and not vice versa, that people start to run into problems. If I hear another person say, 'Yeah, I don't really want to go to the club tonight, but I am going to go,' it's going to make me sick! Look, do what you want to do, and do it with confidence. Don't make yourself miserable by going out because it's the only thing you've done for the past few years and it's the only thing you know, or because you feel like you have some sort of investment in it. Or even worse than that, because you feel like there are no alternatives. We are the gay people shaping our community for not only us, but for the generations that will follow. Don't be afraid to make alternatives.

Chapter 8

The Numbers Game

You sure ask a lot of questions! But they really made me think, so thanks.

Gareth in Boston,
twenty-eight-year-old medical student

One of the challenges in putting a book such as this together—or writing any kind of book or in-depth article—is getting people to open up and tell you what they really think. Obviously, I didn't have too much trouble; you've already heard some of the saucy, cynical, or insightful comments I was privy to over the two years I worked on this book. To be completely honest, through the online survey and personal interviews I conducted, I gathered more material than I could have ever used and still gotten this book boiled down to a reasonable length; it sits in a stack beside me, in a pile about a half-foot high, with pages that number in excess of 1,000. As I was telling my publisher the other day, I could easily have left out every quote and comment you've heard up to this point, started all over again, and come up with pretty much the same result.

Still, scores of gay men told me they just didn't have the time to answer a twenty-five-question survey and do it any justice at all, and several who did take the time would give me only a brief thumbnail sketch of their attitudes about age and aging. But not to worry, my age-related poll took only about five minutes to fill out and by the time I took it offline about 2,000 people had responded.

Before we get to those results—and some related quotes and commentary I'll post with them—let me offer a few explanations and disclaimers. To take the poll, all you had to do was enter the reelingyears.com site, click on the poll link, and register your age.

That would take you to the question page, where you would read the question and enter your response. (I also took in a number of printed-out polls and entered those results on the site myself. There were no hanging or dimpled "chads" to worry about.) Respondents were divided into five groups: Group A is made up of those thirteen to twenty-three years old (approximately 400 responses); Group B is comprised of those twenty-four to twenty-nine (~400 responses); Group C is thirty to thirty-nine (~450 responses); Group D is forty to fifty-nine (~400 responses); and Group E is sixty years old and over (~350 responses).

Oh, I can already hear you screaming. How are thirteen- or fourteen-year-olds in any way comparable to those twenty-one, twenty-two, or twenty-three? All I can tell you is this: I came into contact, both online and off, with an amazing number of young gay kids who utterly astounded me with their comfort level in identifying themselves as gay, and with what they had already gleaned about gay life from the Internet, television, the movies, and magazines (not to mention what they'd already learned from friends, family, or in some cases, older gay men). Many of them were already sexually active or actively planning to become so at the earliest possible opportunity.

I also met dozens of gay men in their late teens and twenties—and thirties, and forties—who were utterly clueless when it comes to what being gay is all about . . . whatever that is. As we've already heard, many of them are deeply closeted, not sexually active with other men, and many are planning to remain so, for a wide variety of reasons. For what it's worth, it feels to me like the numbers sort of balance each other out; the longer, more in-depth responses in the surveys I received and interviews I conducted certainly give me that confidence. (Long after the poll was conducted, the folks at SMYAL told me that they use a thirteen to twenty-one age range for the purposes of their organization, since that's the age when most guys come to sexual awareness. So there.)

Once again I want to remind you that I'm not a professional pollster. Considering how often professional pollsters make a hash out of predicting elections, that may not be such a bad thing. But this is by no means a "scientific" poll; I really have no idea what margin of error might be included in the mix. I can only tell you again that, as weeks went by, the various percentages stabilized and the results remained stable, even as more and more people responded.

In any case, any poll is an arbitrary animal, whether we're talking about divisions according to age, or the individual interpretation of even the simplest question. Just think of these polls as a general guide to what gay men are thinking these days. I hope you'll find them as intriguing and informative as I did.

Let's crunch some numbers.

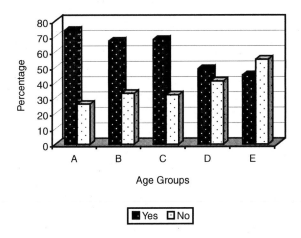

FIGURE 8.1. I have rejected someone's advances, in person or online, *only* because I thought he was too old.

- Older gay guys always want to teach me this and teach me that . . . but I have yet to find an older gay man I can look up to.— *William, twenty-three, student, Ohio*

- When I was a young man I thought it was great fun to shoot down older people who were interested in me. The shoe is on the other foot now, and it ain't so much fun anymore.—*Ari, thirty-four, human resources, Philadelphia*

- Old guys . . . they gross me out. Who likes wrinkly old balls?— *Brian, eighteen, student, Texas*

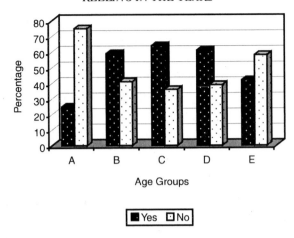

FIGURE 8.2. I have rejected someone's advances, in person or online, *only* because I thought he was too young.

- If he doesn't have hair on his chest, I don't want him. You don't find a lot of hairy eighteen-year-olds.—*Jonathan, twenty-nine, actor, Hollywood, California*

- I know they think I should want them just because they're young. Oops, wrong number. Call me back when you've done something with your life, and your conversation isn't limited to Nintendo.—*George, forty-one, manager, Oklahoma City*

- I see older guys all the time that just look so cool and centered. I'm actually very attracted to older men, but when I try to talk to them I get a little tongue-tied, and it's like they just laugh at me.—*P.J., twenty-three, college student, North Carolina*

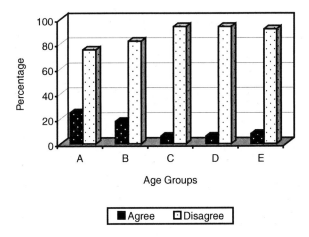

FIGURE 8.3. Older guys shouldn't date younger guys.

- Love of any kind is all too rare these days. If two people find a way to be happy together I say God bless 'em, however old they are.—*Darren, fifty-one, insurance agent, Massachusetts*

- I couldn't care less what other people think about my boyfriend's age—he's thirty-three—because we are in love and support and trust each other in everything we do. Our friends see this and appreciate it because they're not the judgmental, jealous gossip queens who wouldn't know what a meaningful relationship was if it plowed them up the ass.—*Joel, twenty-four, investment manager, Washington, DC*

- My dad doesn't even know I'm gay. He'll kill me if he finds out my boyfriend is twenty-five.—*Jason, seventeen, student, Michigan*

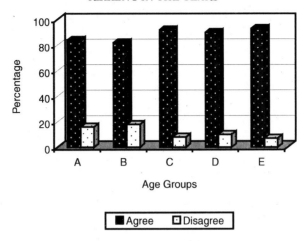

FIGURE 8.4. I think it's OK for someone "older" to date someone who's eighteen or above, as long as they're both in love.

- As long as everyone's legal, sure, why not?—*Johnny, twenty, student, Penn State University*

- True love knows no limits, whether it's age, class, race, or religion. We need less barriers, not more.—*Matt, thirty-two, salesman, Lake Mead, Nevada*

- I was thirty; he was seventeen. We waited for his eighteenth birthday, then went to town. Well, actually we stayed in that night.—*Stu, thirty-two, Florida*

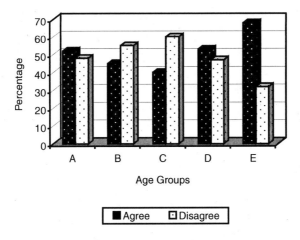

FIGURE 8.5. I think it's OK for someone older to date someone younger, even if he's not eighteen yet, as long as they're both in love.

- I dated someone for three years who was underage when we met. There were a lot of jokes made about us, and me in particular. External validation does matter to some extent in a relationship, and we were deprived of that in many respects.—*Markus, twenty-nine, human resources, San Francisco*

- I was involved with someone who was underage. He was seventeen and I was twenty-one. It scared me to get with him but I did it anyway.—*Jay, twenty-four, graduate student, New York City*

- There's just way too many older men, flitting from boy toy to boy toy. For God's sake, guys . . . just keep it in your pants—and his—until he's old enough. You give the rest of us a really bad name.—*Frank, forty-nine, social worker, Tampa*

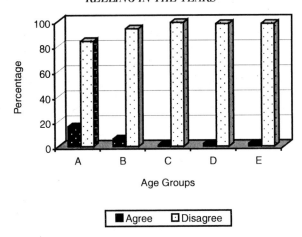

FIGURE 8.6. Older guys don't have anything to offer to younger guys.

- I think older guys have *a lot* to give to younger guys when it comes to overall life experience. Younger guys just need to get up from their trick long enough to listen.—*Elliott, twenty-four, graduate student/instructor, Fresno, California*

- We have been through all the rejections and failed relationships. We can help them put things in perspective. We have dealt with straight society, family, etc., and can help them to resolve issues in that area. Some of our experiences may be dated, but they still hold true for many younger individuals out there today.—*Bob, fifty-two, actor, Belgium (formerly Philadelphia)*

- I think the experience of older men is invaluable. Young guys need to know that they can have a "normal" life, that having a partner and a home and a family is completely possible. I wish when I was growing up that I had had older gay friends to let me know that being gay was so much more than finding people to have sex with.—*Mike, forty, government worker, Utah*

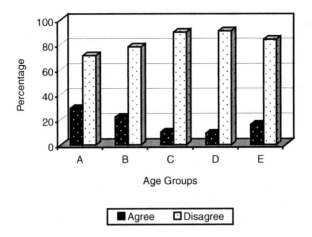

FIGURE 8.7. Young guys don't offer anything for older guys, except maybe sex.

- Do I find younger men physically attractive? Of course I do, but that doesn't mean I have to find a way into bed with them. Mostly I just like to watch them, admire their energy and industry, and recall the days when I was like they are now.—*Howard, fifty-seven, retired, New Mexico*

- If he's like five years older than you, it's all good. After that it's like you just know he's trying to find a way to get you naked.— *Marc, twenty-one, student, Seattle*

- Older men aren't the only ones with ideas. I am seventeen and have a lot of insight.—*Brian, seventeen, student, no location given*

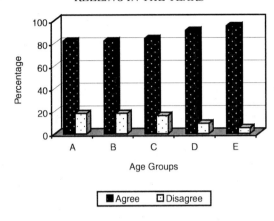

FIGURE 8.8. I think gay culture is friendlier to younger guys than it is to older guys.

- I hate to say it, but I do feel marginalized by my age. I feel angry about it. I try to defy that feeling, but when I go to bed at night alone, I often feel very, very sad and hurt.—*Richard, fifty-two, clinical social worker, Washington, DC*

- I think gay culture is very youth centered, but I'm not sure it's any more so than straight culture. Gay culture can be warm, accepting, and pleasant to me, but it can also be very cold, distant, and harsh.—*Allan, twenty-one, retail manager, Baton Rouge*

- I guess gay culture is driven by youth. I'm kind of on the fence about it, so I don't have a problem with it yet. Ask me again in about ten years.—*Rick, thirty-one, advertising director, Seattle*

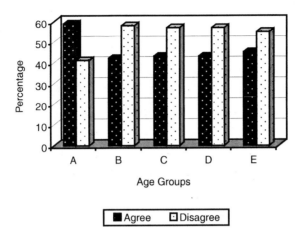

FIGURE 8.9. The gay community doesn't value underage youth.

- Kids these days have it better than any other generation of gays before them, but we could be doing a lot more for them. We need more groups to reach out to these kids wherever they are, before they start to feel too isolated.—*Johnnie, thirty-five, nightclub owner, New York City*

- I think older gay men are pretty much invisible when it comes to addressing the concerns of young gay people.—*Andrew, twenty-four, travel agent, Alabama*

- I don't think anyone cares about young gay people. It's like the world is all about "don't ask, don't tell" when it comes to being gay, and if young gays need help who can they turn to? They turn to each other, or no one, because most of the time the older queers just want ass and the young ones know that. There are no places for young gay guys to go. There's just nothing out there.—*Teej, twenty-three, student, Denver*

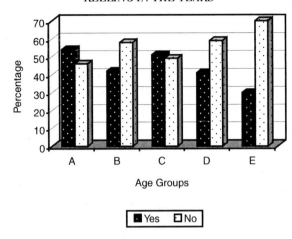

FIGURE 8.10. I have experienced some kind of antigay harassment or violence.

- In high school after my "good friend" outed me, I dealt with regular threats of physical violence, my car was vandalized, and I was actually getting death threats on my home answering machine. The school didn't do anything, except label me a "problem" and send me to alternative education.—*Tim, twenty-two, student, Rocky Mount, Virginia*

- Not for quite a long time, not since I've been an adult. But being a gay teen in high school was hell.—*Adam, forty-two, insurance sales, Northeast*

- If I could delete all memories of my teen years and high school out of my mind I would. I had a horrible time with being teased and have been called every gay-bashing name in the book, even at my job . . . but that which does not kill us only makes us stronger.—*James, twenty-six, student, Fairfax, Virginia*

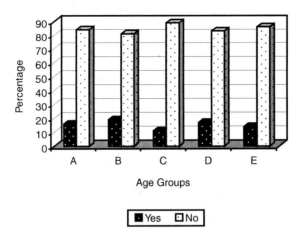

FIGURE 8.11. I've experienced some kind of gay-related family abuse.

- Not abuse, exactly. They just kicked me out and haven't spoken to me since. And we're talking like twenty years, now.—*Cliff, forty, realtor, Akron, Ohio*

- I was expecting it, to be honest. I thought my dad might hit me, my mom would slap me, that my brothers and sisters would hate me, not want me to be their little brother anymore. But other than a rough few weeks, they've all treated me the same since I came out, which was exactly five years ago. Next mission: bring home the boyfriend!—*Dan, twenty-four, student, Midwest*

- My parents took it pretty well, but my older brother didn't. He's not abusive to me, like he never tried to hit me or anything, or say anything bad. He just doesn't talk to me anymore.—*Chad, sixteen, student, Marietta, Georgia*

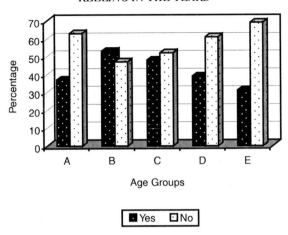

FIGURE 8.12. I am totally out.

- I came out at the end of eighth grade when I tried to commit suicide because the pressure of being in was just too much. I
  needed to be myself. Now everyone knows. It's cool.—*Brian,
  seventeen, student, no location given*

- Depends on what you mean by totally. Family? Yes. Friends?
  Yes. Job? Hell, no. Too many 'phobes here.—*Carl, thirty-eight,
  lab tech, northeast Pennsylvania*

- Last year the local television station covered our Gay Pride Parade, and there I was, at six and eleven, dancing down the street
  like a big ol' girl. If the world didn't know before (and I'm pretty
  sure they did!) they do now.—*D'Arcy, twenty-five, florist, San
  Diego*

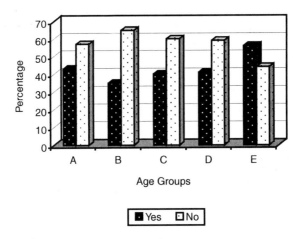

FIGURE 8.13. I am out, but only to friends.

- I wish I had the balls to come out to my family, but so far no dice. Just a few of my close friends know, but I haven't told my sister yet. I just know she'd have to go running to Mom. The girl can't keep her big trap shut.—*Kenny, twenty-seven, graduate student, UCLA*

- I am out to a growing circle of friends, mostly gay. I am otherwise "in" to family and business colleagues. Being "in" is becoming increasingly frustrating, inhibiting my social interests and the friendships that I am enjoying more and more.—*Tom, fifty-two, education administrator, Pennsylvania*

- I'm kind of in and out. I am out to some of my friends, and to my gay friends of course, but I'm not out to my family because I'm scared of what they'll think or do.—*Joseph, eighteen, student, Tallahassee, Florida*

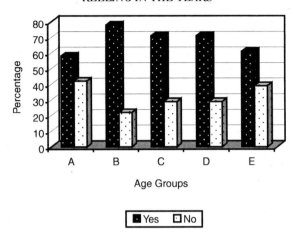

FIGURE 8.14. My family knows I'm gay.

- I came out to my siblings around thirty-five, but my parents still don't know. Well, I'm almost sure they do know, but they just don't talk about it. Come on . . . I'm forty-four with no wife, not even a girlfriend. They're not stupid, just silent.—*Mike, forty-four, human resources administrator, northern California*

- I haven't told my parents, but they damned sure know I'm gay. It's like we have a "don't ask, don't tell" thing. I'm sure they're OK with it . . . or maybe it's made them so deathly ill they can't talk about it.—*Daniel, twenty, music store manager, Roseville, Michigan*

- Coming out was easier than I thought it would be, but acceptance is something else. My older brother, who is now deceased, was gay as well. The thought of "oh, no, another one!" went through my family like a wildfire. It's not exactly a welcome topic of conversation at most family gatherings.—*Chris, thirty-two, interior design consultant, Kenner, Louisiana*

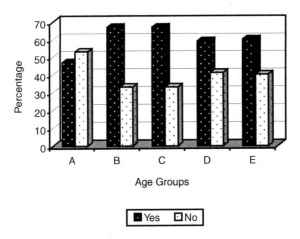

FIGURE 8.15. I've gone to watch or taken part in Pride Day celebrations.

- Of course I go to Pride. It is important to be seen and heard; I think there is more to a Pride parade than just a giant social gathering and place to cruise. The more active we are within the community on a public level, the more likely we are all going to get the results we are hoping for.—*James, twenty-six, student, Fairfax, Virginia*

- We do "gay pride" every time we go to the grocery store together. We don't need a parade or Pride event to try and validate who we are.—*Wayne, thirty-six, insurance salesman, Kutztown, Pennsylvania*

- Pride, *schmide.* It used to be about a cause—now it's about someone making money off of us. My partner and I still go, because on some level maybe it's still important that straight people know we're out here, but it's not like it used to be. Then again, what is?—*Henry, forty-nine, airline pilot, Chicago*

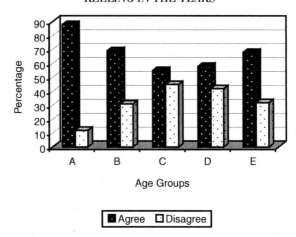

FIGURE 8.16. I believe the Internet makes being gay easier.

- Almost all of my contact with other gay people has been through the Internet. I'm not one for "cruising." Without the Internet, I would simply have no idea where to meet people.— *Theo, twenty-four, student, Southeast Asia*

- Well, it sure makes it easier to get laid. And I suppose it gives you a lot more access to information, and other gay people for friendship and support. Myself, I like looking at porn a lot, and there's more dick online than one could ever find in person. You don't even have to get up.—*Tom, fifty-four, artist, Province-town, Massachusetts*

- I met most of my gay friends from the Internet, and that's how I've met all of my boyfriends. I didn't know where else to start. Yeah, a lot of the guys you find online can be pretty scary, but it's worth it because I've met some really nice people along the way.—*Seb, twenty-one, student, Seattle*

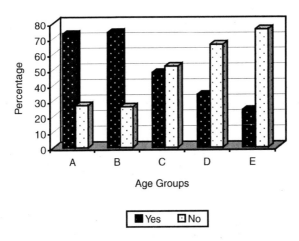

FIGURE 8.17. I like to go out clubbing/dancing.

- Where else would I go on a Saturday night? It's not going to be a movie at the local multiplex. That's for the straight boys and their girlfriends with the bad makeup and hair. And I'm far too fabulous to stay home.—*Frankie, twenty-two, retail worker, Newark, New Jersey*

- I don't go to bars or clubs anymore. I'm currently in a relationship with someone who believes the only reason men go to bars is to find someone to have sex with. I don't share this opinion, but our relationship is not "healthy" enough for one of us to do something different than the other wants.—*Mike, forty, government worker, Utah*

- None of my gay social life centers around bars and nightclubs. I wish a little of it did.—*Tom, fifty-eight, retired, Northwest*

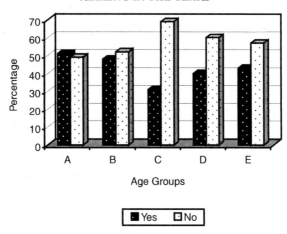

FIGURE 8.18. I hope I'll meet a guy when I go out socially.

- None of us like it very much when people come up to us and try
  to start conversations. We like to keep our little clique intact. If
  any of us want to meet someone, we go out alone. But we never
  go out alone.—*Josh, twenty, student, Cleveland*

- My first boyfriend tripped over me coming out of the bathroom
  at a club—that's how we met. We weren't together long, maybe
  a few months, but I was really in love with him. Even though it's
  been ten years since, every time I go out I still think "please let
  some cute boy trip over me tonight."—*Rick, twenty-nine, factory worker, Pennsylvania*

- I don't go out and meet people. Or rather, I don't go out looking
  to meet people. I'm at a weird point in my life where I don't
  know what I want.—*James, twenty-six, sales, New York State*

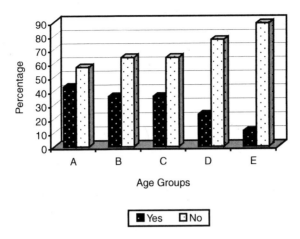

FIGURE 8.19. I occasionally use recreational drugs.

- I am a social drinker, but I don't understand drinking to the point of a drunken stupor. I have no experience with [drugs] but I am unequivocally against altered states of consciousness.—*John, twenty-one, student, Nashville, Tennessee*

- Lord, those days are so far behind me. There was a time when there wasn't anything I hadn't tried. All the popular drugs of the day, I gave 'em a whirl. These days these kids have so many more temptations, so many more drugs to play with, and from what I hear they're a lot more dangerous than the things we played with.—*Ethan, fifty, shop owner, Albuquerque, New Mexico*

- Call me stupid, but I just don't get the whole point of drugs. I don't have any friends that use drugs . . . well, none of my good close friends do. I don't know when I've ever been around anyone who has. I certainly have no desire to try them.—*Lee, nineteen, student, Marbury, Maryland*

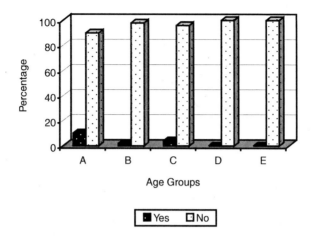

FIGURE 8.20. I have not yet had gay sex (I am a virgin when it comes to men).

For my purposes, "sex" here is defined as any prolonged physical contact involving the genitalia of you or your male partner, clothed or unclothed, where the expressed or implicit intent was the physical satisfaction of both/either. With all due respect to our former president, penetration of the nether regions is not required; blow jobs, hand jobs, frottage, it makes no difference *how* you got your nookie, as long as you got it (which is just how life should be).

- I realized I was gay at twelve or so, but didn't act on it until I was nineteen. Thank God for those Army roommates!—*Jay, twenty-seven, professor, northern California*

- I'm not a virgin when it comes to sex in general, but I am when it comes to any kind of sex with men. Unless you count my fantasies—I'm no virgin there. But no, no sex with men. I'm married, with kids, and deeply, deeply unhappy.—*Pete, thirty-two, house builder, Kansas*

- My parents asked me if I was having sex when I came out to them. I told them no. That was last year. Tonight I took your poll, and in a way I guess I lied to them, since I've been sucking dick since I was thirteen. But no one's been "back there" yet, and they ain't gonna be anytime soon!—*Tommy, eighteen, student, Delaware*

TABLE 8.1. Initial Sexual Experience by Age and Age Group

Age (Years)	Age Group (%)				
	A	B	C	D	E
12 or younger	14	16	16	22	19
13	7	6	6	8	17
14	3	2	1	7	12
15	6	6	6	6	7
16	11	9	4	4	4
17	11	7	7	6	3
18	19	7	11	5	4
19	7	5	10	5	2
20	6	8	4	4	3
21	4	9	5	2	2
22	0	6	2	4	3
23	2	6	3	3	2
24	—	6	2	2	1
25	—	5	1	1	2
26	—	—	3	2	2
27	—	—	1	2	1
28	—	—	3	1	2
29	—	—	2	1	0
30 or older	—	—	9	15	14

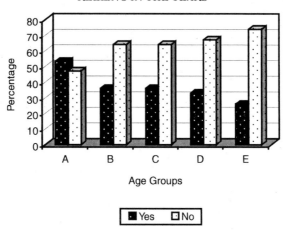

FIGURE 8.21. I use protection whenever I have sex.

- I am forty, poz, and I only have sex with other guys who are poz, so I figure what's the point?—*Steve, forty, office worker, Los Angeles*

- I think young gay men need to start being more safe. It really doesn't take anything away from sex. You really need to help prevent the spread of STDs so they can be put under control and brought back to a minimum. And for those of you who know you have something and still go unprotected, *that's fucked up!* There's definitely something wrong with you if you do that.—*Derek, eighteen, student, Providence, Rhode Island*

- I always try to use protection when it comes to anal sex. I know they say that you can get HIV from blowing a guy, but I've just never believed that. It might be true, sure . . . just seems like there wouldn't be anybody left if that was the case, though.—*Dave, thirty, retail manager, Austin, Texas*

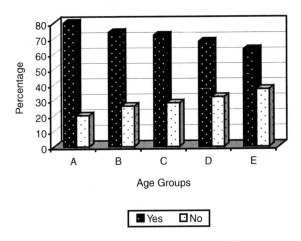

FIGURE 8.22. I worry about getting HIV/AIDS.

- It scares the shit out of me. It's like someone waiting there in the dark looking to shoot you, and you have no idea where the bullet might come from.—*Randy, twenty-seven, musician, New York City*

- If it happens, it happens. At least the drugs are better now.—*Al, thirty-four, warehouse laborer, Baltimore, Maryland*

- Strike me dead for saying this. I almost wish I had the opportunity to get any kind of STD, I've been in a dry spell for so long, manwise. Seriously, I would worry if I was having sex, but you can't get sick from masturbating. In my case, it would have to be some kind of an immaculate infection.—*Ted, fifty, music teacher, Illinois*

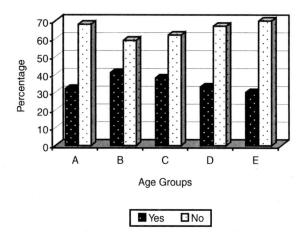

FIGURE 8.23. I am in a monogamous relationship.

- I've never looked at anyone else, and neither has he. Or at least I've never caught him looking, and it's been almost five years now.—*Stuart, thirty-five, web designer, Burlington, Vermont*

- We're about to celebrate ten years together, and I'm still just as excited to come home to him as I was the night we met. I can't imagine my life without him.—*Nicholas, thirty-nine, physician assistant, Phoenix, Arizona*

- We've only known each other for about a year, and so far, so good. We've decided to move in together and I'm scared. I love him so much. I just don't know what it will be like living with a boyfriend for the first time in my life.—*Lucas, twenty-eight, delivery man, Houston*

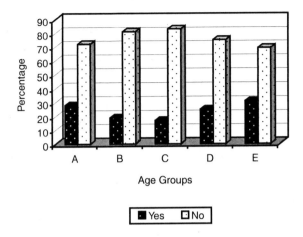

FIGURE 8.24. I prefer being single.

- I'm too young to settle down with only one guy. I've learned that the hard way. As soon as I pick one, I see another I want. It's worse than shopping.—*Lee, twenty-four, student, Hartford, Connecticut*

- Living alone is like a slow death for me. It's been fifteen years since I had a real boyfriend, and I miss having the same arms around me every night.—*Brad, forty-seven, insurance adjuster, Indianapolis*

- It took me a long time to learn that love and sex weren't always the same thing. I used to want to have sex all the time. Now I'd settle for loving one guy and having him love me in return. Being single sucks.—*Ryan, thirty, cook/kitchen worker, New Jersey*

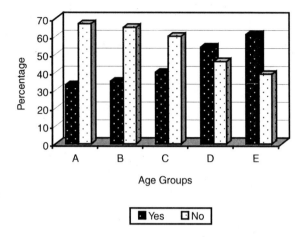

FIGURE 8.25. I would have sex with someone without a serious relationship.

- I'm a nineteen-year-old male in college and my hormones are racing! People randomly hook up here all the time.—*Kyle, nineteen, student, North Carolina*

- I only have casual sex with my partner. I mean, as long as my partner is there with me when we have sex with another guy. I'd never do it behind his back. . . . Wait, this just isn't coming out right. You know what I mean.—*Paul, thirty, mechanic, Hattiesburg, Mississippi*

- When did sex of any kind stop being serious? Wake up and smell the danger, guys!—*Carlos, forty, social worker, Miami, Florida*

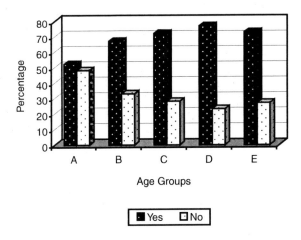

FIGURE 8.26. I will have sex on the first date.

- Sex on the first date is like licking the bowl after making cookies.—*Erik, twenty-three, office temp, New York City*

- Whatever happened to getting to know someone? Whatever happened to the idea of romance? Am I just living in the wrong time?—*Ken, thirty, sales manager, Anaheim, California*

- You better believe I'll have sex on the first date. At my age, there's no telling if I'll live to the second.—*Ray, seventy, retired, Palm Springs, California*

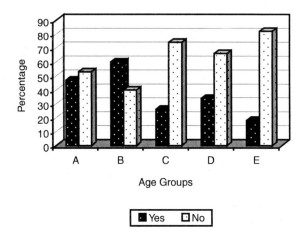

FIGURE 8.27. I have joined a gym or work out regularly.

- I've never worked out just to look younger. Most of my efforts are just aimed at looking good with what I've got.—*Larry, fifty-seven, retired, east Tennessee*

- Right now I've still got the same body I had in high school. I was always a jock boy and people tell me I could be an underwear model, so I guess that means I look OK! I don't really work out that much anymore, though. I should get my ass back on track, before my ass gets saggy. Guys usually don't like that much.— *Tyler, twenty, student, Worcester, Massachusetts*

- All these fat gay guys bitching about being fat. They need to get their butts in the gym and stop eating everything in sight.—*Jordan, thirty, driver, West Hollywood, California*

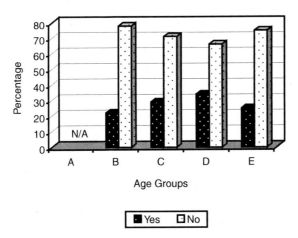

FIGURE 8.28. I have taken nonsurgical steps to look younger (dyed hair, new wardrobe, etc.).

- I used to dye my hair and beard, though I haven't for the last three years. I've joined a gym, which was a pretty wise move . . . but I'd only like to lose about fifteen years. I wouldn't want to look much younger than forty.—*Jeff, fifty-five, college professor, Washington, DC*

- I have all my hair and teeth, and I tend to dress in what I like rather than what happens to be fashionable. Comfort is my keyword. No dyes or anything like that for me, thanks.—*Alan, sixty, brokerage analyst, San Francisco, California*

- I've considered electrolysis to get rid of my beard density, and I've thought about cosmetic dentistry. So far I haven't done any of that, but it really distresses me to see gray hairs appearing, along with wrinkles around my eyes. It's hard for me to see myself as "older." When I put on a Gap T-shirt I'm afraid people will think I'm trying to look younger. I just want to look the age that I feel.—*Lee, thirty-two, projects manager, Atlanta, Georgia*

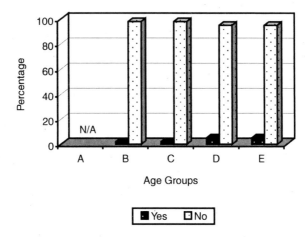

FIGURE 8.29. I've had or would consider plastic surgery (liposuction, hair implants, face-lifts, etc.).

- Wouldn't even consider it. My lover (twenty years junior) would kill me if I flattened out a single wrinkle. He thinks it's sexy.—*Jeremy, forty-nine, municipal worker, Cincinnati, Ohio*

- When my deep red, wavy ponytail started thinning I thought I'd have to go get hair implants as soon as I could afford it. Now my hair is buzzed and I wouldn't wear it longer if it were still thick, red, and wavy. Too much trouble. And I look good bald. Not as handsome as Yul Brynner, but damned good.—*Jack, sixty-three, retired, West Texas*

- Only my plastic surgeon knows for sure. And he's sworn to secrecy!—*Russell, forty-eight, entertainment industry, Los Angeles, California*

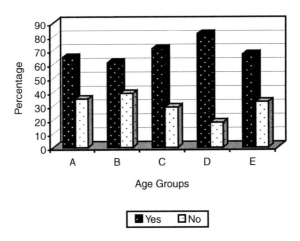

FIGURE 8.30. I am thinking about retirement, saving, investing.

- I try not to think too much about old age. I will worry about that when I get there. I had started putting some money aside when I was working, but now that I'm back at school saving is kind of a luxury. Right now I figure my best investment is keeping my health and staying fit.—*Patrick, twenty-five, graduate student, North Carolina*

- My golden years are here, with a man I love, in a committed relationship, out and open to all, with all the funds to keep us just as we'd always hope to be kept. Not many are that lucky . . . well, there might have been a little bit of skill involved.—*Don, fifty-nine, retired, Palm Springs, California*

- It really digs at me the way I encourage everyone else to save and invest for the future, when I have a hard time making my own ends meet. These are just really difficult times.—*Barry, thirty-eight, accountant, Lexington, Kentucky*

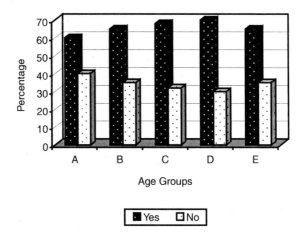

FIGURE 8.31. When I retire I'd like to live near gay men my age.

- Gay life wears you thin. You get jaded at a pretty young age. The thoughts of saving money so you can retire with a partner are so far off, it's incomprehensible. By the time you do retire, most likely the last thing you want is to be confined to any retirement community, gay or straight. Perhaps at that point it's time to spread your wings and be more independent.—*Tim, twenty-three, media planner, Boston, Massachusetts*

- My friends and I joke about this all the time. We've made a pact with each other, that those of us still alive after seventy will sell all our houses and condos, and we'll buy a big house that we can all live in together. We'll hire a few hot houseboys to bring us cocktails on the porch. We'll sit in our rockers and tell all the secrets about people that we can still remember.—*Gordon, thirty-six, massage therapist, Lansing, Michigan*

- Life is a lot more about being a person than just being a gay person. I wouldn't mind having other gay men in my age group around to shoot the shit with when I'm eighty, but God help me if that's my only company when I'm pooping in my pants.—*Jim, fifty, banker, Louisiana*

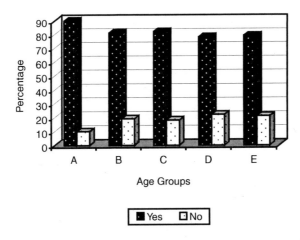

FIGURE 8.32. I am happy with my age.

- When I was seventeen I couldn't wait for eighteen. When I was nineteen I couldn't wait for twenty-one. Now I'm looking at thirty, and I'm trying to figure out where the hell my youth went.—*Byron, twenty-eight, writer, Minneapolis, Minnesota*

- I never knew life would be this good on the other side of forty, but that's how it turned out. A loving partner, a great job, a nice house. I should probably be knocking on wood when I say this, but it's never been better.—*Rick, forty-two, business owner, South Carolina*

- I'd like to be twenty-two forever.—*Josh, twenty-two, student, Berkeley, California*

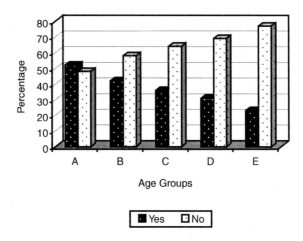

FIGURE 8.33. I fear growing old.

- Sometimes I think I'll die in my bed alone and that scares me to death. Our gay friendships are so important, especially once we get older, because our friends become our real family, by default.—*Matty, twenty-five, music industry, New York City*

- It's a little late for that now, don't you think?—*Sam, sixty-five, retired, Las Vegas, Nevada*

- Maybe it's just the rebel inside of me wanting to break away from home, but ever since I can remember, I've always wanted that "middle age" feel. I don't know. I have to say I'm extremely eager to reach my late twenties/early thirties. I can't wait to have my own place, my career, and my own life. I may not know exactly what I want to be, or study, but I'm confident I'm going to succeed, and have fun with it.—*Dave, seventeen, student, Miami, Florida*

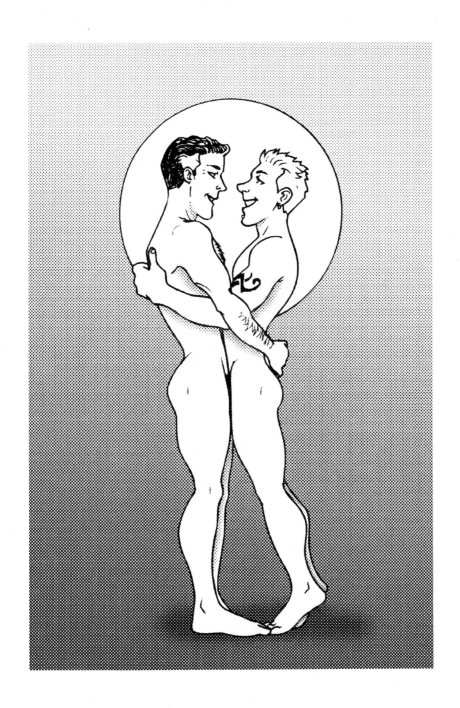

Afterword

I woke up first that morning, as I usually did; Andy was a very deep sleeper, and at his age, usually needed a few more hours of sack time than I required. Easing out from under his arm I rolled out of bed, then stumbled over to my computer. It was my habit—and it still is—to check for any important e-mails or messages before I've even taken the first wizz of the day; I just never know what might be waiting in my mailbox, sent to me by my numerous night owl or early bird friends perched in different time zones around the world. After that, I planned to make my way to the kitchen, make us our ritual breakfast of cereal and coffee, before waking Andy and getting our day started. Outside it was a brilliant, sunny Tuesday morning, with the deepest of late-summer blue skies; gazing out through the bedroom window, I was hoping there might be time for us to squeeze in a nice long bike ride before I was off to work.

I had to blink a few times once my eyes drifted back to my computer monitor; seemed like someone was already IM-ing me and it was hard to see the message. My eyes finally focused: it was my friend J. R., telling me to turn on my television, turn on my television right now. I turned, fumbled for the remote, found it, pressed "power," and in the space of a second, forgot about the coffee, the cereal, the bike ride, work, even my morning wizz.

"Andy. Get up." He told me later it wasn't like I'd shouted, but there was something in my voice that snapped him out of his slumber. "What's up?" he asked, rolling over, sleep still soaking his voice. "New York is burning," I told him.

To call that day surreal doesn't do it justice. There's no single word that can adequately explain how anybody felt on September 11, 2001; it was such a cascade of shifting emotions. We'll remember where we were, what we were doing, when we first heard the news, saw the towers burning, found out about the Pentagon, the plane in Pennsylvania. As for Andy and me, huddled together in front of the television for most of the day, we were stunned, sickened, scared shitless, especially after learning that the airliner that crashed into the Pentagon had pretty much passed over my apartment on the way to its deadly rendezvous; I live just eight miles away (talk about hitting close to home). Then we heard those initial—and ultimately inaccurate—reports of as many as *ten* planes still unaccounted for. That peaceful blue sky outside my bedroom window? Now there were fighter jets up there and the sound of those engines roaring overhead made me queasy.

Friends and family kept calling to see if we were all right, just as I made my own anxious calls to friends in New York, trying not to panic when all I could get was busy signal after busy signal. I kept pulling Andy closer, asking him stupidly, over and over again, if this was some kind of nightmare, if this was *really* happening. His only response, and it was likely the only helpful one he could have given me, was to hold me tighter.

Just four days later, on another, similarly gorgeous Saturday morning, we were in bed again when my phone rang. (Funny how you know when it's going to be bad news; for some unaccountable reason, I knew.) I woke to the voice of my sister, choking through her tears, telling me that my father had died that morning about an hour before, right there at his breakfast table in West Virginia. Apparently his heart just . . . stopped. I broke out into tears instantaneously, and Andy, lying beside me in bed, was there for me again, holding me, comforting me. He knew all too well what I was going through; he'd lost his own father when he was only fourteen.

Later that night, I sat with Mom in her den, Andy at my side, as she told me how depressed Pop had been all week about the terror attacks, but his spirits had seemed pretty high that morning; it was perfect weather, he'd said, to get on his tractor and cut the grass. She'd turned away for a second to get some more coffee; when she turned back he was face down on the table. He was gone—she told me. Gone in an instant, after eighty-three years.

Pop was born during one World War and fought in the second, this after surviving the Depression and losing his mother to tuberculosis when he was only nine. He'd seen the Kennedy and King assassinations, Vietnam, the whole sad litany of the middle to late twentieth century that formed the backdrop of my upbringing, but he'd always told me as I was growing up that things get better, they always get better. After September 11, maybe he just couldn't believe it anymore. I know my mom thinks that; to this day she's convinced that on some level, a part of him just said, "To hell with this world, I am outta here."

I mention those twin tragedies—one deeply personal, the other national, yet deeply, personally felt—for several reasons. First, as an opportunity to thank my former boyfriend, Andy, without whom I may not have survived that terrible week. If you've ever read *A Prayer for Owen Meany* by John Irving, or seen the movie based on it, *Simon Birch*—if you haven't, you should—you'll understand why I believe that, in many ways, Andy was a gift from God, from Fate, or from whatever strange unknowable entities out there that shape our lives and fortunes. You're certainly free to think me foolish for seeing some kind of order in the random chaos of life, for finding meaning in chance. After all, we'd known each other for nine months already before that week, and it would be another four months before we broke up. But I know I'm always going to believe that it was no coincidence that he was with me on those two terrible mornings, just four days apart.

I also mention September 11 for reasons more directly related to this book; a bit more than half of the material I collected was compiled prior to that date. I know from personal experience how the fallout from the attacks has filtered through all of our lives in some subtle and not-so-subtle ways. It was an American tragedy, not a "gay" tragedy, though many gay men *were* prominent among the victims and heroes that day. We've all felt the aftershocks; the economic recession, worries about invasions of personal privacy in the name of homeland security, fears of more terrorism, the possibility of war with other nations in the Middle East. It's all created a sense of creeping dread, and it worried me how those events might have colored my respondents' view of their lives or altered their sense of optimism about the future, *after* I'd interviewed them or recorded their stories.

I wasn't able to contact everyone who submitted a survey, or took the polls—by design they were intended to be as anonymous as possible—but I was able to reach many of them and query several other gay men as well in the months after 9/11, *and* in the months after those anthrax attacks in the fall of 2001. Though heartbroken over both events, and just as wary as anybody else over the prospect of even more such heinous acts, only a few indicated that they were going to let any kind of terrorism, foreign or domestic, dictate their lives or plans for tomorrow. "If you do that, the bastards win," might be the best way to sum up the general response. So I feel confident in presenting all you've seen up to this point as an accurate snapshot of their views.

I'm also proud to say I've seen even more of that attitude here in the DC area, where, as I write this, we've just been through a bizarre twenty-three-day ordeal at the hands of a sniper who killed at least a dozen people, most of them in Maryland, DC, and Virginia; one of the victims was cut down in a shopping center parking garage just five miles from where I live. (By the time you read this the suspects, apparently in custody, may well have been tried and convicted; if I know Virginia, they're sitting on death row or they've already walked that last mile.) But through all of it most of the people I know—and many of them are gay men—refused to let "the bastards" change their daily routines. Oh, we modified them, to be sure; you should have seen me running back and forth across the parking lot from my car to the grocery store or doing my "gas dance" while filling up at the pump, so I wouldn't make myself an easy target for an invisible marksman. But I can't say many of us—if indeed, any of us—opted to stay home on a Saturday night instead of hitting a bar or nightclub just because we were afraid of getting shot. "More likely my drunk ass will get hit by a bus on the way to the subway," is how one friend of mine put it.

There may yet be some kind of delayed response to all of these ordeals, or some unknown, unnamed ordeals to come; maybe in a few years it'll be easier to find a clear pattern or change in attitudes that's had a discernible effect on gay men's perspectives about their lives, something we can trace back to this awful twelve-month period. If that happens, I promise you I'll be back, my publisher willing, to talk about them in future editions.

It's also not just in passing—now there's a really bad pun—that I talk about my father's death. (Trust me, he would have enjoyed that play on words. He was funny like that.) I've heard it said that no man is *truly* a man until his father is gone, because until then he never escapes the shadow of the man who brought him into the world. I don't really agree with that, but I will say that a parent's death does bring your own mortality into closer focus, and makes you look at where you are in your own life, especially once you've hit middle age. For a gay man who is estranged from his father, your dad's passing can be a deeply regretful occurrence; so much bitterness left unexpunged, so many words left unsaid. I am fortunate that while my parents and I had that same "don't ask, don't tell" policy about my sexual orientation you've heard other men speak of—they knew full well why I was kicked out of the Marine Corps two years early, long before the actual "don't ask, don't tell" policy was put in place—their underlying love and affection for me was never in doubt. It was at their home in West Virginia, after all, that I landed when Uncle Sam gave me my walking papers, and though I was relieved to make my exit for DC after five years of putting my life back together in those backwoods hills, I'll never be able to thank them enough for coming to my rescue.

And I'll always be grateful that my last living memories of my father are of his eighty-third birthday party just three months before his death. You should have seen him that day, a king on his throne, surrounded by scores of sons, daughters, grandchildren, nieces, nephews, friends, and his wife of fifty-four years. "They're kissing my ring, or kissing my ass," is the way he put it, to great laughter all around.

Even his passing was something blessed. His greatest fears, he often confided to my mother, were either that she would go first and he'd be left alone, or that he would be stricken down, then linger in a hospital for months or years, tubes stuck here and there, monitors beeping and flashing, trapped in a netherworld between this one and the next. That's not what happened. One second he was talking about mowing the lawn on a crystal clear September morn; the next he was knock-knock-knocking on Heaven's door. Not a bad way to go out. If there's any such thing as a good death, that's it.

As for Mom, well . . . she's a strong woman, grief stricken still, to be sure, but inside my mother is a resilient broad from the old school. Pop might have had a stern exterior sometimes, but he was always the softie, emotional insides always warm and mushy. He wouldn't have lasted much beyond her demise. Nine years younger than Pop was, and tough as nails besides, Mom's going to be around a bit longer, mark my words.

In writing and researching my first book, *Sissyphobia: Gay Men and Effeminate Behavior,* I found myself confronted with a dearth of published material on the topic; up to that point, there had been no single, published work on the topic of why some gay men behave in effeminate ways while others don't, or why society has, to put it bluntly, such a major bug up its ass about men who have a swish in their get-along. In a way, that turned out to be something of a God-send, since I was consequently a lot freer to explore the opinions of "regular folks" and not spend so much time wading through the opinions of those who spend too much time breathing the rarified air of academia.

But with *Reeling in the Years: Gay Men's Perspectives on Age and Ageism,* I had exactly the *opposite* problem; there is just *way* too much stuff out there, in the form of published books, articles, Web sites, experts, organizations, you name it, all dedicated to several of the various topics this book touched on. For instance, I discovered that for all their differences, and for all the specific challenges they face, young gay men and older gay men certainly share one thing in common: a number of advocacy groups helping them fight their fights—even the most cursory Web search turns up dozens upon dozens of local, national, even international groups one can contact online—not to mention scores of journalists and writers willing to publicize their plights. Readers of more traditional, academic tomes might be put off by the fact that I only sparingly quoted from such experts or their works, but please remember: I was sitting on more than a thousand pages of material from my own surveys, interviews, and polls, filled out or shared by hundreds of gay men in every age group. It was to them, and their stories, that I felt I owed my greatest loyalty, and the lion's share of space within this book. I hope you'll forgive me for whatever omissions I may have committed, either by accident or design, in giving them that space.

For truly, I was often touched personally by those stories. Who wouldn't be moved by the tale of a teenager bullied in high school, then forced out of his home by homophobic parents? Who can't empathize with an elderly gay man in the twilight of life, contemplating his last few years without the lover of more than four decades? They are all threads in this tapestry of gay life we weave, and sometimes those threads wind their way through our own lives.

But it wasn't just the sad stories I could relate to. Remember Jack in west Texas, the sixty-three-year-old retiree who spoke about how he *almost* ended up with a sixteen-year-old in his room after talking to him at a hotel pool? Just this past summer, I too met a young man at a pool—my apartment pool, to be precise—and as we started talking those first few days, I grew rather certain he was coming on to me. A recent émigré from a foreign country, with what can only be described as a wickedly sexy accent, "T" was small but solidly built, with dashing dark eyes and a huge, white smile. He could swim like a fish—T had been a member of his school swim team overseas, he told me—and favored wearing a Speedo-style suit that only emphasized his obvious, um, endowments. Every time he saw me lying there, soaking up sun, T would come over and plop down his stuff, pull over a chair, and start gabbing with me, striking what can only be called rather seductive poses. It was all ridiculously cute, and utterly charming. I figured him for maybe sixteen or seventeen years old. Jailbait sure, but not *so* jailbait as to make you feel dirty or sleazy about yourself for liking the way that swimsuit clung to him so well.

I wasn't alone in finding T attractive. My ex-boyfriend and current roommate, Christopher—don't ask me how we make *that* work, we just do—phoned me from the pool one morning about a week later to tell me he'd spotted the youngster, too. "I am looking at this young *hottie* and he's wearing a *Speedo*," Christopher whispered slowly and lustfully into the phone, and I could only grin, knowing just who he was talking about.

"You think he's hot, eh?" I asked him. "Um, yeah," Chris replied. "It's like he keeps following me into the bathroom. Every time I go, it's like I turn around and he's right *there*. I swear I'm going to have to jump him if he keeps it up." I laughed, because the very same thing had happened to me a few times.

Later that day Chris and I were sitting side by side, dangling our feet in the water, watching our little foreign friend swimming about, admiring his youthful beauty while at the same time very much amused by that admiration. T saw us, smiled, pushed himself up and out of the pool and came over—I swear there was a swelling in the Speedo, God help me for noticing—and sat down next to us. He got me wet shaking his hair dry, then out of nowhere mentioned that his birthday was coming up the next week.

"Oh, really?" I asked him, trying not to sound too interested, the math already done in my head. *If he's seventeen now, then that means . . .*

"So how old are ya going to be?" I asked him cheerfully. "Fourteen," he replied, and as if on cue hopped up and dove back in the water. I didn't even look up at Chris but I could feel his jaw hanging wide open beside me. "I've been having fantasies about a thirteen-year-old," I told the water beneath my feet. "Jesus, I am going to hell." Not looking at me either, Chris replied. "That's OK, honey, 'cause I'll be driving the bus. I wanted to do him, too."

There's one small postscript to the tale of T. A week or so after his little age revelation, we were clowning around in the pool when a troupe of very pale, rather foreign-looking folks trudged in. Turns out it was T's family and he pulled me over to introduce me. You want to talk about feeling uncomfortable? I was sure they'd instantly see my interest in him—even though it was harmless, or at least, mostly harmless—and peg me for a pedo right off. But no, they were very friendly, extremely polite, and we conversed quite convivially right up until the moment I had to take off for home. That's when T's father stood up, and motioned me over to him. *Uh, oh*—I thought. *Here it comes . . .*

But once again I was stunned (must run in the family). In clear—if a little broken—English, T's father told me he thought his young son was getting out of shape, though why he'd think that is beyond me; he said he wanted me to take T and "work him out hard for the rest of the summer." That would make him very happy, he said, shaking my hand. Has to be one of the strangest days, and strangest conversations, I've ever had (and no, I never did—just in case you were wondering).

So much for dispelling the myth of the chicken hawk, right? But at least I'll admit to you that I can find younger men terribly attractive, even as I recognize and adhere to the legal prohibitions against doing anything *but* admire them. (I do have to wonder what the hell they were feeding that boy, though.) As with *Sissyphobia,* where the subject matter kept popping up in the national headlines and within my own life as I was putting that book together, so too did I constantly find echoes of *this* project in the national and local press, not to mention on the pool deck just across the parking lot from my apartment. It was almost a daily battle to keep up, so many new articles did I find about gay youth or gay seniors, the troubles and triumphs of underage gay kids, the latest health and beauty aids aimed at keeping us youthful forever.

And sure enough, the comments that younger and older gay men make about each other in the *Washington Blade*'s "Bitch Session" show the battle lines remain firmly drawn for some. From the November 22, 2002 issue alone came two:

> Why do so many twinks insist on living out every gay male stereotype except the one about gay men being intelligent and cultured? I have little patience for airheads and none for men who pretend to be airheads just to belong to the herd. (p. E-3)

As if in reply, this comment appears just a few items down:

> Yes, we A&F twinks know all about your million-dollar homes. I've put the hot frothy in your morning lattes, and when you're out of town, I've put the hot frothy into your man while in that same wonderful million-dollar home. (p. E-3)

What terrible wittiness that fellow has; if only he could harness his powers for good, not evil.

Even our bleached-blond buddy Eminem was back, in slightly sanitized form. He performed a duet at the 2001 Grammy Awards with *uber-homo* Elton John—even embracing him at the end to wild applause—and his 2002 musical offering, *The Eminem Show,* only had four tracks that used the word "faggot" or mentioned gays at all, and none of those references were violent. That's progress of a sort, I suppose. In late 2002 his movie *8 Mile* debuted to much critical acclaim; within that film, his character, an aspiring rapper, comes to the aid of an openly gay co-worker who's being harassed by a homophobe. The subplot may have been nothing more than expert marketing at work, but on some level you sort of have to feel like that's progress too, nonetheless. When he raps/sings the lyrics to "Lose Yourself" on the *8 Mile* soundtrack, "you gotta lose yourself in the music, the moment, you own it, you better never let it go," Eminem probably doesn't realize he's speaking to any number of gay klub kids' experience out on the dance floor, but he is, anyway. (And he even won an Oscar for it, for "Best Original Song." How gay is that?)

The beat goes on elsewhere, too. Among the hundreds of comments people e-mailed me over the course of the last two years, a handful stood out: some guys told me that, after having taken the survey, they were already starting to rethink their attitudes about the experience of gay men not in their age group. "I didn't realize how shallow I sounded, until I started writing down what I thought I knew," wrote Jimmy, a twenty-year-old college student in South Carolina. "I kinda came off sounding like a dick." Another e-mail came from John, a forty-year-old who told me he had stopped trying to approach younger guys in clubs a long time ago. "I started wondering when and why exactly I decided to do that, when I started limiting myself by choice. The other night I had a wonderful conversation with a delightful young man and we're having coffee tomorrow. Wish me luck!"

Perhaps my favorite, though, came from a forty-one-year-old named Alfredo. "The other night I filled out the survey you have for the new book you are researching," he writes. "I wanted to tell you about a related experience I had last night. My boyfriend and I met two other couples for dinner. One of the couples, Jason and Phillip, had along their thirteen-year-old nephew, A. J. Seemed like a nice kid. At one point my boyfriend asked him what his favorite TV show was and he said *Queer As Folk,* which took us both by surprise. After dinner on the way out of the restaurant, one of the other people in our group told us that A. J. had recently come out to his family. It just came as a bit of a shock and goes to show how things have changed for gay youth in the last decade. I don't have any friends who have ever said they came out so young, even those in their twenties. I think it says a lot when a thirteen-year-old feels he should come out at such an early age. I can't even conceive of discussing the topic with anyone when I was that age. It looks like things are getting better."

I think they are, too, just as I always believed it when Pop told me that as I was growing up a long, long time ago. Do we have problems and challenges ahead? Damn right, we have problems and challenges. But I think about all the people I talked with for this book—especially the sweet-natured, earnest young people with open hearts and minds—and the people of all ages I meet and talk with every day. Call me crazy, but I can't help but feel optimistic about the future. The bastards are everywhere, sure enough, whether they fly airliners into buildings, shoot at us from darkened parking garages, or use jagged-edged words to pierce the heart of our self-esteem. All any of us can do is our best, as our time on this planet ticks on, not to let them damage or change who we are, what we stand for, where we want to go in our lives, who we want to go there with, or the way we treat each other. We all need each other, more than ever.

Don't let the bastards win. Don't you dare.

Resources

Youth Services on the Web

Sexual Minority Youth Assistance League <www.smyal.org>

National Youth Advocacy Coalition <www.nyac.org>

Young Gay America <www.younggayamerica.org>

Gay, Lesbian, Straight Education Network <www.glsen.org>

National Mentoring Center <www.nwrel.org/mentoring/>

Senior Services on the Web

Pride Senior Network <www.pridesenior.org>

Senior Action in a Gay Environment (SAGE) <www.sageusa.org>

Gay and Lesbian Association of Retiring Persons (GLARP) <www.gaylesbianretiring.org>

General Gay Sites (Information, News, Dating)

PlanetOut.com <www.planetout.com>

Gay.com <www.gay.com>

Activism, Civil Rights

Human Rights Campaign (HRC) <www.hrc.org>

National Gay and Lesbian Task Force <www.ngltf.org>

References

Arnovitz, Kevin (2001). "Gay Scene Dropout." *OUT,* May, pp. 50-51.

Berger, Raymond (1982). *Gay and Gray: The Older Homosexual Man.* Binghamton, NY: Harrington Park Press.

Bergling, Tim (1998). "The Rainbow and the Pot of Gold." *Genre,* April, p. 82.

_____ (1999a). "Bridging the Gap." *HERO,* Winter, p. 24.

_____ (1999b). "We Always Had Each Other." *HERO,* Winter, pp.74-75.

Berzon, Betty (2002). PlanetOut column, October 12. Available at <www.planetout.com>.

Bugg, Sean (2001). "Stuck in the Middle." *Metro Weekly,* July 5, p. 27.

Centers for Disease Control (1997). "Young People at Risk," CDC Fact Sheet. Available at <www.cdc.gov>.

Chester, Craig (2002). "Outtakes." *Instinct,* May, p. 70.

Crain, Chris (2002). "Editorial: Let's Talk About Sex Without Having Any." *Washington Blade,* April 26, p. 38.

Cummings, Peter (2000). "Editorial: Slut." *XY,* Winter, p. 12.

English, Camper (2002). "Trapped in the Body of a Circuit Boy." *Instinct,* June, p. 94.

Goldstein, Richard (2002). "The Double Standard." *The Advocate,* August 20, pp. 62-67.

Human Rights Watch (2001). "Hatred in the Hallways." May. Available at <http://www.hrw.org/reports/2001/uslgbt/>.

Hunter, Elizabeth (2001). "So Many Seasons in a Season, So Many Lives in a Life." *Blue Ridge Country,* December, p. 8.

Kaiser Family Foundation (2000). *Sex Education in America.* Available at <http://www.kff.org/content/2000/3048/SexED.pdf >.

Kelly, Michael (2001). "Girth of a Nation." *The Washington Post,* August 1, p. A17.

Liberman, Vadim (2002). "Meet Market." *Instinct,* May.

McIntosh, Sabrina (2000). "From Victim to Activist." *XY,* November, p. 11.

National Gay and Lesbian Task Force's Aging Initiative (NGLTF) (2000). *Outing Age.* Available at <http://www.ngltf.org/downloads/outingage.pdf>, pp. iv-v.

"Newsbriefs." (2001). *Washington Blade,* April 19, p. 18.

Nguyen, Tommy (2000). "The Man Behind 'Broken Hearts Club.'" *XY,* November, p. 81.

O'Briant, Erin and Moylan, Brian (2001). "That's So Gay." *Washington Blade,* September 21, p. 5.

Parker, Ray (2002). "High Maintenance." *Instinct,* January/February, p. 52.

Schulman, Randy (1998). "Young, Out, and Proud." *Metro Weekly,* April 16, pp. 22-23.

Sessions Step, Laura (2001). "A Lesson in Cruelty." *The Washington Post,* June 19, p. A7.

U.S. Department of Health and Human Services, Administration on Aging (AOA). "Online Fact Sheet." Available at <www.aoa.gov>.

Weinstein, Steve (2001). "The Gay Generation Gap." *OUT,* October, pp. 91-109.

Will, George F. (2001). "Harry Potter vs. the Xbox." *The Washington Post,* November 16, op-ed page.